Crocodiles, Cakes and the Queen's Petticoats

A Collection of Memoirs from

The Women's Institute,

Volume 1

in collaboration with
Queenbee Press

Managing Editor: Miranda Glover
Contributing Editors: David Chesterton, Katherine Williams
Copy Editors: Jennie Walmsley, Lucy Cavendish, Rachel Jackson

This book is published by Queenbee Press, www.queenbee.co.uk

It is devised from the WI Memoir Writing Programme 2011
Written by Jennie Walmsley, in collaboration with the founder members
of Contemporary Women Writers' Club; Lucy Cavendish,
Miranda Glover and Rachel Jackson
CWWC/WI Website Editor: Rachel Jackson

A CIP record of this book is available from The British Library.

ISBN 978-0-9568053-1-7

Introduction

T his first WI Memoir Journal has been a journey into the fascinating lives of more than 50 women and spans the last 80 years. The tales told in these pages not only span time but cultural, social and political eras, each one a recollection drawn from the memory of an individual whose broader experiences influence the telling. Inside this treasure chest are words of wisdom and wonder, of inspiration and aspiration. The stories provide us with detailed insights into the daily lives of women from the 1930s to the present day, so creating a rich historic resource. We are also privileged to meet a host of characters whose apparently ordinary lives are now documented for prosperity, whose effect on the writers herein has been life-affecting, altering and enhancing.

Certain themes replay: the austerity of the post-war years, the influence of teachers and mentors, the wonder of overseas travel before the arrival of the budget airlines, early career experiences, family customs and secrets. Love and loss play their part in some particularly poignant tales. Interestingly, in tone the stories share a certain stoicism, strength of character and empathy where they could readily have fallen prey to self- indulgence, melancholy or maudlin sentiment. Perhaps this has a lot to do with a strength of spirit amongst the collective women of the WI? There is a certain ability, that runs like a seam through the tales, to laugh at one's own weaknesses and to rejoice in the strength and generosity of others.

So how did this collection come into being? A group of women writers who met regularly around their kitchen tables started the process. The Contemporary Women Writers' Club comprises five writers, including two established novelists, who had for years shared their writing around one another's kitchen tables. As the digital revolution took hold, we collaborated to produce our own collections of short stories, The Leap Year (2009) and Ten Past Eight (2011). Publishing them under our own imprint, Queenbee Press and marketing and distributing them on the internet proved both commercially viable and creatively liberating.

This in turn led to an unanticipated level of media interest and invitations to discuss the books at festivals, libraries and clubs. One such invitation was from the WI in Cholsey, Oxfordshire. We shared the story of Queenbee Press and encouraged the women present to tell their own stories, starting with the premise: what story would you like to leave behind for your children to read about you? The evening was a great success and many personal memories were shared. After the meeting we contacted Ruth Bond, President of the NFWI, and suggested she collaborate with us to encourage women across the WIs to create their own writing groups. The CWWC would produce a bespoke memoir writing programme, accessible online, around which local WIs could start their own writing groups. The programme would provide inspiration, hints, exercises, advice and downloadable meeting notes. Queenbee press would publish the resulting memoirs in a book. And so this collection was born.

The project has been a labour of love by the members of the CWWC and their generous co-editors. It began with a rain-soaked journey to Dartington for The Telegraph literary festival, where we interviewed and filmed such luminary memoir writers as Helena Drysdale, Lynn Barber and Fay Weldon for the programme. We then got down to the intensive work of devising and writing the 8-part programme and produced the CWWC website to support the project. When the resulting manuscripts arrived, we garnered the support of two fantastic editors, David Chesterton and Katherine Williams, to help compile the collection.

Before we embarked upon this programme, we asked a very personal favour. One of our own mother's had never before put pen to paper to write a story but had always wanted to do so. We asked her if she would test the concept and follow the programme to write a memoir. She wrote the following piece. We think it shows the power and importance of writing from one's own life. We felt it only right that the collection should be prefaced by her memoir, to show the lasting power of the written word.

We hope you find as much enjoyment in reading these memoirs as we have had in helping them reach the light of day. And, if you haven't already, we'd encourage you to write your own story.

Lucy Cavendish, Miranda Glover, Rachel Jackson and Jennie Walmsley

2011

The Contemporary Women Writers' Club

Snapshots to Share
Lindsay Chesterton

My first memory is of lying under a mosquito net, looking at the fireflies. My mother had put them inside my net because I was afraid of the dark. Why couldn't she just have left the light on for me?

The reason was that we were in a Japanese Internment Camp in Manila, Philippines where we had been interned in 1942. How did the children have nets? Who were they provided by? I have no idea – one of the many unanswered questions from those early years.

We were in the camp, my father, mother, sister (aged 7) and I (aged 2 and a half) because we had been caught by the Japanese before we could flee to Australia, as so many luckier families managed to do. My father worked for Shell. He had been trying to shut down the oil refineries before the Japanese took Manila. However, they arrived before he was able to do so and we were trapped by the war in the Pacific.

My mother told me that the Japanese had ordered all civilians to report to the University of Santo Tomas so that the foreign civilian population could be listed. Everyone was told to bring enough food and clothing for 48 hours, after which it was assumed we could go back to our houses. Before we went to the University, my mother buried all her jewellery in the garden as a precaution. Sadly, when she looked for it after the war it had been stolen (how strange to think that, 70 years later, some woman is wearing it, with absolutely no idea of its history).

The 48 hours turned into three long years. I think that, as very small children do, I accepted it as a normal way to live. We had a small shack (apparently built by my father, as others also had done for their families). This, at least, afforded some privacy. We were allowed there during the day but were separated at night – the women and children in dormitories on one floor of the building and the men on another.

The only furniture I remember in our little shack, which was somewhere in the shanty town that had grown up in the University grounds, was a table made by my father. And a small, broken, china figure of a Dutch girl which my mother had found in the mud (my sister still has it to this day). The table had an oilskin cloth on it and I remember cutting a little strip off it to wrap round the doll. I also remember being smacked for doing so! Funny how all children remember perceived injustices.

We had a mango tree outside our shack as well. How eagerly I remember the four of us watching the one small mango ripening. My mother said, "Tomorrow, tomorrow it will be perfect and then we'll pick it". The next day came and – the mango had been stolen in the night. The disappointment was crushing, particularly for my mother who had desperately wanted her two small girls to have a treat.

I don't know how they managed to feed us. For a time the Filipinos used to put food through the wire for us but that was eventually stopped by the Japanese. The Red Cross parcels, so kindly sent, were very seldom distributed. People who had brought their dogs and cats into the camp, thinking they would only be there for the promised 48 hours, were reduced to eating them in desperation. There was, in any case, no extra food to feed them. My mother always said thank goodness we hadn't had a pet to bring in. She was soft hearted and thought she couldn't have brought herself to kill it. I think she would have changed her mind towards the end of our captivity when food rations were virtually stopped and the Japanese seemed to be trying to starve us all to death.

Water had to be boiled and always seemed too hot to drink and a thirsty child of three or four finds it hard to wait. I remember whinging about it for which, of course, I now feel ashamed.

I know my parents gave us the lion's share of whatever food there was. My mother nearly starved and weighed only six stone at the end of our enforced stay and my father wasn't much heavier.

I recall being sent, with my sister and lots of other children, to sit under trestle tables and gather up the potato peelings that were being dropped by the women peeling potatoes for the camp kitchens. It seemed like a game to us but I am sure they were put to good use by our mothers when we took them back to the huts.

As for us as children there was, I suppose, a degree of normality. I played with my friends, my sister played with hers. We still know three of them now and meet for a reunion once a year. The Japanese had apparently allowed the internees, most of whom were Americans, to organise schooling for the older children, teachers being among those captured, of course, as well as a make-shift hospital.

We small ones did just what small children do now, kept close to our mothers and ran about with our friends up and down the long dusty paths of the shanty town. The sight of a Japanese guard would send us scurrying back to the safety of our huts, having first bowed, a rule which was insisted upon.

I don't think my sister and I played together much. She was at school and, being four years older than I, seemed very grown up. I think, now, that it must have been much harder for her. She must have been far more aware than I of the dangers that faced us all.

So, life limped on, a huge daily struggle for the adults, a battle of survival for us all. Two Americans escaped and were brought back and shot in front of the internees. Food became even scarcer, the guards more brusque, people more debilitated and hope fading. There were those who died of malnutrition and disease. The Japanese cut down and cut down on the food given out. The war in the Pacific raged on, the Americans sweeping down towards

Manila although I was, naturally, unaware of any of it.

I do, however, vividly remember, as the Americans got closer, the stray shells (I don't know whether they were from American or Japanese guns) hitting the camp. The men's quarters were hit – my mother stood outside the building in total shock, holding me in her arms with my sister clutching her hand. And then, best of all, seeing my father coming down the steps towards us, dazed but not hurt. Unfortunately, not all were so lucky.

Just before liberation, we all fled to the compound and sat cowering and terrified with our backs to the walls for protection. The heavy guns were pounding while Manila, called then The Pearl of the Orient, went up in flames all around us. The Americans had apparently been warned by a Japanese informer in the camp (subsequently shot dead by the Japanese themselves when he was found out) that plans had been made to blow up the camp as the Americans got nearer. Everyone was to be killed. My parents told me later that bombs were, indeed, found placed strategically, ready to be detonated.

After the Americans finally took the camp and the Japanese either fled or surrendered, General MacArthur came in. What an amazing thing. I can remember it now, his promise of "I shall return", the crowds cheering, realisation that we were finally almost free setting in, no wonder we thought he was wonderful.

When the Americans pulled out to continue the fight, the Australians were deployed to look after us until arrangements could be made to repatriate us. We children loved them – so tall, so blonde, so well fed. They carried us on their shoulders, gave us sweets (what are they, we asked) and chewing gum. We must have looked like starving raggle-taggle gypsies as we followed them about adoringly. Unfortunately, they also gave out tins of baked beans to all internees, with predictable effect.

Eventually we were put onto troop ships and went in convoy to America, a dangerous trip in itself as Japan and Germany were still fighting the Allies. We were warned not to make any noise on deck and told not to throw anything overboard, in case it alerted the submarines lurking below. We children loved it, so much freedom, even though we were all piled in like sardines. After arriving in America, we had a five-day train journey from San Francisco (where my mother wasn't allowed off the train to see her sister, who had been waiting on the platform for ten hours), to Halifax, Nova Scotia where, finally, we caught a boat to England – to home.

Do I forgive the Japanese? No. Not for me, but for my parents. My mother's mother and my father's father both died when we were on our way back, not knowing that we were safe. My mother died when she was 54 partly, I am sure, because of the stress she had undergone.

As for me, the experience left me nervous and physically weak, prone to severe nightmares and sleepwalking, for much of my early years. I was terrified of thunder until well into my twenties which I now think subconsciously reminded me of the guns and flames at the end of our captivity.

Future Christmases were spoilt for me. On Christmas Eve when I was about 4, I woke up under my mosquito net in the women's dormitory and heard footsteps. I was absolutely convinced that it was Father Christmas with lots of presents, as the stories had said. It was, in fact, a Japanese guard on his rounds of the building, rifle by his side. As he marched by in his heavy boots, I shrank back with fright and disappointment. I have never felt the same anticipation and magic again.

So............why have I written this? Because I never asked my father and mother how they had felt, how they had coped and it's now too late. Because I want my children and grandchildren to understand what helped to make me who I am before they, too, say – I wish I'd asked her before it was too late.

Contents

Part 4 - Passions and Aspirations

Part 5 - We Did It Our Way

Part 6 - Inspiring People

Part 1

Growing Up

Boarding School In Tanganyika

Veronica Wood

(Brightwell cum Sotwell)

Part of my childhood was spent in Tanganyika, East Africa where my father worked as a civil servant. At a young age, in the 1950s, I was sent to an "up-country" boarding school.

W ham! I hit the metal bar running. My head swam. I truly saw stars. Across my forehead an elongated bar-shaped welt was already rising. I still clung, with one hand, to the skirt of my grubby white sports dress in which there was a handful of small under-ripe peaches, spoils from a forbidden garden. If we were caught we would be caned.

I was at school; more precisely I was at Mbeya European Primary Boarding School in the Mbeya Region of Tanganyika, now Tanzania, not too far from the borders of Zambia and Malawi. I was there between the age of eight and eleven in the early to mid 1950s, a shy girl, some would say too young to be at a boarding school, which had two long terms a year. But I was not alone, for the school gathered children from the whole Southern region as well as a few day girls and boys.

To reach this outpost from Dar es Salaam where I lived, involved a journey of two nights and a day. We were delivered to the station, when the brief African dusk had already turned to night, like little parcels, to be handed over by our parents and placed, four or more, into the bunk-bedded compartments of the train which snorted hot grey-white clouds of smoke down the platform. Before sleeping we hung out of the windows getting smuts in our eyes, already adjusting to a life away from home. I think we sometimes shared bunks because I remember one occasion when we made a younger girl sleep on the floor in a nest of blankets because she generally wet her bed. The minimal supervision that we had enabled us to get away with this.

The train would chug and snort rhythmically through the night and when it stopped at halts, often to take on water, we were jerked awake to hear the hiss of steam, voices calling in Swahili, and the never-ceasing chirp of crickets, a sound so evocative of African nights. And then on again it would go, picking up a few more children on the way, a pied piper train heading for the uplands.

We were woken, bleary-eyed, in a grey dawn and bundled out when the train pulled into Itigi, a wild west town in the red earth scrubland of central Tanganyika. Two iron rails snaking to the horizon, a scattering of sheds and a small white Rest House with corrugated roof and wide veranda. Here we spent the whole day, the fear of being bitten by tsetse flies, which cause sleeping sickness, preventing us from continuing our journey until darkness fell. We sprawled in the shade of the Rest House; we put our ears to the railway lines to listen for trains. "Don't wander too far, kids," they said. But where to? There was nowhere to go.

At dusk we were loaded into two or three rackety buses. As we travelled, we sang. Two favourites were 'Ten green bottles' and 'We'll be coming round the mountain', familiar songs known to us all. Later we dozed through the long night, with occasional stops for children to vomit onto the verges (for the buses bounced us about unremittingly) or a longer stop when, after discharging a mass of steam from its engine as it had laboured up the escarpment, one bus broke down, and we either waited for a replacement or were herded into the remaining ones, squashed side by side like kernels on a maize cob.

Daybreak brought breakfast at a farmstead outside Chunya and then on again to school where, arriving grubby and tired, we were sent to bed. I remember waking on one occasion to find that my case had been unpacked and that I had missed the first meal, the one where we were allocated places. Throughout that whole term I had to hover at the edge of the dining room waiting to find somewhere to sit down where someone was absent.

The school buildings seemed to sprawl over a vast area - classrooms, hall, dormitories, sick bay, staff houses and the huge sports fields which were partitioned by thick belts of fir trees. There we built dens, and hoped we might meet German spies, for the site was a school and camp when the territory was under German control. No mysterious strangers intercepted us with secret messages but we did turn up the odd wartime relic.

The dormitories were long and narrow with two rows of little beds separated by table-height lockers. The Matron's room was at the end. The beds had hard mattresses which we turned regularly and, like army recruits, we would stand at the end of the beds when our lockers were inspected. Bathrooms had three baths in a row and as so many of us had verrucas, we would have to sit on the edges of the baths with our feet in water coloured purple by potassium permanganate. Warts on hands were also a problem and we hated holding hands with anyone who had them.

At the beginning of each week the girls were handed out white "sports dresses" each with a band of colour on the belt denoting which house we belonged to; I was in Stanley which was blue. These communal garments were distributed according to size and were worn during play-time. I don't remember wearing any other uniform, although later I realised that we did have one.

The curriculum was reminiscent of a boys' prep school in the UK. We were generally called by our surnames and had our own language: to warn friends that staff were approaching we hissed twice, loud and long, "kush, kush", followed by the word "cavey", from the Latin for "beware", a language which we were learning at school.

The regime was a strange mixture of freedom and discipline. Only the kitchen garden was out-of-bounds but even during our sneaky visits there we usually evaded officialdom. Tree climbing was an acceptable pastime. I loved this and was better than the boys, a fact of which I was very proud. We would bag a good seat in the forks where the slender branches met and swing in the wind. Then there was the wheel, a large metal object, 6ft high at least, outer rims joined together by half a dozen bars. Round and round it would go making its laborious way down the slope, a small child spread-eagled within.

On Sundays we went down to the river, a wild, fun place where we roamed freely in and out of the rushing stream, making dams and soaking our white canvas tackies and dresses. One day one of my tackies was carried away by the swirling water and I was somehow able to get away with this loss for the rest of the term, even at the end when I craftily packed the remaining shoe in my suitcase as though it was a pair. My concern at hiding this misdemeanour leads me to think that I might have been worried about getting a black mark. Too many of these could invoke a caning by the headmaster. These were regular affairs. The miscreants were called to his house, and either received a few lashes with the springy cane on their hands or were bent over a chair and given "six of the best". As with so many things considered to be a punishment - and the canings did hurt - there was a certain amount of pride in showing your friends the parallel red welts neatly displayed across your bottom.

As the school area was large, and we were often playing in the fields, we were summoned to meals by the loud and rhythmic beating of an African drum. Mealtimes were strict. We were not allowed ever to leave anything, so breakfast was an agony as we were served with lumpy porridge every morning which I hated and which made me gag. If we were lucky we could get the server at the end of the table to put just a little on our plates and then we would smear it around as though we had had a plateful. Lumpy mashed potatoes and the glutinous mass of tree tomatoes were other unpleasant experiences.

During Easter, although some of the more local children did go home, many of us stayed at school, and on one memorable occasion another girl and I were invited out to a farm for lunch. We were given what I remember as being one of the most delicious meals of my life. I don't know what we had, only that it was a buffet of such variety, colour and taste that I have never forgotten my astonishment and pleasure. Perhaps it was just in contrast to our daily fare.

On Sunday evenings we would go to the headmaster's house for a story. How the whole school was accommodated for this ritual I don't know, but I remember girls and boys sitting cross legged in his lounge before bedtime and being read a chapter or two, while he sipped at his pink gin. This was how I was introduced to the Swallows and Amazons books and I particularly remember the story of "Missie Lee".

Like all children we had our crazes, but access to shop-bought toys was limited and so we had to use our ingenuity and make most things ourselves. Once a year, during the windy season, kite flying was popular and competitive, and we made our kites from paper and sticks and whatever string we could get hold of. Another time paper doll-making was a craze for the girls and I was lucky to have a friend who was a brilliant drawer. I believe she became an artist in later life, and she was able to make cut-out dolls of all shapes and sizes, from babies to teenagers and with all the clothes to match.

We would amuse ourselves in other ways too. We would barter for chameleons from the local villagers. As we understood that these poor creatures could swim, we would put them into the cloakroom wash basins and watch them frantically splash around in the water. One year, when we were perhaps nine or ten, we were taken on a hiking adventure. We passed along winding bush paths, through plots of maize, far taller than ourselves, and through rutted fields of vegetables. In the villages of mud huts and wide-leafed banana plants, scrawny chickens scattered at our approach, and children, with skins smooth and bare and dusty brown from playing in the dirt, ran up to us with curiosity. We were headed for Mbeya Peak and the source of a stream. Our excited anticipation was fed by a delicious rumour: that lemonade would gush out of the hillside into our greedy little mouths. To children fed on a dull and rigid diet the very word "lemonade" conjured up an unimaginable delight. Imagination is a wonderful thing and when we eventually reached the mineral water spring which spurted into a stony pool, some of us were convinced that it did indeed taste sweet and fizzy.

Our day got even better when one poor boy was bitten by a snake and the headmaster's wife, who was escorting us, immediately sucked out the venom and spat. We were fascinated by this repetitive process of suck, spit, suck, spit, no doubt hoping that our companion would turn blue and provoke a real emergency. However he survived and was able to walk back.

When I left Mbeya it was not the end of my boarding school days for at the age of eleven, in complete contrast, I was sent to a girls' boarding school in England. But that is another story.

Red Hat, No Knickers

Rosemary Greasby

(Brightwell cum Sotwell)

*I was born into a farming family in Brightwell.
It was here, in St. Agatha's Church my baptism,
confirmation and marriage took place. In my late
teens I pursued a nursing career in London. Ten
years later I returned to the village with my husband
to continue farming and raise our four children.*

T hunder crashed, and a billowing black cloud chased us as we stumbled and tripped over mole hills and rabbit holes across the Horsecroft and Haycroft, making our way back to the farm. "Wait for me, my legs are shorter than yours." Tomorrow was Mothering Sunday and my sister Gillian aged ten, a big four years older than I was, had been put in charge of picking our posies of cowslips. Gleefully we had gathered the multitude of dainty little blooms, dripping yellow and swinging off their pale green slender stems. A mattress of cowslips stretched the full length of Long Meadow. This was our golden haven situated in the Thames Valley under the protection of the Berkshire Downs and the Sinodun Hills.

My village had now settled down after the losses of the Second World War. The Italian prisoners, who were the labour force on the farms, had all returned to their homes. Elizabeth our new

27

Queen was on the throne. Brightwell was a village of gurgling springs and gardens with redundant wells.

The distinctive brick tower of St. Agatha guarded the parish. Her bells rang out, joyfully exclaiming to all villagers when it was Sunday. The tenor bell would follow solemnly for ten minutes, warning parishioners Matins would commence in quarter of an hour. Five minutes to go, and the Sacristan bell, affectionately known as the Ting Tang, would ting tang merrily, hurrying the footsteps to the Church door. I skipped along, wearing my new brown Clarks sandals with neatly cut out shapes over the toes. My old red sandals would be having the end of the toe area cut out, so I could still wear them for play.

Blonde curls bounced as I swung between my parents' hands. Late-comers to Church were not welcomed. Reverend and Mrs. Walton scared me. The Rector was stern. Mrs. Walton wore black-rimmed glasses and a large black hat. We filed into the family pew, where my grandparents and great grandparents had previously sat. Craning my neck around I viewed the congregation.

There would always be Mr. Crauford Inge from the Manor, Mrs. Annie Foster, and Mrs. Heyworth the schoolmaster's wife. Mr. Heyworth would be in the choir as he was also the choirmaster. I always hoped to see a red hat and quietly giggle as it was a well known fact that 'ladies in red hats' didn't wear knickers.

My sister was a choir girl. I wanted to be a choir girl and wear a flowing black gown and have a star shaped hat perching on my head so all the congregation could look at me as I processed up the aisle. It was an unrealised dream. I was bluntly told I could not sing. As the service rolled around me, up and over me, I stood and knelt and held my hymn book and dreamt of being a choir girl.

Dreaming was interrupted with 'Our Father who art in heaven', which I was able to chant, and then I would listen to the Nunc Dimittis and the Magnificat. When we reached the words 'He hath filled the hungry with good things', my mouth watered as I thought about Sunday lunch and the block of vanilla ice cream which would soon be evenly sliced before being carefully sandwiched between two wafers.

I look back wearing rose-coloured spectacles. I see the 'Darling Buds of May', not the reality of long, hard hours of work in order to make a living. Auntie Alice and Uncle Jack were tenant farmers on the Mapledurham Estate. Whittles Farm was a lonesome settlement snuggling into the Chiltern Hills. The dark farmhouse kitchen - the hub of the house - was where shafts of sunlight leapt from the hills and streaked through the small square window above the sink.

When we made our frequent Sunday visits to Mapledurham (whether by invitation or my mother's "we were just passing by," made no difference) the welcome was profuse. Cakes miraculously appeared on the large farmhouse kitchen table, chocolate, fruit, and Victoria Sponges with a central crown of glistening white meringues filled with fresh cream straight from the dairy. There was no refrigerator but the walk-in pantry was cold enough to give rise to goose pimples.

It was isolated, but full of life. Auntie Alice and Uncle Jack had four daughters in quick succession, Pamela, Angela, Sheila and Paula, all with their long, enviable plaits. Also a large golden Labrador called Judith and Darkie the New Forest pony, whom I eventually inherited.

Some 22 cats roamed Whittles farm but only the favoured few were allowed over the threshold. Bread and milk wobbled from side to side of the pan as I gingerly trod across their farmyard desperate not to spill the delectable supper for these feline friends. Blacks, Gingers and Tabbies appeared from all directions, over stable doors, under gates and from behind staddle stones. Squatting, I watched the furious competitive lapping until the bowls all sparkled. Then the cats returned to their favourite sheltered haunts for the licking of paws and washing of faces in the fading sunlight.

Some would stretch out and laconically watch me in the paddock learning to ride. I went from bouncing like a sack of potatoes to learning the skill of a rising trot – straight back, heels down and Darkie and I were like dance partners waltzing around the paddock.

Back in Brightwell, smells of newly-baked bread often drifted through the kitchen door. Crumbs needed to be dusted off my green cable-fronted cardigan as I crunched my way through the freshly baked tommy loaf – this was a 'dog end' of dough left over from the morning work at the bakehouse. These little loaves were handed out free to any passing child, but as I lived opposite I had an unfair advantage.

Sitting on the wall swinging my legs, munching a tommy loaf with Grampy next to me, was a frequent pastime. Grampy suffered from dementia and would enjoy breaking into song to any passer-by. "Come and sit down on the sofa, love, and kiss me once or twice" or "Daisy, Daisy give me your answer do …I'm half crazy all for the love of you." My mother would cringe with embarrassment, but it didn't worry me. Three times a week he would buy a small bar of chocolate for me, my sister and three cousins. No wonder I enjoyed sitting next to him whilst he packed and chewed his pipe and sang.

On their way down to the farm, Shady (Shadrack being his baptismal name), Midge, with his built up boot, Whip, who always wore a sack tied around his waist, and Duke would all stop and talk with him. These village characters all worked on the farm, from driving the grey Fergie tractor to cleaning out the pig sties.

Living opposite the bakehouse was a great childhood privilege and the envy of perhaps more needy children. The enormous, traditional coal-fired ovens used by three previous generations of bakers were an asset to the villagers, for apart from the daily fresh bread, large joints of meat could be cooked after the morning bake.

Queenie, Stan and Stan the younger all ran the business. To recover from the heat and hard work, Queenie would spend

seemingly hours standing outside just smiling and nodding. I think
she enjoyed watching me play 'pretend ponies' as I sat astride
the high wall with its coping ridge. This was my horse and the
adjoining smaller wall was my pony. Queenie's arms were neatly
crossed and tucked beneath her bosoms and she always wore what
seemed to be the same floral wrap-over apron. Her dark brown
plaited hair was neatly folded over the top of her head. I had no
idea of her age. I thought she was old, but there was not a grey
hair in the intriguing plaits. Stan would often come and stand by
her, wearing his flat cap and camel serge apron.

Bread was delivered to our back door three times a week, even
though we were only divided by the village road. My mother
frequently had the audacity to complain to Stan, after he had
lugged his large rectangular wicker basket full of cottage loaves
to the farmhouse, "The crusts are black and far too burnt, Stan."
They often were, but we were used to them. "The air holes are
ridiculously large" – she thought paying for air was a waste of
money, but Dad loved it that way, the larger the holes the more
butter he could use to fill them.

Our dairy farm didn't produce butter, but it supplied the village
and all the surrounding villages with a daily delivery of fresh milk
on their doorsteps. The farm was not a 'free for all' playground – it
could be a dangerous place. Being allowed to help gave us an air of
importance. I would clutch a bendy stick and walk in silence with
my uncle. A sharp swish of tails interrupted the silence. Monica,
Phyllis, Daisy, and Daphne rhythmically lumbered along the well-
trodden track with the rest of the Friesian herd, moving in a well-
engrained routine from the lush spring grazing of Rushy Meadow
to their familiar milking parlour in the traditional buildings of the
Dairy Farm.

Collecting the household milk was my daily job. The twisted metal
crate clanked with empty bottles as I sauntered down to the dairy.
The dairy, which had a distinctive smell of cleanliness, contained
large tanks of fresh frothy milk. As I waited to collect my newly
filled bottles I played a game of pretend ponies, using three milk
churns and a length of rope for the reins.

31

Daily milk was needed for our household - father, mother, sister Gillian, myself and Smoky the cat. Five pints were consumed each day. Custard, blancmange (white and pink), rice pudding, porridge and milky drinks were all part of our regular diet. Gently I would place in the crate five chunky glass bottles full of fresh white milk, each topped off with rich golden cream and crowned with a glistening silver cap. Scarlet writing on the side of the bottle boldly advertised 'Everex Bros', Brightwell Dairy Farm. Lugging them home the full length of the drive was hard labour for a little girl. Every few paces I would stop and change hands as the metal handle dug red grooves across my palms.

I am a dairy farmer's daughter who loves cows yet dislikes milk. One frosty morning a hatred of raw milk that was to last all my life overpowered me. This had nothing to do with poor Daphne or Daisy but with a monstrous cast iron stove situated in the school classroom. On that wintry morning, the compulsory government child's allowance of milk filled the stubby bottles standing to attention like toy soldiers, surrounding and guarding the hot circular furnace where the milk gradually warms and thickens, warmer and warmer as break time approaches. The forced consumption of this nauseous sweetness and the shining globules of fat - some floating and others fixed to the side of bottle - remain clinging to my memory. I soon learned the art of taking a deep breath and downing my third of a pint in one go, followed by dashing to the playground whilst reaching for fresh air. The playground was full of laughter and I skipped through my formative years, chanting rhymes such as 'Brightwell, Sotwell, Merry Mackney, lousy old Cholsey is worse than all three'. One day the 'Big City' called and lured me. When the dazzling lights faded I returned to farm the Sinodun Hills with my husband. The Dairy Farm has now been replaced with large houses. But my grandchildren can still fish for minnows in the meadowlands crisscrossed with waterways - and Gillian and I will never forget how wearing a red hat can make a little girl giggle.

Transition Through Childhood

Jill Fenn

(Burghill)

Born in London in 1932, I lived in Surrey from the age of five. I missed a lot of schooling due to the war. I taught art and ran my own bead shop for 25 years. Now retired, I have three children and one grandchild. My hobbies are gardening, book club, genealogy, walking my dog and gold work embroidery.

Faster and faster went the wheels of the tricycle: little white boots moving up and down, up and down, the pedals turning with single-minded determination. Now the wide tree-lined black promenade began to slope downhill and I was travelling faster still. Not for one moment was I afraid. A steely determination was driving me forward. I had to reach my destination and nothing was going to stop me.

I was oblivious to the frenzied cries of my poor Granny, "Jill, Jill, wait, wait for me, come back, come back!" And soon I was out of sight and a frantic grandmother, hurrying as best she could, stopped now and then to ask the old women seated on the park benches if they had seen a little four-year-old speeding past on her tricycle. "Yes, yes that way," they replied. My grandmother was not usually in sole charge of me, but today was different - very different. Although I was unaware of it at the time, my mother had been taken into hospital five days before in labour with my brother, and still had not given birth. Granny must have already been consumed with worry, and now to add to her problems she had lost her only granddaughter.

The family had moved from their Surrey home to a flat overlooking Battersea Park. Daily, my mother and I crossed the road into the park through the big black iron gates, passing the gaunt hurdy-gurdy man and his starving monkey and the gold-tipped railings. It was an idyllic place for a small child to roam, with wide, flat, tree-lined paths, perfect for cycling in safety, and a lake, ducks and acres of neatly manicured grass and no shortage of friends to play with. Mothers with toddlers sat on the green painted iron benches and talked in hushed tones of royalty and death and of an American woman whose name was only whispered, while the children threw balls, and skipped, and talked of things that only children understand.

The sun always shone as I clutched in my hand a paper bag full of the leftovers from breakfast. Leaning over the low hoops of railings, I threw the crumbs towards the orange-billed ducks waddling on the grassy edge or into the water where the tail-in-the-air ducks dived and swam. I existed then in a mixture of reality and the imagination of a four year old fuelled by the stories of Kenneth Grahame's 'Wind in the Willows' and the works of A.A. Milne. I knew some of their poems off by heart. Battersea Lake was the 'backwater' of 'Ducks' Ditty' and the surrounding grass was its 'rushes tall'. The trees of Battersea were home to 'Wol', and at their feet prowled a 'bear of very little brain'. 'Eeyore' was being miserable by the lake and I probably thought I was Christopher Robin. Battersea Park was my familiar playground, my back garden. No wonder it held no fears for me even though I had not set eyes on Mummy for five days and Granny was nowhere to be seen.

Speeding down the wide promenade, I passed the regiment of professionally-trained nursery nurses, wearing their belted and buckled uniforms like a badge of honour, marching with their heads held high as if on the parade ground, their highly polished shoes showing as much 'spit-and-polish' as any member of the forces. They guided their charges with pride in their immaculately maintained prams, each a status symbol as much as any car would be today. Navy blue carriage built chaises, high, elegant wheels and matching hoods kept their occupants warm and snug in winter. In summer the babies were bathed in jungle - cool light from the green lined canopies, the fringes blowing coolly in the breeze.

Now that I was nearing my destination, I was excited with anticipation. I went down the slope and out of the sunlight into the shade of the tall leaf-laden trees. For a moment, the sudden change of light confused me. Where was it, that dark, black, smoke-belching, fire-eating giant that I had expected to see? What had happened to the acrid choking smell of tar, the flames and the heat? Where were the crowds of small children, peaking from behind Nanny's skirts, half excited, half afraid, watching this black monster with its vast wheels moving slowly and deliberately across the concourse flattening all in its path? Now all was empty and desolate. The steamroller had gone. Suddenly I was alone, frightened and missing my mother. I turned, looked up and there was Granny, relief on both our faces. "I thought I had lost you. Come on now before you give me any more frights: and you've got a baby brother waiting to say "hello" to when we get home."

Back in the flat, a tall woman, the 'monthly nurse' bent down towards me holding a bundle in her arms. Even at four, I realized that some comment on my part was called for but all I could see were folds of a woolly blanket. "He's very nice," was all I could manage and returned to my toys. But from that moment, my world had changed. Now I was to share a bedroom with the new nanny. Not for us the brown uniformed Norland Nurses – we had to make do with Mother's Helps from rural Ireland. Young, naïve and inexperienced, what knowledge they had of childcare was probably gained from caring for their younger siblings. My mother trained them and provided their uniform. When they left, which they did all too frequently, the uniforms went with them. At night, I woke to hear Nanny's homesick sobbing and to see my dressing-gowned mother sitting on the side of the bed struggling to comfort her.

What could my mother know or understand of this young girl's loneliness, hundreds of miles away from the Connemara of her childhood, of the peat fires of her family thatched cottage, of the rocky open space surrounding it and the smell of the sea and the wide-open sky above? London must have been a terrifying place, with its strange ways, its noise and bustle, its trams and buses and above all its smog. These girls were floundering in a strange and unfamiliar society. They arrived as obedient little Catholic girls in awe of the parish priest. Their social lives revolved around the church. But it was here that they met older and more experienced girls and it was not long before, the bright lights of London began to have their attraction, all homesickness forgotten. More exciting forms of employment than nappy washing soon attracted them and off they went. A new nanny would arrive, new uniforms would be ordered, and my mother would begin the training all over again.

On one occasion I was given a sixpence owed to the cook and told to take it to her in the kitchen but she never received it. Mother and Cook talked and puzzled while I looked on in silence. I gave no answer to the repeated questions and so the mystery might have remained forever. The tale was often recounted but never solved. Many years later, by now a granny herself, my mother was swapping amusing stories of children with her friends. Turning to me, she said,

"I gave you the sixpence to give to the maid."

"Yes, I remember. I did give it to her."

"Well, she never received it. To this day I don't know where it went."

"Oh! But I do!"

There was a sudden hush, all eyes turned in my direction.

"You know where it is?"

"Yes. I've always known where it was."

"Why didn't you tell us at the time? What did you do with it?"

"It's probably still where I put it!" I said with a laugh.

"Where?"

"In the key hole!"

The keyhole! What keyhole?

"The kitchen door."

"Why? Why would you do that?"

"I posted it!"

"Posted it? What do you mean?"

"Posted it to the maid, pretending to be a postman. The postman put letters in a slot in the door. So I did the same. I put the sixpence in a slot in the door."

"You swore you had given it to the maid."

"Well, I had, if you asked the postman if he had given the letters to you he would probably have said 'Yes' wouldn't he?"

My mother looked at me with blank amazement.

"I suppose so but it's not quite the same."

"It was exactly the same to a four year old. That's how I had worked it out with a child's logic. So we were both telling the truth."

Silently gazing at each other, none of them could think of a reply to such innocent common sense. Then laughter broke the silence. The 'mystery of the missing sixpence' had been solved.

There were many attractions around London, but the one I most vividly remember is the visit to my father at Watney's Stag Brewery at Victoria, where he was head brewer. We would pass through the great arched gateway, across wet cobbles smelling of farms, to the foot of his private iron stairs where, clambering up to his office, we would be greeted by an unfamiliar figure clad in white overalls. My eyes ran across the glass-fronted mahogany cupboards filled with pipettes and other strange shaped bottles. On his large wooden desk were other weird implements. One looked like a very large thermometer. It reminded me of the contents of the white-gaitered doctor's bag for the inoculation of my baby brother. I was fascinated by the great old stone building, full of dark corners, strange sounds and even stranger smells. Everywhere was wet and steamy. I stared down through iron gratings and open metal walkways onto the churning, steaming vats of beer below, a cauldron of thick, bubbling, grey froth. Occasionally a thin feral cat would brush past in the gloom, as dark and mysterious as any witch's familiar. The noise of glass bottles crashing and rattling on their moving conveyor belt echoed around dark corners, gangplanks and stairs. It was a world where one could believe in witches and goblins, magic and mayhem.

However, it was not long before the outside world began to penetrate the cosy family life. Gathering round the radio, grown-ups began talking, whispering. When they handled a coin with the king's head, "He's dead," they said. I was given a mug with another king's head, then a blue chocolate tin with another king and a queen as well. A party, a new coat, "Just like the princesses," they said. They spoke of waiting for someone to open a bridge - but he only cut a ribbon. The security of family life and my own make-believe world were giving way to a puzzling reality of adults who spoke in hushed voices of things only half understood.

Leaving behind the attractions of the ducks in the park, the hurdy-gurdy man with his chained monkey, dancing classes, visits to the zoo, shopping at Harrods and all the other excitements London had to offer, the day came when we left to return to Surrey. Soon I started school, walking each day with pride in my royal blue blazer with the silver star embroidered on the pocket. My life had settled into a secure routine again, but it was not to last. On a holiday one summer the news was disturbing. The country was at war. My much-loved nanny, Julie, this one from Holland, decided to return home. My mother tried to dissuade her, but to no avail. I have a picture of the two of us sitting affectionately side by side on the sand, contented and at ease. She was the last of my nannies. Two days later, she was gone. We never heard from her again.

Nits

Joy Millernas

(Stock Harvard)

My love of words began when I was a small rebellious child and continues today. Reading took me into a magical world away from the weary conditions of post-war Britain. I live in an Essex village. My hobbies include watercolours, gardening, studying and enjoying my six grandchildren.

I felt hot. The sun was shining through the tall glass window and I could see the dust motes dancing in the air. If I concentrated on them and not on the flashes of light coming off the steel comb as it rose and fell, I could perhaps control my churning stomach. It was just after dinnertime and the queue of children snaked all around the school hall. A hint of stew, floor varnish, sweaty plimsolls and chalk lingered in the air.

It was early summer 1953, the year of the Queen's Coronation, and I was 10. A school trip to the Isle of Wight was to take place for the classes soon to depart to secondary education. Those of us who had never experienced a holiday before were twitchy with excitement. It bubbled under the surface of our daily life. In Greenwich, where I lived, a holiday to most children I knew meant spending a few days with relatives, hop-picking in Kent or a Sunday school outing if we were lucky. Preparation for our school trip included learning the geography of the island, complying with the clothing list which only allowed three dresses for a fortnight, and a head inspection by 'Nitty Nora' the school nurse, which was now taking place. Her comb was dipped into a bowl of disinfectant between heads and it was now coming nearer to me.

It was over. I had been pulled closely to the nurse's body and could hear the crackles her starchy uniform made and smell the Lux soap she used. My head had been pushed to one side then the other, hairline inspected and hair combed through with the torture implement. My hair was short, so the experience was over quickly, but those girls with long plaits had to unravel one to allow exploration of the long strands. For once I didn't envy their flowing tresses, and my pulse rate gradually slowed.

I couldn't understand why I got so upset about this procedure. Maybe it was the way my Mum and other mothers said things like, "Keep away from that Pat Jones, she's not clean." Pat looked alright to me, her cotton dresses were clean and her socks didn't have 'spuds' in them like mine sometimes did. So maybe mothers could see things we children couldn't. After all, they're renowned for having eyes in the back of their heads.

I thought I could forget about it all now but my exuberance didn't last long. Later in the afternoon I was called quietly to one side by my teacher and given a brown envelope to hand to my mother. I felt the contents held some kind of awful news, and I imagined all sorts of scenarios. Perhaps I had the dreaded ringworm in my head and I would have to go around sporting a large spot of gentian violet painted on my skull. As I neared home I dragged my sandals and scuffed the toes so that the leather lost its colour. Anything was better than handing over the envelope. My friend Claire, a plump girl with a kind face, whose smocked gingham dresses were always stretched tightly across her chest and Peter Pan collars curled up under her chubby chin, was sympathetic.
"Perhaps your Mum hasn't paid up properly for the holiday."
"Yes she has because I take it in every week."
"P'rhaps it's because you're tiny and don't look big enough to go."

"Maggie Brown's smaller than me – she didn't get one."
We explored and exhausted all avenues and I knew eventually I had
to go indoors. The letter was opened. I watched my mother's face
blanch, and my heart started pumping again. What was wrong?

No explanations were given. I was given sixpence and sent
immediately to the local shop for a shampoo. This came in a small
paper packet, the contents of which were dissolved in warm water.
Water had been boiled in the kettle on the gas stove, the only source
of hot water in our household except on washdays and bath night
when the 'copper' was lit. My head was scrubbed hard and I
thought my eyes would soon pop out under the pressure of
Mum's fingers.

Newspaper had been spread in advance covering the kitchen table.
My mother produced a small toothed comb, and my head was
bent forward over the newspaper and combed through in every
direction. The newspaper was inspected repeatedly, and then she
walked her fingers through my soaking hair.
"What are you looking for, Mum?"
"Nits," was the reply, and her tears began to fall. "I don't know
where you've picked them up from - I try to keep you as clean as
I can."
I certainly didn't know, but at last I knew what the problem was.
I suddenly heard a crunch as Mum's nails pushed together. "Got
one," she exclaimed.
My hair was left to dry. Water dripped onto the towel encasing my
shoulders. I didn't like flipping nits if they caused this much trouble.

The nightmare continued. At school Nitty Nora inspected my
short blonde hair again and my head was given the thumbs down.
Those blooming nits were still there. Another envelope was issued,
but this time for the Cleansing Station. More tears erupted from
Mum's eyes.

In preparation for this event I was scrubbed from top to bottom,
standing naked in an enamel bowl of warm water placed in a
corner of the kitchen, a small dark windowless room off the

scullery in the old terraced regency house we rented. Bodies were not to be seen in this state, and our scullery had a glass roof. Occasionally Randy Dan from next door could be seen at an upstairs window peering down when we bathed there in our tin bath, and Dad would go outside and shake his fist up at him. Mum wasn't having any of that this time, especially not with nits around.

I was told not to tell anyone where I was going. The shame began to envelope me and I became nervous. Could people see these things in my head? Would my friends still speak to me if they knew I had them, and would they call me dirty too? After all Mum had said only dirty people got nits, like poor Pat Jones.
I rebelled against going.
"Don't want to go."
"You've got to."
"Why?"
"Because I say so. Don't keep on. You're doing me nerves in."

These nerves seem to come up frequently. I knew Mum had a hard time of it and she struggled to make ends meet. In winter her hands would turn white with cold because she didn't have any gloves. I vowed that when I started work the first thing I'd buy would be a warm pair of mittens for her. My dad drank a lot and that caused arguments and a continuing air of tension, and my brother Donald was away in a TB sanatorium. Betty, my elder sister by 12 years, had been away with TB too, but was now cured, married and living in the upstairs top two rooms with her husband and new baby. I wondered if I'd get nerves when I grew up.

I certainly felt nervous now at the Cleansing Station. I held on tightly to Mum's hand as we walked in. It was a low, dark, one storey building. The windows were covered in frosted glass reinforced with wire. The walls were painted a muddy green colour, and the building smelt of disinfectant mixed with a peculiar acrid undertone. This was probably due to the various creams and potions that were applied to impetigo, ringworm, scabies and, of course, head lice.
We sat in the waiting room on benches attached to the walls. Just

as my name was called, Beattie Cox from the next road walked in, alone. She was the youngest of a large family whose mother had died, and they were struggling to keep things going. She saw my mother's anguished face and said "Don't worry Mrs Hunter, Joyce will be alright, the ladies will look after her." I was pleased to see Beattie because it meant I was not the only one with these blasted crawlers living in my hair, and she had obviously been there before.

Mum was not to be comforted. This place epitomised everything that she had fought against, the shame of being thought 'dirty' by her working class neighbours. In this post-war era where people had little money, lived in cramped conditions and often hand to mouth, pride was taken in keeping what little possessions you had clean. There was an unspoken standard that housewives adhered to usually involving soap and water. Bed linen was boiled and 'blued', curtains were hung in neat folds, children were scrubbed, shoes were polished and dirt was the enemy. Nits were dirt. Her tears were now falling like a tap that wouldn't stop dripping. They ran down her face and into the crevices of her mouth which was opened in a silent wail.

I was fed up with this. Why was she crying and moaning? I was the one with the little bleeders in my head. This indignation carried me into the next room, where I was met by two stout ladies whose bodies were enveloped in huge white pinafores that crossed over their ample chests. They reminded me of my aunts who were all the same shape. I was led to a huge butler sink attached to the wall and sat on the stool provided. My head was again washed, pummelled and covered in an evil smelling lotion. A final wash and rinse ended my ordeal.
In the waiting room Mum was given a small bottle of lotion. "Now, Mother, if she starts scratching her head put this on immediately."

The bottle lived on a crowded shelf in our scullery. It was needed occasionally whenever I was spotted scratching my head. I hated this stuff: it smelt awful and I was sure that when I sat cross-legged on the hall floor in Assembly everyone else could smell it too. One day in Assembly the ginger-haired boy who sat in front of me had an insect crawling in his head. I watched fascinated and felt reassured because obviously his nits were much bigger than mine.

Mum's shame and nervousness continued and I was told to report to her any time I felt an itch in my head. A few weeks later we were on a bus to take us to Blackheath where two of my aunts lived. These were weekly visits where my mum could chat and get sympathy or advice from her sisters. She was the youngest of seven surviving children and most of the family still lived in the Greenwich area.

The red double-decker bus was full to the brim. The only seats left were at the front of the lower deck which Mum took, while I was squashed on the bench seat at the back near the conductor. I was looking at his machine that punched holes in the bus tickets when suddenly I felt an itch. What should I do? The school journey was getting nearer and I definitely didn't want to be excluded. I decided that I must obey the instructions I'd been given. So I shouted out, "Mum, me head's itching again."
The bus went quiet. Heads turned and all eyes were on me. I could see Mum's face redden from where she sat. Oh no, I'd done it again. I'd have to put up with all that weeping and wailing again. It wasn't my fault they liked my hair, was it? I was dragged off the bus at the stop, and I thought as I was heaved along by the collar of my blazer, that it would be good, sometimes, to be bald.

Say 'nits' to me now, and I itch!

A Close Call
Jenny Harris
(Hawkesbury & Horton)

I am 66 years old and live with my husband Tony in the Cotswolds. We have a daughter, Victoria, who teaches in London. I have always loved writing, and an A Level in English Literature in 1998 led to a degree course with the Open University, from which I graduated in 2008.

The black kitten yawned and opened his startling blue eyes wide. My mother and I lay with him on my dad's bunk feeling ill and weak. At last the wind had dropped and the ship had stopped its constant pitching and tossing as it battled through the waves. We had set sail from Portland Bill in Dorset a few days earlier in sunny weather, but as we headed north for the Scottish islands, storm clouds appeared and the sea became rougher and rougher. My father, who was a Royal Fleet Auxiliary captain, spent most of his time on the freighter's bridge, and my mother and I lay together on his bunk being sick, with the small ship's cat keeping us company. What had promised to be a rare holiday for Mum, Dad and me had turned into a bit of a nightmare - in more ways than one.

The year was 1953, which saw one of the last polio epidemics in Britain before the life-saving Salk vaccine was introduced in 1955. What I later discovered had distressed and worried my mother and father terribly was the fact that a sailor who I had been sitting next to on the ship had died a week later of this dread disease which killed and crippled so many.

Mum had noticed that while we were in the throes of seasickness I had been running a high fever, so on our return home she called in the family doctor. I couldn't understand what all the fuss was about, as I just felt slightly under the weather. However, the diagnosis was positive, and he too was seriously concerned and arranged for an ambulance to come to take me to the City Isolation Hospital in Cardiff, a few miles from where we lived in Penarth. My aunt and uncle who lived near us were called, and my dear uncle Don, a great big man, wrapped me in a blanket and carried me into the ambulance, not caring for himself but only for me. The neighbours all came out and stared. It was unusual in those days to see an ambulance at close quarters. I can remember now how scared I felt. It was two days after my ninth birthday.

Being alone in the Victorian wilderness of the Isolation Hospital was a frightening experience. I was put into a room of my own and left to my own devices for a while. Then a team of doctors and nurses arrived with a clanking trolley and told me they were going to give me an injection. I was instructed to lie on my side with my knees tucked up while they bustled around. Then the doctor warned me that there was going to be a pain. However I had expected nothing like the pain I felt and I started to cry and then to scream. The doctor said, "We've got to be firm with this one nurse, hold her legs," and continued to try to insert the needle for the lumbar puncture. It was a harrowing and agonising experience. After that, whenever I heard a trolley come near in hospital, I would break out into a cold sweat for fear that the procedure would be repeated. Of course trolleys were always being pushed about the wards, so this became a fairly constant anxiety.

My distress was compounded when my mother and aunt and uncle came to visit and were allowed to come no further than the bottom of my bed, because of the disease I could be carrying. Needless to say, they were as distressed as I was. It must have been very hard for my mother, as my father was still at sea and my brother

Michael, who was seven years older than I, was farming some way away in West Wales. I was in a side ward on my own but I can remember a boy in a bed in the main ward jeering at me and calling me a 'cry baby'. Hospitals were very different places in those days and the doctors tended to be brusque with children and accorded them no special consideration.

Eventually however I was moved to a more pleasant ward facing open countryside where I was to stay for three weeks. I was lonely, as again I was in a room on my own and was only allowed out of bed occasionally. But the nurses were kind, and I read and did jigsaws to occupy my time. There was a little girl next door to me who I used to chat to sometimes, but a nurse said, "Don't talk to her love, she's got TB," and indeed I had noticed she had a terrible cough.

Fortunately, I had always loved books and was a good reader at quite a young age. The first thing that I had noticed (and which cheered me up on reaching the hospital, albeit for a very short time) was the fact that there were Enid Blyton Secret Seven adventures in the bookcase in my room – my favourites. Mum and my aunt and uncle visited regularly and would sneak Rowntree's fruit gums to me, which made me laugh as sweets were banned in the hospital for some strange reason. I used to write to Mum (and she to me) and still have one of the letters that I wrote to her that she kept until she died:

Dear Mum,
I am now in Ward 9. Sorry I have to use a brown pencil but I cannot reach my other one. Yesterday a bee stung me and left his sting in but luckily a nurse was with me and she called another one and pulled it out. I am feeling better now and stiffness has gone I don't know whether I spelt it right. Oh well there is not much to say, come on Sunday. Give everyone a kiss for me.
Love Jenniferxxx

I don't remember feeling any different physically, and now and again a doctor would come in to check my reflexes etc. which would provoke another anxiety attack. Eventually to everyone's great relief I was allowed to go home with the proviso that I took things very easily. It was so good to be back home. Uncle Don had made a new leather saddle for my rocking horse, Cactus, as a welcome home present with real stirrups, which I was thrilled with. Father came back from sea on a flying visit, and so did brother Michael.

My mother often sent Mikey parcels to the farm where he worked with a few treats for him. She was shocked and upset when she received a letter from the farmer's wife asking her how she dared to send food that may be infected with polio into their household. It shows just how much the disease was feared and also how little it was understood.

No physiotherapy was offered, but my mother was told that I needed to exercise regularly. Penarth is a seaside town and there was a pitch and putt course on the cliffs. Mum was marvellous. Every day for some weeks she and I walked down to the cliffs which was a good mile's walk in itself and then played pitch and putt which I enjoyed greatly. We also went to visit my dear Aunt Lil (my mother's other sister) in Suffolk, and I can remember enjoying the lovely rolling countryside and the rich red ploughed autumn fields.

The recovery process was a slow one and I suffered from severe headaches for a while. I had lost weight and muscle tone and my legs were now quite wasted. The tendons had been shortened by the disease so I was to walk for evermore on tip toe (equinus foot). Photographs taken before and after the illness show a very different girl - although this is something that I have only realised since writing this memoir. In the past 50 years I have visited various consultants regarding the advisability of having the tendons in my legs cut, which would enable me to walk properly again, but their views have differed and most have been against the idea.

Salk introduced his lifesaving vaccine in 1955. Yet polio is still a disease endemic in some third world countries. I am now 66 and because of a lifetime of walking on my toes have increasing problems with my knees and hips. These, however, are only minor problems compared with what others still suffer. It was a close call, but I was one of the lucky ones.

Emotional Baggage

Mais Appleton

(Brightwell cum Sotwell)

*I am a wife, mother and grandmother, now living in
South Oxfordshire. I am an enthusiastic WI member,
keen gardener, diarist and quilter. I love the theatre
and concerts and have travelled extensively,
especially loving the Middle East.*

I am standing in the crypt of Winchester cathedral looking at an
Anthony Gormley sculpture. It is a figure with its arms crossed,
its fingertips touching its shoulders, looking down at water that
comes up to its knees. It is beautiful, but why am I thinking about
the Anderson air raid shelter that we had in our garden during
the war? I think it's the dark and damp and a slight feeling of
unease. I was born just after war was declared and as we lived on
the outskirts of Portsmouth there were constant bombing raids. I
don't exactly remember going down into the shelter, but my mother
later said that if they thought there was going to be an air raid,
she would put me to bed there. If I had to be woken up and taken
down later I would create "merry hell" and make everyone even
unhappier. It made me think how much the past still lives with us
and affects us. I much preferred sleeping in the Morrison shelter
in the front room even though the floor was hard. It was like a
large, heavy steel table with wire mesh sides. Often my much older
brothers shut me in there like a caged animal when I was being a
nuisance and played table tennis, or "ping pong" as they called it,

on the top. Another way to keep me in my place was to hide on
the landing in the black out and shout "Boo" when I went "up the
stairs to Bedfordshire." I still don't really like going up the stairs
at night.

It was the front room where we reared day old chicks on the lino
in the bay window under an ultra violet lamp to keep them warm.
Rhode Island reds, White Leghorns and Light Sussex were the
breeds we had. Every morning I would rush downstairs to check if
any had died in the night. I loved their vulnerability, their fluffiness
and frantic cheeping in my hands. When they were older and
outside I used to catch them and stroke the hard ridges of their
wing feathers until their feeling of slight panic subsided and they
relaxed in my arms. To stop them being bored I devised a chicken
Grand National, poking canes through the netting across their run.
Then I'd get inside and chase the poor creatures from one end to
the other seeing them scramble over the jumps. The bit I loved
best was lifting the lid of the hen coop and picking up the warm
brown eggs lying on the straw and taking them into the kitchen.
When I hear the gentle chook, chook of contented chickens
scratching in the dust, the years disappear and I smile.

Being a late arrival and my brothers being off their hands, I
suppose my parents wanted a week on holiday on their own and I
would be sent off to stay with all manner of relatives, friends and
strangers. There was a week touring in Scotland and another in
Wales. One year I spent the whole week sitting in the grandstand
at Lords from where, at least, I returned with all the autographs of
the Surrey, Middlesex and Australian cricket teams. I still can't
remember who my minders were. When I was six the Reverend
Clough, of the local Methodist church, was taking some of his
congregation and their families to Swanage on a camping holiday.
I was sent too. Our first view of the site was a collection of army
bell tents. We had to collect our canvas palliases and fill them with
straw, which were then placed six to a tent, toes to the central pole.
I can't remember what covered me but it wasn't my comforting
blankets, eiderdown and woven bedcover. The first night it rained.
The cold, the dark, the dampness, the trek to the latrine which was

a plank with a hole in it over a ditch behind a hedge. No walls, no door, no privacy, and no toilet paper if you'd forgotten to take it with you.

I was lonely, frightened and desperately home sick. It was such a long week. A few years later I went on another camping holiday with my parents in Cornwall. That involved a flooded tent and more misery. The last attempt to discover the joy of life under canvas was in Pembrokeshire with my husband, retracing his time in the TA with the Royal Artillery. I lasted a couple of days feeling violently sick. We went home and I discovered that I was pregnant.

I've never been near a tent since!!

I was always happy to stay with my grandma Wilkins in her terraced house in Portsmouth and share her bed with its feather mattress, lovely when you got in at night , but a bit lumpy in the morning. With the presence of the Royal Navy, Royal Marines and Army there were about twelve cinemas in the city and five were within walking distance of Gladstone Street where grandma lived. We often went three times a week. I was completely in love with the silver screen. The anticipation as you went into the cinema and took your seat, and then watching the Pathe news, two films and all the adverts, and you could stay and watch it all again if you wanted to. I saved up my pennies to buy the Picturegoer magazine, and cut out photos of all my favourite stars and stuck them in my scrap books. Every Saturday, with my pump-water straight hair extra carefully plaited, I walked to Cosham High Street and the magic world of Woolworths. I was quite convinced that that was where Hollywood talent scouts hung about, and at any moment one of them would tap me on the shoulder and say, "Will you take us to see your mother. We'd like you to be the new Margaret O'Brien." But they never did!

My mother didn't approve of the cinema. "Waste of money." However, she did love the theatre. We often boarded the number 31 Southdown bus and went to the King's theatre in Southsea. There I discovered pantomime, ballet, Gilbert and Sullivan operas

performed by the Carl Rosa company, the musicals of Ivor Novello and the lovely John Hanson as the Red Shadow in The Desert Song. We always sat in the "gods" right up at the top.
The seats cost 1s 6d and if you got a place in the front row, although it sometimes made me feel a bit sick and giddy, you could see everything.

Every Thursday, when I arrived home from school, there was always a large, bread pudding waiting. My mother would cut a generous slice, and with my music case in one hand and the comfort of the warm, fruity, spicy pudding in the other, which slightly helped to allay any worries about not having done enough practice, I would set off up Portsdown Hill for my piano lesson.

Being surrounded by grown ups, I knew the songs of Frank Sinatra as well as I knew my nursery rhymes and he is still my favourite singer. One of my brothers used to play all his latest hits on the piano from music printed half size to save paper as part of the war effort.

When he left home I inherited it and entertained, I thought, the patients of the doctor next door who were in the waiting room which adjoined our front room. Whilst chatting in the queue in the Co-op my mother was often told which pieces people they liked best. Frank went down very well. Bach wasn't so popular.

Scents of flowers bring back more happy memories. Hot sunshine on wallflowers is one of the most intoxicating scents I know. My mother planted them down beside the front path. In the back garden were the sweet peas and chrysanthemums that my father grew along with his giant dahlias. He gave me the job of making bunches of them which he gave to friends and neighbours. On Sunday afternoons he would take us out for a drive in the country as a treat. The car was used strictly for business the rest of the week. It was a Morris 8 – ATP 499 – odd how such trivia stays with you. If we went up a steep hill we had to get out and walk, and occasionally we even had to push it. We usually ended up at the cricket field in Soberton surrounded by hedges of honeysuckle.

If I catch a scent of it now I'm sitting in the back of the car outside The Bold Forester where we went after the match, with an orange squash and a slightly soggy packet of Smiths crisps with salt in a twist of blue paper.

Whenever I hear the words "That's the way to do it" I shiver and see a little creature with an overly painted face and a pointed nose and chin that almost touch. It has a red felt hat and a pair of clacking feet that dangle over the edge of the puppeteer's stripey booth. When all the other children were sitting watching the Punch and Judy show I would hang back until my mother pushed me forward. "Go along and sit down there with the rest of the children. You'll enjoy it. It's funny". I sat down and shut my eyes. I didn't quite dare to put my fingers in my ears and shut out the voice, but at least I didn't have to watch Punch, with his stick, beat his wife, his child, the policeman and the crocodile. I never understood why everyone thought it was so funny. I still don't.

Perhaps one of the most treasured memories concerns my father. He used to say every year on his birthday, "I've had a good life you know. Not many days when we went without food." I remember, what seemed to me, a sparsely laid Sunday tea table some time in the late forties. There was a bowl of winkles which my father would have picked in Langstone Harbour – it was my job to put the pins on the plates to eat them with – a dish of tinned pilchards, a plate of bread and marg, homemade raspberry jam, some homegrown lettuce, tomatoes, radish and cucumber and some of my mother's rock cakes. Friends had come and later they would have a game of darts and then some games of cards. Maybe rummy, pontoon or sevens. He sat at the end of the table looking around and smiling at everyone saying, "Well, here we all are together about to enjoy this feast. Aren't we lucky?" I could almost imagine my mother's "Huh" as she flounced out into the kitchen to get the teapot.

She would be saying that it wasn't a feast, any fool could see that. And why were we sharing the small amount we had with these people in these days of rationing? She could never understand his positive attitude.

We carry a lot of emotional baggage with us through life. If we're sensible we try and leave the bad bits behind and keep going with the lovely things and pass them on. I can overlook the fact that my children love camping and go at every opportunity. They may even love Punch and Judy. But they do keep chickens, grow sweet peas and make music and bread pudding.

I agreed with my mother all those years ago but later I came to see that my father was right. The quality of the tablecloth and cutlery is immaterial, as is the quantity of the food. What matters is the joy of gathering around the table and sharing, not only what's on it, but friendship, laughter and love.

Now And Then

Barbara Slough

(Marlow Bottom)

*Married with two sons and three grandchildren,
I was born in Southall in 1946. I attended Ealing
Grammar School and worked as a secretary.
The family lived in Iver Heath before moving to
Marlow Bottom in 1984.
Always interested in community activities, I joined
the WI in 2002.*

The birth of my granddaughter, Madeline, three years ago, started me thinking. What a different world she has been born into from my post-war London. No-one around her talks mysteriously about "the men who didn't come back"; she won't wonder why there are gaps in the streets where houses used to be; her mother doesn't burst into tears every time it thunders.

As a small child growing up in West London, I took it for granted that if there were a thunderstorm, my mother would hide under the table, after she had covered all the mirrors and closed the curtains. Bombs, it seemed, would shatter all the glass so it was best to cover it as some form of protection. She had been a firewatcher during the war and although she had never backed away from that duty, she never got over the fear that had grown in her during those years. Even 20 years later, I would telephone her "just for a chat" if there was a thunderstorm, although by then she would make a cup of tea instead of diving under the table.

Madeline showed me her latest toy recently. It's an app on her Daddy's iPad. She showed me which icons to touch and how to stroke the screen to make her virtual cat purr or yowl or repeat what she says to it. She giggled because she can make the cat say, "You are beeyootiful". I had a doll which said "Mama" if I turned her upside down.

We do have some toys in common though. She loves playing tea-parties with her dolls just as I did. However, I had a china tea set which I was only allowed to play with if I had been extra good. It was very pretty and Japanese in design. One day I was playing with it in the kitchen when the whole ceiling suddenly crashed down. It must have been weakened during the bombing and chose that particular moment to collapse. I was completely unhurt but not one piece of my tea-set survived.

Families stayed close together in those days. I grew up with my grandparents and aunt, uncle and cousin living in the house opposite ours. My cousin and I had a lot of freedom, even when we were quite small. I suppose after the trauma of war, peace must have meant safety to our parents who felt nothing bad could happen now.

We used to get sent on errands together – probably to ensure that we got things right. Our grandmother had a paraffin burning stove for extra warmth, as there was no central heating and some rooms didn't have fireplaces. We were despatched to collect the paraffin in cans – bet 'Health and Safety' wouldn't allow that these days.

A cousin several times removed worked at Nestle and would occasionally give us a brown paper bag of chocolate rejects. No hand-made chocolate from Harrods could ever equal the anticipation of biting into one of those misshapen lumps of chocolate and wondering what would be inside – with luck it would be fudge or strawberry cream, but if I was unlucky it would be that nutty one.

We had a sweetshop at the end of the road, but we were forbidden to go there. The sweets were all unwrapped and the whole place was definitely not hygienic. When our grandfather sneaked us some pennies we would walk casually down the road and then duck into the forbidden shop. The really naughty purchase would be a twist of lemonade powder, measured out with a tin scoop, and a packet of sweet cigarettes. We would dip our fingers in the lemonade powder and lick them. By the time the powder was all gone, our fingers were "nicotine" stained and we could smoke our cigarettes just like the grown-ups. Strangely enough, neither of us smoked when we grew up, but I still love sweets.

Another errand had the opposite effect. Round the corner (near enough that I was sent on my own) was Maddens corner shop. I hated it. It was dark and poky and old Mrs Madden sat behind her counter and peered at me through wire-rimmed spectacles. I was convinced she was a witch and would cast a spell on me. Her son served the customers and he was small and bent and very creepy. The only thing my mother bought there was vinegar. It was stored in barrels and I had to take an empty bottle so that the vinegar could be poured from the barrel into a metal measuring jug and then through a funnel into my bottle. The smell of the vinegar used to make me feel sick and I couldn't wait to get out of there. 60 years on and I still can't eat anything with vinegar on. How anyone could ruin fish and chips with it I can't imagine.

The fish and chip shop, however, was a culinary paradise. We didn't go out to restaurants, so our only experience of food other than that cooked by our mothers would be fish and chips for a special treat. Sometimes though, those sneaked granddad pennies would buy a twist of crispy bits from the bottom of the fryers. Twists of newspaper that is, with salt but no vinegar!

Shopping for food is another aspect of life that has changed beyond all recognition. Madeline's weekly groceries arrive in a van in baskets, ordered online by her mother. Or sometimes they go for a trip round a large supermarket where everything you could possibly want is there for the choosing. We hadn't always had a fridge and very definitely no freezer, so shopping was a daily chore. Bread went off before it could all be eaten, so bread pudding and bread and butter pudding were an essential part of the week's menu. Meat came from the butcher, milk was delivered by the milkman and extra had to be fetched from the dairy. Fruit and vegetables came from the greengrocer who put things into brown paper bags and twisted them round by the corners so nothing could fall out. Try as I might, I couldn't master that twist. The grocery was divided into dry goods and other things. We had to queue at both counters, so that butter, cheese and ham came from one, and tea, sugar etc. from the other. Dried fruit was measured out into purple paper bags and tea was measured from tea-chests into oblong packets – no teabags. Biscuits were exciting. They were in tins at the front of the counter and were weighed out into bags and you could choose how many of each sort you wanted. At the end was the magic broken biscuits tin and if I was very good, a small bag was given to me to have in the garden. This manna from heaven was only shared with my cousin if he had been very good and I was feeling generous.

Even if there had been supermarkets, we didn't have a car to bring the shopping home. In fact, on Sunday afternoons we would walk to the Great West Road (better known now as the A4) to see the cars go by. What a sight they were, they went so fast – probably all of 40 mph. For an extra special treat we could go to London Airport to watch the planes take off and land every half hour or so. There was a viewing area with a sandpit to play in when we got bored between flights. For the really rich, which we weren't, there was a joy ride in a small plane to see the airport from above. Imagine that these days. We went everywhere by bus or train or even trolleybus. Steam trains of course. One of my favourite walks was to go with my father to the local railway line where we would stand on the footbridge while the trains thundered underneath. My mother would be cross when we got back because I would be all covered in black smuts and smell of smoke.

Of all the rooms in the house, the kitchen must have changed the most. I used to help my grandmother with the washing. There was a big concrete copper in the corner with a wooden lid and I would use a stick to poke the washing down into the hot soapy water.

That stick was worn smooth and white and somehow felt almost
soft and I loved it. All the hot wet washing was then hand-rinsed
in the sink, and the best bit was doing the whites with blue-bag
water. My job was to swirl the blue-bag around until the water was
the right shade of blue – it made patterns as it swirled. Then the
mangle! This was a monstrous contraption in the yard with big
wooden rollers, a wheel on top to increase the pressure, and a wheel
with a handle on the side to turn the rollers. It took two hands to
turn those rollers and if the hands were small, it took four! We had
to be very careful though, fingers could easily get squashed. Shirts
had special treatment. They had to be folded so that the buttons
were down one edge and then fed through very carefully so the
buttons were outside the rollers – one slip and all the buttons would
break. Ironing was another huge undertaking. Everything had to
be ironed, no easy-care fabrics then. The irons were flat irons and
black. They were heated on the stove, and my grandmother would
spit on them to make sure they were hot enough - the spit had to sizzle.

Cooking was more time-consuming too. There was brawn made
from a pig's head which was boiled for what seemed like days. I
could never eat that brawn because I had seen his ears, and that
made him a person. I helped with the Christmas cake too. I
rubbed the skin off the almonds in a basin of hot water and
grated a whole nutmeg. When the cake came out of the oven my
grandmother would cut a slice out to make sure it was cooked
through and then put the slice back. On Christmas Day when the
cake was cut I held my breath waiting for someone to get the slice
which had already been cut but it never happened. I think it was
glued back in with all the brandy with which it was fed. My special
treat was the left over bit of pastry after the Sunday lunch fruit pie
was prepared. It was put on a piece of butter paper on the shelf in
the oven and when it was cooked it was cut it half and spread with
butter which melted all over my hands and chin. This was a treat
from my grandmother and I was not allowed to tell my mother
because she would have said it would spoil my appetite.

Some things however, don't change. Madeline has a scooter, a little
trike, teddies and dolls, a girly bedroom, but most importantly, just

as I grew up secure in the love of my parents for me and for each other, Madeline is safely wrapped round in the love of her parents and the extra special love of two wonderful big brothers.

Pre-War Memories
Jean Ley
(Marlow Bottom)

Born in 1931 in Woodford Green, Essex, I attended Woodford County High School and later Westfield College, London from which I graduated with a degree in Modern Languages. After a life involving much travel, I settled in South Bucks and am married with a grown-up family. I am also a proud graduate of the Open University.

I have only a few vivid memories left of my early childhood in the 1930s. That's not surprising since it was some 70 years ago. There are such enormous gaps in between these memories that it is difficult to make them into a coherent story. However, one memory stands out above the others because it marks a transition in the circumstances of my life.

On the afternoon of 9 September 1939 I was sitting in an apple tree when I overheard a conversation between two villagers which impressed me for its quiet urgency, although their country burr confused its meaning for me. "Oh yes," they said, "It's true, we heard it on the wireless."

At the age of eight I had arrived that day as an evacuee from the suburbs of London and had thrown myself eagerly into the exploration of my new surroundings. Even the long walk past the apple trees down the garden to the strange wooden-seated toilet inside a lean-to shed was an adventure to me.

Talk of imminent German air raids was rife in the weeks before the Declaration of War, so my father had bicycled into the depths of the Essex countryside and had rented a Georgian cottage for us in the village of Stansted Mountfitchet, which in all probability now lies under a runway of Stansted Airport. But then, as if preserved in aspic, it was still an archetypal English village with artisan tradesmen in the main street and surrounded by a farming community. Our cottage shared with several other houses a water pump in the backyard and had no electricity or gas. A rickety old stove had to be coaxed into heating the hot water we used once or twice a week to fill a tin bath for the whole family to wash in. All great fun for us children, but not for my poor mother.

I was a distinct outsider in the village school among the farmers' children and was in awe of the cane-wielding teachers. Lessons were ridiculously easy except for the copperplate writing lessons. My easy-going suburban school had taught 'kick-ups', not the curvaceous shapes and loops of the cursive style I was now expected to adopt. To this day my writing is an untidy mixture of the two systems.

The countryside was my adventure playground. Sometimes I played with the children of the big house up the road – at least I could understand what they said. Often I was given lumps of dough to fashion into plaits and shapes and allowed to 'help' in the bakery, where loaves made from dough that had risen in large wooden vats were baked in the brick oven built into the bakery wall and sold to eager customers attracted by the gorgeous aroma of freshly baked bread.

Village and country life was a new world for me and I could have had no conception of the dark shadow that was about to be cast over us all, and of the consequences of that broadcast announcement.

My memories of life before this transition are much sketchier. I was born in 1931 in a brand new semi-detached house in the fast-expanding north-eastern suburbs of London on the edge of Epping Forest. So new was this suburb in fact that there were no other children of my age living near to play with and it was extremely quiet. I was regularly sent out into the garden to play on my own.

There was no plethora of books with conflicting advice on how to bring up and socialize small children in those days. My toys were the few books around our house – I can remember playing at libraries – and a pile of vinyl records that I played on an old wind-up player using steel needles. They were my father's treasured possessions. He must have been an admirer of operatic tenors. I played and danced to recordings of Enrico Caruso, Richard Tauber and Peter Dawson. The sound of their voices is engraved on my memory.

These games were solitary and until I went to school at four I had little contact with other children, at least that is how I remember it. I think it was not considered necessary by my parents that I should play much with other children. Not surprisingly, my first day at school was daunting. I have a vivid recollection of being dressed in a scarlet and grey uniform that day. The two school teachers who founded the school had chosen bright red for the uniform, a stroke of genius as it turned out, because it became known for miles around as The Red School.

I was deposited in a classroom containing about 20 children sitting at double desks in serried ranks facing a blackboard on which were written simple addition sums. We had to copy the sums into our squared maths books and fill in the answers for ourselves. No explanation and no help at all, in more or less complete silence. A slightly older boy who shared the desk with me and whose name was Norman (I remember that clearly) turned to me and said, rather haughtily, "Don't you know how to do add-ups?" It was my first put-down. At the time I just stared back, but have thought of many smart answers since.

Despite this rocky beginning, school was a happy place, although I always found it difficult to make friends and tended to be a loner. Our house was so new, the road outside was not yet metalled. Apart from my father's company car, there were few vehicles of any sort, with the exception of the tricycle of the 'Stop me and Buy one' Walls seller of iced lollies, and the occasional knife sharpener. Very rarely too we heard the raucous cry of the rag and bone man who came by on his horse-drawn dray. There were few vehicles on the road and no planes in the sky either. It was very peaceful and dreadfully quiet.

My mother and I walked to the shops frequently, since we had no refrigerator. This was about a ten-minute walk, but it took more time to buy items from separate grocers, greengrocers, butchers, bakers and confectionary shops. When we asked for a pound of sugar in the grocers, for instance, the assistant shook out a white paper bag, placed it on the copper balancing scales and weighed out the loose sugar. The same with other commodities like tea, flour, rice, etc. Butter was cut off a large lump, patted with paddles into shape and weighed the same.

Getting in the shopping was a lengthy business. On the way back, if we espied the infamous Sylvia Pankhurst walking on the pavement on the same side of the road, my mother crossed to the other side to avoid having to pass the time of day with her. This always puzzled me and it was not until many years later that I discovered this must have been because she was a communist and ardent feminist, and refused to marry the Italian anarchist who was the father of her child. Divorce, or anything that smacked of marital infidelity or irregularity, was taboo. In fact there was very little discussion about relationships at all. Awkward children's questions were met with either embarrassed silence or fairytale explanations.

I was aware that in many ways life was quite hard for my parents. My father worked a six and a half day week and I saw relatively little of him. Apart from frequent shopping, my mother had to contend with a house without central heating or refrigeration. She had open fires in the living rooms to tend, and in the kitchen she had to grapple with an obnoxious Ideal boiler on which the supply of hot water depended. Washing clothes was another heavy chore to which most of Monday was devoted. Outside in a shed was a huge iron mangle for wringing the clothes. On rainy days these were dried and aired on pulleys in the kitchen.

On Mondays we always had 'bubble and squeak' for lunch to finish up the remains of Sunday's roast dinner. The only entertainment – apart from gossiping, and a lot of that went on, especially on the telephone because local calls were cheap and untimed – was the radio, or wireless, as we called it. I remember being woken up at 9 o'clock one evening to listen to Gracie Fields, who must have been at the height of her fame. I had no idea who she was, but I did understand that her broadcast was an important event for my parents.

Social life for them revolved around the friends they made at a local tennis club. The tennis was incidental, an excuse to spend Sunday in the open with friends and their families. The weather seemed always to be fine, the clubhouse welcoming and in the distance there was a cricket match in progress with the sound of bat on ball and desultory clapping.

For several years running we went on group holidays with tennis club friends. I still have faded black and white photos to prove how enjoyable those holidays were. Many of these friendships lasted for the rest of my parents' lives, long after they were capable of playing tennis, and we still have contact with the children of the original tennis club members.

So these are some of my memories of my early life in a new suburb of London. It was a quiet, uneventful and rather boring life, and was to come to an abrupt end that day in September 1939 when I overheard the conversation from my perch in an apple tree. Although we stayed on as evacuees in rural Essex for several months during what later became known as 'the phoney war', we returned to the relative comforts of suburban life, to my mother's great relief, just in time for the Blitz that started in earnest in 1940.

However, my few months in Stansted had taught me that other worlds existed outside the restricted suburban world I had lived in up till then. Such was the pace of change from the mid-twentieth century onwards, I would be able to experience and explore worlds further and further afield and take advantages of opportunities for travel and knowledge undreamt of by my parents.

Part 2

No Place Like Home

The Lake Of Stars
Lesley Dore
(Brightwell cum Sotwell)

I was born in Malawi and came to Britain with my husband in 1967. Brightwell has been our home for 35 years and our sons were brought up here. While lecturing at Abingdon College I taught A level English at Denman College, and continue to tutor courses there in writing and literature.

If you look at a map of Africa you'll see a string of lakes lying down the right hand side. The most southerly of these is Lake Malawi, and its waters cover a fifth of the country that bears its name. Three-hundred and fifty-five miles in length and in parts fifty miles wide, it was "discovered" by the missionary explorer David Livingstone in 1859. He called it "a lake of stars" and found it "pleasant to bathe in the delicious waters, hear the roar of the sea, and dash in its rollers".

Almost a hundred years later this lake became my playground too, for my parents moved to the township of Salima, and bought land on the lakeshore eleven miles away, a three-acre plot of virgin bush covered with tall trees and tangled undergrowth. It lay towards the end of a large bay and looked across the water towards the blue hills of Cape Maclear. The far side of the lake, some 22 miles off, was seldom visible, so that sky and water merged seamlessly on the horizon. The beach was good too: where the vegetation ended fine,

69

yellow sand took over and sloped gently into the water, which here was shallow and free of reeds. It was perfect for swimming and safe for children.

On the other three sides of the plot lay a forestry conservation area where building was prohibited, and although there were other residences owned by Europeans dotted along the bay, most were holiday homes and only sporadically inhabited. There were no public services - no electricity or piped water or sewage system; no telephones, no mail deliveries. The residents of the large African village further along the bay lived in traditional mud huts with grass roofs, grew mangoes and maize, and dried fish on racks in the sun. At night they beat drums to scare away the hippos from their gardens. Their lives were different from ours, little changed since Livingstone's day, and their presence did not alleviate the feeling of isolation that the lake engendered. It preoccupied us, filled our days with its sudden storms, breathless calms and bloody sunrises. We watched it, listened to it, talked about it.

Once we owned the land we had to start from scratch, and our first home was a grass shack where we camped at weekends to escape the heat and dust of Salima. Of course it was hot at the lakeshore too, but there was that vast expanse of water in which to swim, and usually a cooling breeze.

By mid-day the sand was red-hot and my sister and I would stand in the shade gathering courage before dashing "Ow! Ow! Ow!" across it. Since the shallows were tepid we'd wade out and dive into the cool depths, drifting there, submerged for as long as our breath would hold. Our labrador, a stronger swimmer than us, bounded through the waves and set off across the lake until he became a black dot on the horizon. Above us in the navy-blue sky the black and white fish-eagles soared, suddenly rocketing downwards to snatch a glittering fish from the water, then retreating to the tree-tops to call to their mates, an eerie, desolate sound. Later we'd lie on our stomachs in the shallow water and be tickled by the pretty painted fish as they sucked at our skin. Buster, returning from his swim, barked and frolicked around us until we threw sticks for him to retrieve, a game he never tired of.

Occasionally clumsy dhows, vestiges of the Arab slave trade, struggled across our bay, seeking the wind to sail to Mozambique. Their sails dipped haphazardly into the water and the wooden masts creaked as they rolled from side to side. In contrast the dug-out canoes, fashioned from tree-trunks, slipped silently and elegantly by. Two men dressed in loin cloths stood in the narrow aperture, one propelling the canoe forward with a pole, the other poised, a fine net in his hands, watching for nsipa, the tiny, intensely silver fish that moved across the surface in flashing, tinkling shoals. As a shoal approached, the fisherman would leap into the water, throwing the net across them, and then pull the struggling mass into the canoe behind him as he climbed aboard. It was a graceful performance, perfectly timed - man in harmony with nature - ancient - and so the movements would be repeated, both men standing upright again, their bodies glistening in the sun.

Darkness came early and we'd light a fire on the beach to keep off the mosquitoes. I'd make a hollow in the sand and sit hugging my knees and staring out as the moon rose over the lake, throwing a path of gold across the water. When it was a full moon I'd see Kalulu the hare quite plainly on its surface, and think how magical it would be if I could step on to the path and walk up to join him. Then came the night, a black, black sky, and dazzling stars that tumbled and fell and sang, it seemed to me, so vibrant and busy were they.

But the path I took next led not to the moon but to boarding school. Erica and I, now eleven and twelve, had to join our older sisters in Zimbabwe. For nine months of the year we were away.

Every week there'd be an envelope on the letter board addressed to me in my mother's beautiful italic script, letters for my sisters, too. She wrote to each of us every weekend, commenting on our letters home and giving us news of life in Salima. There was the orphaned duiker she was struggling to rear, bottle-feeding it 3 times a day on powdered milk; Buster having his rabies inoculation when the Government vet came to do all the dogs in the area, and the citrus orchard my father was planting, stocked with trees imported from South Africa.

At the lake a wooden chalet replaced the grass shack, and the household left Salima to take up residence there. After the foundations were laid for the main house an uncle from Suffolk arrived to help with the family business, while my father supervised the building. He strode around the site in his khaki shorts and topee while Cristo planed roof timbers in the shade of the mopani tree and Sinoodi the bricklayer, stoically suffering the thirst of Ramadam, watched the spirit level the Bwana placed on the completed course of bricks. He knew that the work would have to be redone if it wasn't perfect.

In October 1954, Aunt Margaret came to visit us at school.
"Your Daddy's been up to mischief," she said. "He's had a fight with a crocodile."
We were incredulous, appalled.
"Where? Where? There aren't any crocs in our part of the lake. They've all been shot out!"
"In the water in front of your house," she replied. "He's in hospital, but he's all right."

From home, there was silence. And then this letter came:
"My darling Lesley,
Now Daddy is home again and I haven't got to dash up to Lilongwe Hospital any more, I can settle down to writing you a proper letter.
I expect you have been wondering what on earth happened to our Daddy, haven't you? Now you shall hear the truth. It's a horrible story, but he is home and walking around so you have no need to worry.
We were bathing at night, as we always do. We were standing waist deep in water. Daddy knelt down to wet his shoulders when a crocodile grabbed his thighs. Daddy was very brave and very calm. He put his hands in the crocodile's mouth and tried to open the jaws. He couldn't - so he dug his thumb into the croc's eye. It let go, Daddy got to his feet - then the crocodile attacked again, getting Daddy below the waist. Daddy called for help - he didn't call before - and I rushed to hold him. I knew at once what had happened and screamed to Uncle Fred to come to our aid. Uncle Fred held on to him while I dashed to get the lamp on the shore. I was half way back when Daddy and Uncle came staggering towards me. I wanted the lamp because I knew I had to blind the crocodile to make it let go, and I was afraid that if I felt in the dark

for its head it would pull away from my touch and take Daddy with it. But when I went for the lamp Daddy fastened one hand on the beast's nose, and with the other hand dug his thumb into one eye. The croc released him for the second time and Uncle helped him to the shore. We rushed him to Lilongwe and got him attended to.
That's the whole story. We are, of course, very lucky to have a daddy alive today. He saved himself by his amazing bravery and by not losing his head. He has some nasty wounds from the croc's teeth - that's all.
Now let's talk of happier things."

My mother didn't elaborate on the details - the dreadful tug-of-war that had taken place in the dark water; how she'd ripped the sheets from the bed and wrapped them round his waist in an effort to staunch the blood; the scramble to reach a friend at the far end of the bay who could drive my father to the nearest hospital 66 miles away across difficult roads. Crocodiles don't have long teeth but they have a great many of them, and the wounds were shocking. It was months before he'd completely recovered.

Some years later I sat with him in the sprawling brick bungalow that now stood on our land - every room had views of the lake - and I remember him saying, "My experience with that croc has taken all the fun out of swimming for me." It's the only time I heard him refer to it. He would never tell the story – except, as it turned out, by royal command.

In 1960 the Queen Mother, visiting the far-flung outposts of her daughter's empire, flew into Salima, and my parents were invited to lunch. Afterwards she rested with her aides in a pavilion built for her on the beach, and someone, no doubt seeking to let her know that this paradise had a darker side, told her about my father. The visit ended and the guests lined up to say farewell. She stopped in front of my father.
"I hear you fought with a crocodile, Mr Smith. Please tell me about it."
He couldn't refuse. She listened to the story.
"You're a very brave man," she said.

On this the Queen and Mrs Smith were in complete accord.

The Odd-Numbered Houses

Sandra Grainge

(Brightwell cum Sotwell)

*I am writing my story for my grandchildren and
to share highlights of childhood fun in post-war
Bracknell before it became a New Town. After a
professional and family life in Surrey I now live in a
South Oxfordshire village where I hear echoes of
a long-gone way of life.*

The words of the nursery rhyme "Boys and girls come out
to play, the moon doth shine as bright as day" remind me
of my childhood spent in a Victorian terraced house in Bracknell
while it was still a small Berkshire town. By chance, all the children
in the terrace lived in the odd-numbered houses and the youngest
child in each family slept in the back bedroom. These were my
friends and partners. We could see each other when we leaned out
of our bedroom windows.

Before the telephone age, we still needed to make sure we were
in the right place at the right time, as we made our play plans,
we shouted out of our windows from one house to the next to
confirm details, often to the annoyance of the adults who lived
in the even-numbered houses. Obviously not satisfied that this
was efficient enough, we invented a homemade telephone system.
Each child had a tin: mine at number 5 was a cocoa tin, Ruth from

number 3 recently reminded me that hers was a treacle tin. We couldn't remember what sort of tin David used in number 1. We do remember the strategy for getting the communicating string from one house to another. The length was measured out along the yard; it was then tied to a borrowed clothes prop and stretched up to each window in turn to be anchored there. An earlier method had been to attach the end to a stone and throw this up to be caught by the future telephone operator. There were obvious dangers with this unsatisfactory method. In our memories the phone system worked.

We lived as if we had infinite freedom to roam together and explore. An escapade of apple-scrumping in the policeman's orchard demonstrated our lack of fear. We saw no one, but the message arrived home before us, that if we wanted apples, we had only to ask.

From the older children we learnt folk-lore which followed the plants' seasons: anemones, celandines, hidden primroses, bluebells, fragrant violets and dog roses; games with convolvulus that popped Granny out of bed, honeysuckle sips, bull rushes, blackberries, hazel nuts, shiny chestnuts and Christmas time holly. We saw, smelt, picked and sometimes ate. Stinging nettle rash was cured by soothing dock leaves. Did they really cure or were they just cool and comforting? At the annual fete I won a prize for a pot of gathered flowers, given not for skill but the luck to choose flowers that did not wilt immediately after the early morning picking.

Summer time was heralded by the arrival of swifts and cuckoos when, despite nights spent scratching mosquito bites that parents covered in messy calamine lotion, we delighted in being outside. We children emerged at bedtime to sleep behind our respective houses. Tents were home-made, an old rug was spread on the bricks with great enthusiasm, although experience taught us that these were hard to sleep on. A wooden clothes horse tipped on its side was covered with blankets to shelter the rug and pillow. The evening was full of giggles and frights of the night with dark patches where the beam from our torches did not reach. More excitement was caused by the blunderings of the occupants of the even-numbers where children did not rule. One of these was a willing collaborator; she was a renowned cook and would treat us to midnight feasts. Crumbs dropped outside were soon devoured by cheerful sparrows that inhabited the yards of all the terrace houses. I only really valued their constant chirruping when they were no longer a part of my daily sounds.

After the war, inland children seldom went to the coast. Petrol was rationed and families did not travel far. Sand, sea, and boats were the stuff of legends and dreams.

To me, the seaside was where my beloved Rupert Bear had holiday adventures. In my favourite, but now banned, story, he went to tropical Coon Island, where he was feted by locals dressed in white night gowns, their curls skewered up onto the top of their heads. When he arrived Rupert was garlanded with exotic flowers and presented with a huge platter of tropical fruit and I wanted to be there. At this time, bananas returned to the local shop. The taste was disappointing and the bright yellow skins did not live up to the cartoon image of joke slip-ups for the unwary.

Eventually there were outings to the sea on two chartered trains. Excited children were identified by a blue or red ribbon badge. Everyone was going. Early at the station we saw the "special" steam in and stop for us. Sick with excitement and lack of sleep I had no enthusiasm for the bag of buns and sweets I was given on boarding. The long train enabled us to wander safely along the linked carriage corridors, while the rhythm of the wheels was intoxicating as we raced nonstop through fields and towns on our way to the sea. Usually we went to Bognor Regis, but once the trip was extended to include a boat to the Isle of Wight. The train went straight to the dock where we boarded the ferry. After rolling about and finding our sea legs, we expected to meet foreigners when we landed.
In our daily life the older children had an important role; my brother, a gentle giant, was the largest threat we could offer as defence. He was wise and creative; he made my much envied first transistor radio which was housed in a lunch box. I could hear

it under the bed covers, very special because none of the terrace houses had electricity. Ruth's older sister was the fashion expert and care giver. She mopped up tears, put on bandages, tied shoe laces and hair ribbons firmly and probably got the blame for our exploits. These older beings enriched our lives and prevented bullying. We belonged.

Why did I always get wet in any available water? Memorably, the collection of plants for my brother's university project was once the cause. The message was that he needed to have the roots as well as the flowers, and I fell into a stagnant pond when winning him the trophy of a rare plant. Friends helped. "Grab a hand as we reach from the bank and we'll give you a pull."
"That mud smells awful!"
"I'm not leaving this plant behind!" After assisting me to emerge from the mire in my dirty smelly clothes they escorted me home as I proudly carried my trophy, a foxglove with roots, which was larger than me. I was surrounded by a circle of children as we processed down the small town High Street. Did we really think I wouldn't be seen? Or smelt for that matter.

The terrace was on the route to Ascot races, and each June cars raced past from dawn till dusk. Local schools closed for safety and only the foolhardy tried to cross the road. We sat at the roadside to collect car numbers just as our older siblings collected train numbers. We became discerning: huge lists shrank as we chose to grace our pages with only Rolls Royce, Bentley and Jaguar. Good behaviour was rewarded with a trip to Ascot Heath to see the Queen drive down the course from Windsor. To me the colour of her hat was fashion. After our brief glimpse of the Royal party we saw the horses: beautiful flashes of shiny brown or dappled colour that thundered along. "Having a flutter" was for those from the even-numbered houses and we giggled at the thought. We were protected from the dangers of "riffraff" and the Heath vagabonds, though to us the tic-tack men and travelling performers looked fascinating.

Books told us of the exploits of Enid Blyton's Famous Five and Arthur Ransome's children in boats. We children from the odd-numbered houses had bicycles. The terrace cavalcade of wheels consisted of different sized tricycles, a neighbour's borrowed bike, a sturdy "sit up and beg" and one modern roadster. There were few cars about as our troop set off to explore for the day. We went anywhere with accessible water, fallen trees or a recreation ground.

We spent wet or winter days in each other's kitchens playing inherited board games. Ruth's hand painted snakes and ladders board was framed to hang like a picture when not in use. As we played the dice smacked noisily onto the glass and prevented any cheating. Tiddlywinks had us in hysterics as we occupied floor space and got in everyone's way. When all the grownups tired of us we wheedled our way into David's shed, the only one in the yards. It was at number 1 where his family ran the end-house sweet shop and general stores. We huddled among empty boxes that smelt of tobacco and soap powder. In this den we created fantasy stories, planned future exploits and had access to the easily climbed fence of the neighbouring overgrown pub garden. We hid in the jungle as we searched for balls lost from our game of improvised squash that we played against the house wall between the bedroom windows. Because the even-numbers got in the way we only played when the long-suffering neighbours were in a favourable mood.

We happily anticipated Bonfire Night as we saved pocket money to buy fireworks. Shopping and choosing was a delight of descriptive labels, each requiring a decision about the size of the bang versus the prettiness of the explosion. We had rockets, Catherine wheels, jumping jacks, bangers, fountains, coloured matches, sparklers and, best of all, fireworks that could be held in a gloved hand. These were selected with great care and then stored lovingly until the big night of November 5th. We hoped for a dry evening when the villainous Guy Fawkes was burnt on the biggest bonfire. One year, in the excitement, I dropped one of my lit fireworks into the storage tin; no one was hurt but in the dark garden multi-coloured fireworks lit up fast fleeing figures as plumes of sparks shot in all directions. Another time we fearlessly put lit bangers under an old army helmet and cheered as it rose magnificently into the air. Christmas celebrations began with the gathering of holly and fir. We raided the known places and dragged back our trophies to be trimmed and decorated with much-loved tree ornaments and angels made from shiny paper and chocolate wrappings that we scrounged from everyone's sweet ration. Cotton wool was used as snow on the branches and every candle holder was placed so carefully for artistic value. Each house was festooned with paper chains, holly was balanced behind every picture, and we all claimed to have the best tree.

The terrace children experienced a kinder approach that succeeded the Victorian maxim of "children should be seen and not heard". Parents were strict but did not exclude fun or freedom, and there was a lot of laughter, creativity and self-help. A few shared sweets went a long way and the sherbet dip would last for ages. In my house the regular dosing of children with castor oil had long been abandoned but some of the others were not so fortunate.

This world changed in 1951 as the Bracknell New Town Development began. I still remember the adults' distress as we viewed the plans; there was no appeal against compulsory purchase of our homes. This eventually resulted in the dispersal of our community. Street-wise London children arrived in school to extinguish our rural ways. Everyone's finances improved but the old ways were gone. The terrace was pulled down and so I was among the last to grow up with the glorious freedom to enjoy the fun known to generations of children who had access to the countryside.

A Very Strange Day
Christine Cooke
(Marlow Bottom)

I was born in 1945 and grew up in a terraced house in inner London. I obtained a degree in English from Nottingham University, then a further teaching qualification. I have taught English to adult education classes, immigrant groups and in secondary schools. I am married with two grown-up daughters and two grandchildren.

The second day of June, 1953, had seemed just the same as any other day to my seven year old self at first. I'd got up, got dressed and come downstairs as usual. But that was when everything started to go wrong.

It shouldn't have been there, it should have been in the middle of the wall, not squeezed in the corner by the chimney breast. "It's just for Coronation Day," smiled my mother, sitting down beside me and giving me breakfast.

"Ssssshhh." A man's voice on the wireless told us that we were listening to the Home Service and that this was the news. Two men had conquered Everest, the highest mountain in the world. And, of course, it was the day of the Coronation. Mother obviously thought this was exciting.

I was intrigued. Was that what people did when there was
A Coronation, climbed a mountain? Was that what always
happened? Apparently not, which was even more puzzling. What
was the connection then? There must obviously be a connection,
but what was it? Coronations and mountains, coronations and
tables. And then all our chairs arranged in the space created by
moving the table, all facing the television set in the corner.

The television set was shiny, gingery brown wood, standing on
the floor facing into the room, with the small greenish grey screen
set into the top part of it and sloping back slightly. As there were
only three of us - Dad, Mother and me - since big brother was
doing his National Service, this new arrangement of the room was
completely mystifying.

It must have been some time later that the first people arrived.
With no telephone to check in advance if people were at home, it
was quite normal for my various relations simply to turn up on a
Saturday or Sunday, just as we too might decide to drop in on one
of them on the off chance that they would be at home. That was
why the 'front room' must always be kept tidy and why there was
always home-made cake in a tin, and bread and sardines ready for
sandwiches.

This wasn't a weekend but it was a holiday, and if Dad wasn't
there, that was also quite normal as he often had to work when
other people were at home. What was really strange about this day
was that nobody went into the 'front room' but gathered around
the television set even though I knew there was nothing to be seen
at that time of day except something called a 'test card'. It was a
relief when Auntie Ethel and Margaret arrived. Margaret was my
cousin. Three years older than me, she knew everything, and with
no brothers or sisters of her own, delighted in explaining the world
to me. Not that I was going to ask anything yet – no need to look
stupid if I could work it out for myself.

There obviously was something other than the test card on
television, because all the chairs were by now occupied by people,

and the people were now intently watching the screen and listening. It must have been very interesting because at one point Auntie Ethel slid off her chair and crawled forward, under the impression that she would see a bigger brighter image of Princess Margaret that way. I couldn't see anything at all as I was by now in the far corner of the room, sitting on the floor. All I could see was everyone's backs, and the chair legs.

By the time Margaret came round to join me, I was ready to admit defeat.

"It's putting a crown on someone's head. Princess Elizabeth's. Then she's a Queen."

"Is that how you get to be a Queen? Can I be a princess when I grow up? Would I have to marry a Prince to be one? Why does it take so long to put the crown on her?"

I can't remember what my cousin said by way of an answer. Whatever it was, it can't have satisfied me, because I do remember that feeling of unease, of a safe routine disturbed, of an inability to make sense of what was being said. Whatever it was that was happening, it must matter, but I couldn't make it connect with anything I knew or understood.

Then people were calling me, pushing me forward, pointing out what was happening on the screen. What I could see were lines of uniformed men marching in formation. Actually, since the camera must have been placed on a balcony or other high point, it was a square shape made up of lines of flat cap tops, but even I could work that one out. Of course I could, and I didn't need anyone to tell me that they were the Air Force, because I knew the uniform.

"That's Peter," they were saying, "That's your big brother," and I remembered all he had told us about how strict the training was, how proud he had been to be selected for the parade, how very, very fussy they had to be to get their uniform just right and to be perfectly in step. So I wasn't at all surprised to see that the Air

Force lines were so much straighter than those of the Army or Navy. And what was more ....I knew what a Coronation was.

The clouds of confusion now cleared, I was ready to accept any other divergence from my usual Tuesday routine, so put on my 'best' shoes without question in the middle of the afternoon and dutifully trotted along the road with my mother to the factory building at the corner of the street.

Ours was not a manufacturing area, but small industrial units existed in many places then. Walking along the pavement on a normal weekday, the clatter of dozens of typewriters could clearly be heard from the typing pool just the other side of the wall. On this Tuesday they were silent however, and whatever normally occupied the hall into which we were directed had been cleared away to make room for ....the party.

The entrance door opened onto a platform from which steps led down to the main area. Seen from above like that, the whole area was a jiggling, hopping, jumping, mass of children. Long trestle tables down the sides of the hall were spread with sandwiches, iced cakes and jellies. Mother disappeared – probably to cater for our guests at home – and kindly adults led me down the steps to join in the games. As usual, I was rubbish at the games, but also as usual, I enjoyed the tea.

It was Dad, home from work, who came to collect me, and one of the men helping at the party who handed me a pile of presents as we went to leave; a mug with sweets, a medallion and a book of the Coronation with a cream hard cover embossed with a crown and with lots of photographs, some even in colour.

"But I didn't win anything," honesty forced me to protest.

"That doesn't matter," he smiled. "These are for everybody."

So we walked home, carrying my precious party presents, to a house safely restored to its normal arrangement and empty of visitors.

One afternoon at school the next week, the tables were pushed together, large grey sheets of sugar paper were handed out, powder paints mixed up in jars and distributed around the classroom, and we were told to paint a part of the coronation procession, so that all the pictures could be joined together to make a frieze round the room. There was a lot of competition to paint the horses, the Queen or, especially from those lucky ones who had been given a little model of it, the coach itself. But I knew what really mattered. Happily I filled my piece of paper with lots of men marching in uniform, paying particular attention to their caps. One of them had dark brown hair because he, of course, was my brother. I knew what made a Coronation.

I still have the mug, a rather scratched medallion, and the book, with its label no doubt typed by one of the 'pool' girls.

"Presented to
Christine Russell
on the occasion of
The Coronation of
Her Majesty Queen Elizabeth II
2nd June, 1953
Malyons Rd. Coronation Party."

Snapshots of a Northern Terrace Life

Jan Wood

(Much Marcle)

*Recently retired as a Headteacher I now live with
my husband in Herefordshire. I am a governor
at a village school and through our book group
we decided to re-establish our local WI. I love to
travel, enjoy my art studio and garden, but ultimate
happiness is entertaining family and friends.*

My selected memory is my early childhood during the 1950s. Since choosing this topic it is living with me, feeding my thoughts and imagination with events, emotions and experiences that have been buried deep inside for the last fifty years. It is swirling in my mind and has been difficult to give some order to my thoughts as they seem to want to spill out.

A small group of laughing, yelling children kicked a rusty old can down a terraced street. The neat rows gave a cosy feel all clumped together. Doors were always open in the houses that were homes, other houses were rubble, empty shells, a remnant from the wartime bombing raids a few years earlier. These skeleton buildings became our dens, secret spaces and climbing frames where we played with the bricks, rubble and broken glass. Imagine health and safety today looking in on the little girl in her dress and cardigan, bow of ribbon and white socks covered in a film of grey from a play session.

The two up two down was ours. The gas lamps and khaki paint had been removed to give a modern feel for the young couple at number 18. *'My Secret Love'* by Doris Day was the first 78 record bought for the new radiogram that took pride of place. *'Rock Around The Clock'* blasted from the shiny wooden box as the young couple, Mum and Dad, jived around the living room. I clapped for joy watching my parents having so much fun. It's a tradition that has stayed with us, reflected in the fun I've had with my own children and now my grandchildren. That shared love of music and dance is still a huge part of our family.

When I was a small child all my school writings would say, "My Mum is very tall and she wears beautiful dresses." She wasn't that tall but always wore very high heels, bright nail polish and the latest hairstyles. The beautiful dress was because she was a ballroom dancer and I remember stoles, evening bags and those shoes. She had a modern outlook on life and her philosophy for me was 'Dream Big'. My bedtime song each night was *'Swinging on a Star'*. She loved the latest gadgets and had one of the first fitted kitchens, courtesy of my Dad who could make or fix anything.

Thursday was a significant day. I never knew what I was coming home to because it was the day she completely transformed the room with a different layout and sometimes even new furniture. To this day I like everything to remain in the same place! It was also the day that my Dad returned from working away. Thursday nights were treat times and I'm sure the chocolate bars were bigger then; Mars Bars cut into slices, liquorice, dib dabs, wagon wheels and Terry's chocolate mis-shapes in brown paper sacks.

In winter time, the coal fire was warm and comforting while we toasted crumpets for tea. My shiny blue and white spotted Dorothy bag adorned with a metal West Highland terrier was no more that a twisted, melted plastic lump after the roaring fire had done its work. I had attempted to feed the flames with a sweet paper and let go of my pride possession instead - something even my Dad couldn't fix, although he did manage to retrieve it. Fuznag, the cat, named by my Dad's friend Len, a goldfish and Timmy the budgie, who had a very short life, shared our loving home.

A sense of community pervaded the space around us and the
characters who inhabited it. Families of five, like the Oldfields,
whose daughters were my friends. I can see their formidable but
lovely Mum Rhoda in her pinny and scarf turban standing with her
hands on her hips calling them in for bed time, wielding their spoon
of cod liver oil and malt. I did my best to avoid being included
in the line up. Gran Rylatt, the wise old woman, the oracle that
seemed to know all the answers and gave support to all the young
families. She was there when my Mum called for help when, as a
four year old, I had trapped my fingers in the wheel of her green
bicycle with the red tartan child seat - but unfortunately not there
when I broke my arm. My awareness not yet fully developed, I
ran and tripped, as I was sure the dust cart would run me over as
it tried to pass me in the narrow space. After a trip to the hospital,
and a plaster cast, the itchy green band holding up my arm was
substituted for a soft silk headscarf. Her grandsons, Kenny and
Norman, accompanied me to the Queen's coronation street fancy
dress party, two Black and White Minstrels (not very politically
correct these days) to my Little Red Riding Hood. James and Jean
Parrott, the plumber and the amazing housewife, my Mum's friend
and the greatest butterfly cake maker. I remember being taken to
their house during the night when, aged six, my brother decided
to make an appearance. My Dad sold his car, a Singer Bantam, to
buy a Silver Cross pram and I was now an older sister.

Children can be so cruel about things that are different. We used
to follow a lady that lived in the next terrace when she did her
shopping. She always wore a smart hat and covered her face with
a net and lint combination because she had no nose. I never knew
why, but we made up all sorts of stories never realising how much it
must have upset her.

Summer nights would ensure that social gatherings went on into
the evening. Chairs outside, darts matches, card games, monopoly,
discussions, cups of tea or things more daring once the children
were in bed. Whole families getting together as if we had all come

out of deep sleep, emerging into the glorious sunshine.

This paved the way for our summer performances. Curtains across a washing line depicted a stage that stayed right through the school holidays. We made up and then later wrote plays, had a wealth of props and entertained with weekly performances. I didn't fight to be the Princess with the beautiful dress, as I always wanted to be the hero, probably fed by the literature I collected. My Dad made sure I had a mixed diet, so along with Enid Blyton and Bunty, I had the Eagle comic, Moby Dick, The Three Musketeers, Black Beauty and The Arabian Nights. This love of literature has remained with me thanks to my Dad and a few teachers along the way.

Other summer time memories include the swimming pool, the park and the cinema on wet days where there were always two films, a feature and a B movie. I saw Oklahoma three times in one sitting. I remember the ice cream man on his bicycle ringing his school style bell, gob stopper competitions, aniseed balls and the forbidden bubble gum in waxed paper. The sticky coconut covered toffee apples perched high on their wooden handles were always worth the scraped knees as we climbed over the red brick wall to get to the old lady who sold them to us for pennies. Cats cradles, skipping games, hopscotch, marbles, roller skates and later Hoola Hoops all kept us occupied. There were outings to the seaside where we'd take early evening trips in the car or train journeys for the whole day. One Penny platform tickets allowed you onto the station to print your name on a metal strip if a trip wasn't planned.

School holidays were spent at my grandparents' house. They had a large garden and Granddad was a keen gardener. I had my own flower patch and took dahlias wrapped in newspaper home to my Mum. They also had a bathroom, which was a luxury then. I had friends over to stay and Grandma would bake with us and make tents and scrapbooks. My friend Maxine and I caused a scare when we decided to take our dolls for a very long walk. When it was discovered we were missing we enjoyed a thrilling ride home in a police car.

The radio blared out Children's Hour and the television set enticed us with Watch with Mother, Picture Book, Andy Pandy, the Flower Pot Men, Rag Tag and Bob Tail and, my favourite, the Wooden Tops. I can still see my brother running as fast as he could from the house next door as he didn't believe their TV had the same programmes.

Illnesses like chicken pox and whooping cough were commonplace as the first immunisations were not available until 1955. When I had a bad case of the measles the local shopkeeper, Mr Curry, sent a tin of iced gem biscuits to aid my recovery. The tin was pale blue and covered with fairies and elves. Once empty my Mum used it as a sewing tin, showing it to my children when they were small.

School days were happy times. The red bricked Victorian building of the infant and junior school was within walking distance and all my friends attended. My very first teacher was Miss Appleyard in her green tweed suit, and there were counters in tobacco tins and a sand pit in a large wooden box. Miss Taylor, my very favourite teacher, was with us for two years and read the 'Magic Faraway Tree' stories to us over and over again by popular request. As I got older and aspired to be a monitor and pass my eleven plus exam my inspiration was Miss Bergwitz, the Headteacher. I used to love to be her helper and imagined myself sitting at her desk. I always wanted to be a teacher and role played from an early age - it always seemed to be part of me. So, no career angst, just a sense of motivation to reach my goal.

As the sixties loomed, embracing modernism and leading an age of reform, the social policy concentrated on slum clearance and new housing stock. Our area was highlighted and this familiar environment would be no more in this new age. We were to move to a brand new house on an estate, other families to different areas of the town. I had my new uniform, my strongly smelling leather satchel that I jumped on repeatedly to look more lived in and a life of new beginnings as a new era stretched in front of me. Even though the house was to be demolished my Mum insisted that it was to be cleaned from top to bottom before we left. Our last evening was spent on the floor of the sitting room all on one mattress full of excitement and apprehension while we waited for the removal van. The strength of that emotion comes flooding back every time I hear, *"Waiting for the Moving Van to Come"*, a song by the American singer songwriter David Ackles. Those sparkling windows were broken before we had even left the street.

A Year Of Celebration
Agnes Allen
(Hawkesbury & Horton)

I was born in 1950s Paisley, Scotland, one of 11 siblings, one adopted. I am the 'one in the middle', having an understanding of both generations of children. I remember we were a family who walked everywhere, mainly because we could not afford the bus fare.

My mother had a magical way with children and always knew the right things to say and do to make a child feel calm and loved. Margaret started life in Paisley, Scotland. She was born in 1920, the seventh child of an Irish mother and Anglo/Irish father. Her parents suffered the tragedy of the death of their then youngest child just before Margaret's birth. She told me that she felt her mother did not love her. With hindsight, I can understand that her mother was suffering grief from the death of her daughter and had difficulty coping with a new baby. However, it affected my mother and therefore our family for all of our lives. She loved us all deeply as children, but found it harder to show her emotions as we grew older. She was always afraid of rejection.

As we grew up we jointly decided that we would always demonstrate our love for each other. Because of this the last thing we say, either on the telephone or in person, is - I love you. As for my mother, she was always hugged and told the same by every one of us. Eventually she grew to like the hugging. On her deathbed she made a point of saying I love you to us all individually. It felt sad but wonderful.

My father, Joseph, was a man who lived in fantasy, who never really wanted to grow up and accept responsibility. His father had died of a brain haemorrhage aged 47. Joe was the only boy and at 14 he was required to give up grammar school and start work. He had two older and one younger sister. In 1929 men could earn a lot more than women. He always regretted not going to University and was forever seeking knowledge from books.

I suppose you would say Joe was a self-taught man. He was very clever and had encyclopaedias and reference books which we could use. He encouraged us to find answers to questions for ourselves. He had a quick wit and was full of stories. This ability came into its own with his children. We loved him telling us his made-up stories at bedtime. Sometimes he would include us in the story which was very exciting to hear as a child. At other times he would sing to us until we slept. He was the opposite of my mother in that he was expressive with his emotions and we loved the excitement of his personality, the fun of his tricks and jokes.

Our family life was based on annual celebrations, or so it seemed to me at the time. My father loved to sing and had a good tenor voice. Mum was always shy, even in front of us, and didn't like to perform. The year of celebrations always centered on New Year, which was important to us as a family. It is only with the hindsight of maturity that you realise what you had and have lost forever. We will never have that time again. That is why, as adults, our family has the philosophy that 'everything is a memory'. Even if stuck in the rain on holiday, if you are with people you love you can have a laugh, and that's what we've done...

My older four brothers and one sister were born within a year or two of each other. There was then a five year gap and I was born in 1950. Then another five year gap before my younger three sisters and one brother arrived. Much later, our parents adopted another boy. To "make up the football team" according to Dad, with him as coach and Mum as referee. There were only two months in the year where we didn't celebrate a birthday. Mine was in February. Sometimes my birthday would be at the beginning of Lent, which I disliked - although it could mean that I would have pancakes.

By Easter the weather had usually become warmer and at last we could walk a bit further afield. Easter was the only time that the whole family attended Church together. Normally we would go to Mass at different times as Mum was usually busy with cooking, cleaning etc., and would go at a later time. As Catholics we always had to 'fast' before communion and were absolutely ravenous by the time we got back home from Church. A communion wafer and a boiled sweet don't go far.

I think we must have created 'The Brunch' as that's what we always had late Sunday mornings after Church – a combination of cereal and cooked breakfast with toast, followed by biscuits or bread and jam. As there were so many of us, there were two sittings. At Easter there was extra as we had special boiled eggs and, if we were lucky, a chocolate egg also. There were two lots of eggs. One fried that we ate with our Lorne square sausage, slice of Ayrshire bacon, tomatoes and toast, and the other boiled which we decorated and saved for egg-rolling later – on some occasions we had to borrow Mum's make-up to do this as we couldn't afford paints. Eyebrow pencil and a dab of lipstick worked a treat.

After 'brunch' Dad would take us out for a walk to 'The Braes', to get us out of the house while Mum cleared up and prepared our main meal. The Braes were hills 1000 to 1500 feet high overlooking the town and valley below, looking towards the Kilpatrick Hills and Ben Lomond in the distance. The view is spectacular. This is now called The Gleniffer Country Park and has lots of made-up paths to walk on. In those days we just wandered over the countryside as we pleased.

We carefully chose our spot at the top of a small hill where we could safely roll our eggs down to the bottom. It was important that it was not too rocky as we didn't want those eggs smashed to bits. As you can imagine, there were sometimes tears. So, you made sure that you made the right choice. It was always our own decision. Dad encouraged us to think for ourselves.

I remember going to my Gran Allen's house on May Day. At the front of her traditional sandstone tenement apartment was a park with a Maypole. It was great fun eating liquorice and sherbet, or even an ice-cream, whilst we watched grown-ups holding the long silken ropes as they circled the Maypole weaving up and down and in and out. There was a man playing the accordion in accompaniment to their movements. The ice-cream was always Italian as a lot of Italians had moved to the West Coast of Scotland and started businesses of ice-cream parlours, mobile ice-cream vans and fish and chip shops. We loved Jaconelli's ice-cream and Cardosi's chips. Later, we could go round the Maypole ourselves and got into a confusion of ropes and people. It was magic.

A peculiar thing happened before every Whitsun, when we would all be bought new clothes. I don't know why this was and have never found out the reason. It was really exciting to have brand new clothes and be able to show them off. It must have been a struggle for my parents to find the money to buy them for us all.

There was a bad time one year at Whitsun when my father, my oldest brother and older sister were in three different hospitals. They were in a triangle 30 miles apart. Each weekend Mum travelled by bus to see them all. She sometimes took me with her for company. I was six years old. Mum had to get a Provident cheque that year to be able to afford the Whitsun clothes as my father wasn't earning because of his illness. Mum had to pay an extortionate amount of interest on this credit. It really wasn't like today when everyone has credit cards and they are accepted everywhere. You were made to feel poor.

We always looked forward to June as this meant long holidays of seven weeks. The days seemed never-ending as it didn't get dark until 11 o'clock and if it rained it was always at night which was okay as we were tucked up inside. A trip to the seaside meant all the children being carried in the back of a neighbour's pick-up truck. Eventually it came to be August and the time when we had to go back to school. The autumn and winter would soon be with us.

Hallowe'en was one of my favourite times of the year. It meant the house was full of apples, satsumas, nuts and cakes. We used to dress up in the Scottish tradition, not the American version adapted from ours, and visit other people's houses when it was dark, which was amazing for us. It wasn't really that late, it was just the 'nights drawing in'. At their houses we would sing a song, tell a story or joke, or do a trick to earn our reward of fruit or nuts. It was rare for people to give us money and if they did we would be disappointed.

Bonfire night was not a tradition we celebrated when very young as my parents felt it was anti-Catholic. We used to envy others their fireworks and bonfires with baked potatoes. Eventually, my parents relented and we were allowed to visit a community bonfire and have firelighters, a banger and Catherine wheel to give to an adult for the show.

We couldn't wait for December and Christmas. Most of our time was spent in Church. The rest was to have family time together. My parents could not afford a lot of presents and I remember my favourite was my first watch, a Timex, when I was nine. I put it on to wear to Church and 'show off'. I loved that watch and had it for many years. One year my father and I made presents of purses and wallets for all the family. We had an old leather settee which had to be thrown out. However, the back of the settee had been against a wall and the leather was good, so we used this with tartan lining to make the items. My dad marked out a pattern and we glued on the lining and cut it out. We then punched holes around and put twine through and finally put on covered studs. It was wonderful to see the expressions on their faces when we gave them our presents. After my father died, Mum gave me his wallet as a keepsake. It was the only original item left from our craft work.

Finally, we come to New Year's Eve. The house was cleaned from top to bottom. All the curtains and bedding had to be freshly put up and on to meet the New Year. Mum always made a load of ginger wine for us to have (non-alcoholic). She also made a great spread of cakes and shortbread for us to eat. When old enough, we were woken up before midnight to come and join the celebration and would be given a glass of ginger wine and a piece of Madeira or Dundee cake. After singing Auld Lang Syne and wishing each other A Happy New Year we would all enjoy the 'family party'. Starting with my father and progressing down to the youngest we would perform our party piece. This could be a song or story, a joke or dance, playing a musical instrument or even playing a tune on your teeth. The only person excused was our mother. Dad made her a cup of tea. This was always a part of our lives at every celebration.

This is not the end. It was the beginning of our family traditions, stories and songs passed on from generation to generation and now at the great, great grandchild stage – happy days.

All Appeared New, And Strange

Esther Large

(Brightwell cum Sotwell)

I grew up in a Quaker family near Birmingham, with my parents and two older sisters. I am very grateful that my parents saw education as the way out of poverty and ignored the neighbours who said, "It's no good educating girls, they'll only get married."

Born in 1932, I have two memories of myself as a very young child. In one my mother is holding me in her arms and I have one arm round her neck. She is standing and talking to my father who is also standing. They begin to argue, probably about money, which was in very short supply, and I see myself leaning to put my other arm round my father's neck as well. This effectively stopped the argument for the time being.

In the other, my mother is wearily pushing me home in my pram, after doing the shopping. I start to play one of the oldest games known to babies. I throw my teddy bear out, quite confident that she will pick him up for me. After a few times she loses patience, tells me off and puts my teddy out of reach. I am surprised that she is not enjoying the game.

In those days, wives did their housework in the morning and then changed and went out to shop in the afternoon. One day she tidied me up and dressed me in a frilly white dress, a hand-me-down from a cousin, and then went to get washed and changed herself. Getting bored, I wandered out into the garden and found a heap of soot, which my father had collected after sweeping the chimney. He had left it there so that the harmful chemicals in it would disperse and it could be safely spread on the garden. When my mother was ready, she found me sitting by the heap, sifting the fine soft soot through my fingers. I have no memory of what she said.

My sisters, five and seven years older than I was, certainly didn't want the little 'un tagging after them when they went out to play with their friends, so I played in the back garden by myself. It was a long, narrow garden with a lawn, with narrow flowerbeds near the house and the rest of the garden devoted to growing vegetables. Where the two parts of the garden met, there were three trees. The one in the middle was a crab apple tree and my mother made delicious jelly from the fruit. The other two trees bore Worcester Pearmain and Ellison's Orange apples. I enjoyed the fruit, but I had a sense of grievance about them, because I remembered that my sisters had been allowed to choose which apple trees to have, and I was considered too young for this.

I loved being in the garden, especially when my father was working there. I followed him round trying to help, delaying him all the time. On one occasion when I was "helping", I managed to strike him on the forehead with a wildly flailing hoe. It drew a lot of blood but did not do any serious damage, and as my father dashed off to stem the flow, he said, "You silly little kid," I was devastated by what I had done and rushed to my mother for comfort and reassurance.

Though a dog would have been more fun, I enjoyed seeing all the little creepy crawlies in the garden. I understood that slugs were definitely bad and that ladybirds and earthworms were very good. I was enchanted by the centipedes and millipedes with all their little legs, and also by the earwigs, although I was dubious about touching them. I knew that I must avoid bees and wasps or I would get stung. One day, when I was in the garden on my own, I found two cabbage leaves still attached to the root, left behind after my father had cut a cabbage for dinner. It must have rained and the leaves were full of water. I decided that these would make a good bath for earthworms. I found a nice fat one and gave it a good wash. Fortunately I didn't succeed in drowning it and it returned safely to its home.

Planting seeds in a small patch of the flower border that was to be mine was exciting. I knew that my father grew all the vegetables from these strange little dried up things, some of which were almost as fine as dust. I was given some nice big knobbly nasturtium seeds to plant under supervision. Next morning I rushed out to see if the plants had appeared, but there was no sign of them. I wanted very much to dig them up to see what was happening, but I was persuaded to be patient and eventually the shoots appeared and the plants flowered, much to my satisfaction.

A lot of time was spent watching my sisters and parents to find out how they did everything. Unfortunately, I didn't always understand what they were trying to do. I noticed that my mother spent time polishing the furniture. I decided to try this and found a small bottle of almond oil to use as polish. With an old rag I started rubbing the oil into the upholstered settee. My mother quickly found out what I was doing, but though she paid professional cleaners to deal with the mark, the stain was permanent.

A more dangerous experiment resulted from watching my father light the fire in the morning, before going to work. This fire was not only the main source of heat in the house, but it also heated the water in the back boiler. First he would clear the ashes from the fireplace and then lay the fire, crumpled up newspaper at the bottom, then sticks and lastly small pieces of coal. When lit the newspaper blazed up beautifully, and as this died away, the sticks began to burn and finally the coal caught fire. Just occasionally the fire would not draw, and then my father used the time honoured method of holding a sheet of newspaper over the fireplace to make a good draught and soon the fire was roaring away. While he was out of the room for a moment, and the fireguard was not in place, I tried to make the fire roar in the same way. Fortunately he returned before I set either myself or the house on fire.

Left to my own devices, I did not always get into what others regarded as mischief. I had plenty of toys to play with, though my grandchildren would think I was deprived if they compared the number of their toys with mine. Particular favourites were half a dozen tin clockwork creatures, of which I remember a hare that hopped and a chicken that pecked. I used to try to wind them up so that they would all be in action at the same time. As soon as I had wound up the last one the first would be stopping and I had to start all over again. I also enjoyed my spinning top, which needed vigorous pumping to get it revolving. There was a big dolls house, given by some friends of the family, and I would spend time re-arranging the furniture. I did have some dolls, including a Shirley Temple doll, as well as a doll's pram and cot, but I don't think I found them very exciting. My favourite toy was my teddy bear, Cubby, who always came to bed with me and was loved so much that he ended up in a very dilapidated state.

Family holidays were rare, but on fine Saturdays we would take a picnic to Sutton Park. This is a wild area of some 2400 acres, remnant of an ancient forest, containing heathland, woods and man-made pools. The nearest pool to our home was called Bracebridge, and we usually went there. Here my father taught us all to swim and my eldest sister could swim out to a little island in the middle. The edges of the pool were quite sandy and shallow, so it was heaven for me on sunny afternoons. Sadly, when I went back there as an adult, I found that swimming was no longer allowed.

Other regular highlights in the year were Bonfire Night and Christmas Day. On bonfire night a guy, made from my father's old clothes stuffed with newspaper, was ceremonially burnt on the bonfire. We had a box of fireworks and my favourite was the Catherine wheel whizzing round, securely nailed to the washing post. My mother's task was to keep me at a safe distance from the action, particularly the jumping jacks, and to supervise me when I was allowed sparklers and red, green and blue Bengal matches.

As Christmas approached, my mother always made the pudding, the mincemeat and the cake. We had a chance to stir the pudding before it was cooked, when one or two silver sixpences would be added for the lucky ones to find on Christmas day. Then a fire was lit in the front room, which was only used on ceremonial occasions, and we played games and usually had indoor fireworks: more sparklers and Bengal matches and best of all a grey snake coiling out of a small volcano.

Sometimes my father read aloud to us. He read some of William Blake's poems to me as I sat on his knee, when I was at an age when most parents would have thought nursery rhymes suitable. As a result, Blake's poem "The Tiger" has always been one of my favourites. When he acquired a cheap edition of the Complete Plays of Bernard Shaw, courtesy of the Daily Herald, he would read one of the plays for our entertainment on winter evenings. On one occasion he began to read " Arms and the Man" which I remember as "the Chocolate Cream Soldier", possibly because just when we had got to the point where the soldier was eating chocolate creams in the lady's bedroom, my bedtime arrived and I had to go in spite of protesting, "It's not fair".

In 1939 we travelled to Norfolk by train to stay with an aunt and uncle who ran a poultry farm near North Walsham. Their farmhouse, which was built of flints in the local style, seemed very grand. There was no electricity, so you went to bed by candle light and my aunt had to light big oil lamps for the downstairs rooms. I particularly enjoyed the novelty of sleeping in a feather bed.

Other relations of my mother's were camping on the farm and another family had moved quite close, to escape the anticipated bombing in Norwich. All the cousins were older than me, so I seemed doomed to be the little 'un. The weather was beautiful for the whole fortnight and one day the whole gang of us set out to walk to Mundsley, a good five miles, to spend a day on the beach. We played in the sea and made sandcastles and some even allowed themselves to be buried in the sand until only their heads could be seen. I had never spent a day like it and when we set out on the return journey, I was very glad to ride on the shoulders of my male cousins, who took it in turns to carry me.

After our lovely summer holiday in Norfolk, my next clear memory is of the whole family listening to the wireless on the morning of September 3rd and hearing the dreaded announcement by Neville Chamberlain that we were now at war with Germany. My parents had already lived through one war and feared the worst. I did not understand what this meant, but after that life was never the same again.

Part 3

Breaking Away

Stranger On The Shore

Margaret Sykes

(Monkton Farleigh)

I spent my childhood in Plymouth before developing a career as a social worker and Family Therapist. I worked in Fiji with VSO from 1970-71, and continue to enjoy travel. I live with my husband in Wiltshire and we have three children scattered across the globe.

I held the key to my future in shaking hands and tore open the envelope. "You will be posted to the Social Development and Welfare Department in Suva, Fiji". I read the words again in disbelief. Surely there had been some mistake. The only thing I had heard about Fiji was that it was known for its history of cannibalism. I had never heard of anyone visiting the country. I reached for the Atlas. Fiji, I discovered, could not have been further away from home, tiny dots scattered in the vast ocean, around 180 degrees longitude, thousands of miles away from anywhere. I could not sleep that night, wondering whether, as a 24 year old newly qualified social worker, I had the courage to step into the unknown, so different from my comfortable, white, middle class upbringing in a corner of south west England.

Six weeks later I found myself on a plane for the first time in my life together with four other Volunteers (VSOs). As we stepped onto the hot steamy tarmac we were welcomed Fijian style and presented with a sweet scented "leilei" (garland) of frangipani

blossoms. Maybe things would not be so bad after all. The
gentle lilting Pacific Island singing that greeted us soothed my
misapprehensions.

Alarm bells started ringing, however, as I was ushered into the inner
sanctuary of Shankar Lal, the Chief Welfare Officer, a dapper little
Indian man full of his own importance, who was also responsible
for all the VSOs. The others had been dispatched one by one to
their new homes. I was the only one remaining. He looked me
up and down approvingly, with a glint in his eye. "I have decided
you will stay with me," he said putting his arm around me. I could
smell the garlic on his breath. "I will look after you and bring you
to work with me to train new staff."

I envisaged myself a prisoner of the one person on whom my job
depended. Weary and bleary-eyed after thirty six hours travelling,
the last thing I felt like doing was fighting off advances from
my new boss. With apparent reluctance he took me to a small
flat occupied by New Zealand Volunteers, who had not been
forewarned of my arrival. This was to become my home for the
following year and a half.

Two days later I made my escape from Shankar Lal's office. My
saviour was his Deputy, Mere, a beautiful, lively and articulate Pacific
Islander, just returned from leave. She was clearly the driving force
within the Department. "Who are you and what are you doing
here?" she asked with amazement, seeing me surrounded by piles of
files. Taking charge, she whisked me off, explaining that there were
no new staff to train, but with a staff shortage in the local office, it
would be useful to work there. She explained the whole country was
preoccupied with preparing for Independence celebrations and the
imminent arrival of the young Prince Charles, and there had been
no time to think about what to do with humble VSOs.

I was allocated an office, a caseload of ninety probationers, and was
soon inundated by requests from the British Magistrate for Social
Enquiry Reports on youngsters, prior to sentencing. It became
apparent that much of my time was being used to keep the judicial

process running smoothly. There were times when street children were reconciled and returned to families in the countryside, at least for the duration of court orders, and occasional validation of adoption applications.

One day Mere dashed into my office, as always a bundle of energy, in sharp contrast to the languid pace of tropical life with the mantra of "mataka" (tomorrow). "I have just heard there is a Government boat due to take supplies and check on the copra production of the remote Yasawa Islands. Your passage is booked. It will introduce you to island life"

After five hours sailing, green specks of land emerged on the horizon from the shimmering haze of the South Seas. As we negotiated the channel through the coral reef, a golden crescent of sand fringed by gently swaying palm trees greeted us. Clambering down the ship's ladder, holding my sandals and woven Fijian basket aloft, I splashed ashore to the group of friendly villagers dressed in sun bleached sulus (sarongs), gathered on the fine sand. But the peace of the idyllic scene was short lived. On entering the village, set a few yards back from the shore along a sandy track, excited small children rushed out to see the new arrivals. Taking one look at me, the only white woman, they ran crying in fear seeking refuge behind their mothers' ample backsides. With a jolt I experienced the discomfort of being different, and apprehension about how I might be treated. I felt I might almost have been the first white woman to leave footprints on the unspoiled coral shore.

The village of trim bures made with traditional thatch, encircled a large grassy communal area, with the larger chief's bure at one end, and, of supreme importance to the Fijian community, the larger white concrete church at the other. We were led to the centre of the village for the time-honoured welcome ceremony. As I took my place sitting cross legged in the circle, I anxiously checked to ensure that my new brightly coloured sulu was tied securely in place over my cotton mini dress, to avoid giving offence. The welcome ritual went back centuries and was still strictly adhered to as an essential part of accepting visitors into the village. The gift of yaqona roots was handed over to the chief, who placed them in a large "tanoa" or ceremonial wooden drinking bowl to which he added water and spent many minutes squeezing the juice from the roots. Interminable speeches of welcome were exchanged before the yaqona (grog or cava) was distributed. My reverie was disturbed as I looked up to see a handsome, muscular light brown skinned Fijian with a halo of black wavy hair, crouched in front of me. He carefully ladled grey unappetising liquid, reminiscent of dirty dishwater, into a highly polished, half coconut shell, and held it out for me to take in both hands to drink. Desperate to make a good impression, I steeled myself and took a large gulp as I knew to be the accepted custom. "Vinaka" (thank you) I managed to say without choking on the musty, bitter taste.

A large friendly smiling "marama", Fijian woman, called Mereoni, beckoned me to follow her away from the men who were settling down to talk business and start a lengthy grog drinking session. She led me to her family bure where visitors spent the night. Barefooted, I entered the high, spacious room. The floor was covered with layers of soft, finely woven mats. A double bed was curtained off in the corner where she indicated I would sleep. In my rudimentary Fijian I attempted to object as I would not wish to displace her and her husband, but was soon overruled with lots of laughter on her part, and I felt it would be discourteous to reject this offer of hospitality. Everyone else, men and women, were to sleep on the floor of the bure, which I suspect may have been more comfortable than the hard wooden bed, which also reinforced my feeling of splendid isolation. Displayed in the most prominent place was a photo of our Royal Family, the Queen, Duke and their four children. Otherwise the walls were hung with beautiful masi or tapa, decorative hangings made from mulberry bark and intricately decorated with traditional rust and black designs.

"Do you come from London? Do you know the Queen?" Mereoni asked in Fijian. I was unable to claim Royal patronage, but although this may have been a disappointment, her welcome and hospitality was none the less enthusiastic.

Mereoni, followed by a small tribe of children gradually becoming bolder, showed me around, and with shy giggles from the ever growing crowd, indicated the hole in the ground toilet, and the shower arrangement with large bowl and water jug set behind a small shoulder high wooden screen. Some distance away a crowd of women had gathered around a "lovo", (earth oven) some two feet deep, lined with hot stones, in which had been placed a suckling pig wrapped in banana leaves, which had been cooking for several hours, delicious aromas permeating the village. Another group of women were sitting around under the shade of the coconut palms, sharing laughter and gossip, and weaving beautiful mats of fibrous pandanas leaves, typical of every Fijian home. A young boy shimmied up a palm tree to pick a coconut which he deftly cut with his bush knife, to offer me one of the sweetest drinks I had ever sampled.

As the tropical night drew in, about 20 people gathered in the chief's bure for the evening meal. I was clearly an enigma, and our host was unsure where to place me in the circle sitting on the ground around the white cloths laid out for the communal meal. Traditionally all the men sat at one end, and the women and children at the other. However Government officials were treated as guests. The Chief solved the dilemma by seating me at his right hand, and elevating me above all others to the guest of honour. Thus when the fish soup was served, the first dish was placed in front of me, and to my horror, I saw that in the centre was what I knew to be a great delicacy for the Fijian, a fish's head. I knew that as much as I wanted to fit in, and follow local customs, this was one step too far. To refuse the offering would be an unpardonable rejection of Fijian hospitality. So with some quick thinking I offered it to my host, who, much to my relief, accepted my gift with alacrity.

I was able to show genuine appreciation after this somewhat tense and delicate start. I was introduced to tastes and smells that lingered and I would want to capture and relive in more mundane times. The kokoda (raw fish marinated in lime juice and coconut cream) was superb, the slow roasted pig was the best I had ever tasted, and the rich flavours contrasted well with the dalo (taro), kumala and cassava. Fresh pineapple and pawpaw and mangoes had never tasted so good, as juice dripped down my wrists.

Early the next morning, I sat alone on the white sands and recalled my trepidation of coming to this unknown land. I realised how prejudice develops from fear and ignorance. I had experienced discomfort as the outsider. I had been embarrassed and ashamed that skin colour brought entitlement to privilege. The islanders had developed a culturally rich, happy and healthy lifestyle with a strong sense of community, from so little. What right had we as a colonising nation, to impose our way of life on other cultures and nations? My way of viewing the world was fast disintegrating, and from this moment I began to see things differently, returning to Suva with as many questions as answers.

As we gathered on the shore later that day, I was presented with a farewell garland of delicate shells. I felt honoured to have enjoyed time with some of the most hospitable and generous people I had ever encountered. As the boat sailed out into the bay, accompanied by outrigger canoes, the sounds of the Fijian farewell song "Isa Lei", asking the traveller not to forget precious moments spent on Fijian shores, faded away. I often wondered how long this Pacific paradise would remain untouched by the modern world, but I also knew the island experience had affected me profoundly in ways that would send ripples down the years ahead.

The Rude Awakening
Margaret Wilson
(Rydal)

I am a new member of the WI and this is my first experience of writing. I have had a varied career, nursing, teaching and counselling. I am married with a grown up family and am enjoying my retirement in the Lake District, where I enjoy walking and recreating my garden.

Looking back I wonder, what was it that made me long to be a nurse? I remember the hours of pleading, cajoling, sulking and crying I had used to persuade my reluctant parents to let me leave home. Mum was already missing my two brothers and was reluctant to see her last child fly the nest. Two nurse friends they knew were moving to take up posts at a small fever hospital in Stockport and it was eventually agreed that I could go with them. As I was only 17 I was to go as a cadet.

Cherry Tree Hospital provided care for anyone with an infectious disease. There were three wards. A cubicle block, used for the most infectious patients; a small ward for children with tuberculosis; and a long mixed ward for babies, children and adults.

As I walked nervously through the gates on my first day the hospital seemed dark and forbidding. The butterflies that had been playing somersaults in my stomach began to dance with renewed energy. I was met by a stern-looking uniformed woman, Home Sister. She marched me along to the small plain room that was to be my home for the next twelve months. I was instructed to change quickly and then come down to the dining room.

Lying over the iron bedstead was my uniform. I dressed quickly and, turning, caught my reflection in the wardrobe mirror. My heart skipped a beat - was that really me? There I was in my blue dress, stiffly starched white apron, frilly sleeve cuffs and, perched precariously on my head, the cap. An oblong of stiffly starched cotton that had been transformed by some miracle of origami into a 'butterfly cap'.

Feeling very self-conscious I pushed open the dining room door. I nervously took my place at the long table to be greeted by hostile stares. What had I done wrong? I sat there wondering what to do next. After what seemed an age a nurse entered the room. "May I sit down please?" Nods all round. Ah, that was it. This was the hierarchical world I had entered. A far cry from my childhood imaginings, where nurses would always be kind and caring.

Another cadet nurse, Meadows, started at the same time as I did. Two mornings a week when it was the maid's day off we had to make toast for everyone else. The day started at 7.30am so those mornings it felt like we were up in the middle of the night. Toast was made using a toasting fork in front of the electric fire, no mean feat.

My first day I was assigned to the cubicle block. This was a group of glass-sided rooms surrounded by an open air balcony. I was told that each time I entered one of the cubicles I must don a gown, and for some patients a mask. It all seemed exciting at first. Whenever I left a cubicle I was instructed to wash and scrub my hands with carbolic soap. Even in September it was often cold and rainy, windy days were a nightmare. Cardigans were strictly forbidden.

My duties involved taking patients their drinks and meals. As the most junior nurse I was assigned the most mundane tasks, including the inevitable bedpan duties. Soon after I started an awful incident occurred. Holding a bedpan and its unsavoury contents as if it were some precious offering, I backed through the door. I thought I was entering the sluice. I wasn't. I was confronted by the first naked man I had ever seen. Wrong door. It was the bathroom, and he was just about to get in the bath. I was determined I would never make that mistake again. Horror of horrors I did exactly the same thing the following day. Same man. Mealtimes became a nightmare. I prayed I would not have to take him his meals. I would try to avoid his eyes as a blush travelled unrelentingly up from my neck. How I wished they would send him home.

I arrived at the hospital shortly after the height of the polio epidemic, which hit Britain in the mid 1950s. I had not realised just how devastating an illness it was, until I encountered my first patient being nursed in an iron lung. This was a coffin-like structure which encased the patients from neck to toe as an external bellows forced air in and out of their paralysed lungs.

I had been aware of polio, as a school friend of mine contracted the disease. There were anxious days as everyone waited to hear the outcome. She was one of the lucky ones, and was left with only slight paralysis of one leg. Others were not so fortunate, as infantile paralysis (as it was more commonly known) left many severely disabled. I had been unaware that it could affect the respiratory muscles. Patients nursed in iron lungs were sentenced to a life of inactivity lying on their back with only an adjustable mirror above their face allowing them a view of their immediate surroundings. I was too junior to have any involvement in their care. I watched as nurses spent time carrying out whatever needed to be done through portholes situated along the sides of the machine.

One of the patients was a young lady. The nurses would sit with her combing her hair, applying make up and talking. She was understandably extremely depressed. I admired the nurses' attempts to make her life as bearable as possible. She had frequent visitors but it must have been horrendous for her.
We had three patients nursed in this way, but this young lady is the one that sticks in my mind. I wonder what became of her?

The children in the hospital were mainly suffering from measles, scarlet fever, diphtheria, gastro-enteritis or tuberculosis. They were collected from home by a nurse and brought in by ambulance. No one questioned the effect this would have on them. It must have been terrifying, as the parents were not allowed to accompany them. Visiting was not allowed, although some parents would come and stand at the windows just to get a glimpse of their child. Who knows the long term emotional damage those children suffered.

I was asked by the Sister to collect a child. I donned my long white gown and off we went. When we arrived, the ambulance driver dropped me off while he turned the ambulance round. Children appeared, as if from nowhere, to gaze as I walked down the path. I knocked at the door. No answer. I was at the wrong house. More children arrived. I made a hasty retreat, much to the amusement of the ambulance driver who had realised we were in the wrong street.

Children were nursed in high-sided metal cots for the duration of their stay. One little girl was determined this was not for her. I spotted her climbing precariously over the cot side. Rushing into her cubicle to rescue her, I said, "Oh no, you mustn't do that you could fall and hurt yourself." She looked at me thoughtfully, then said, "Alright, if I hurt myself I would have to go to hospital and I don't want to do that." I don't know where she thought she was.

One evening I was asked by the senior nurse to sit with a little girl who was being nursed in an oxygen tent. I was to report immediately if I noticed any change. I was petrified. The sides of the plastic tent were filmed with condensation, making it difficult to see her. I sat there, eyes glued to her little body, watching the rise and fall of her chest. I was probably only left alone for a very short time but it seemed like hours. I was so relieved when the nurse came back and seemed content that all was well.

How different nursing was then. I was awakened by a loud knocking on my door at 4am. Night Sister needed me to 'special' a child who was very ill. I hurried across to the ward where a 10 year old girl was fighting for her life. I was instructed what I was to do and there were frequent visits from doctors and senior nurses.

I had never seen anyone who was so ill. Feelings of panic and helplessness washed over me. I learnt that she died shortly after the day staff came on duty.

Not many weeks after starting work I was summoned to Matron's office. Apart from her brief visits to the ward, I had not seen her since my interview. My main recollection of that event was of her small, ill-tempered dog. It seemed intent on laddering my new stockings. Matron was a small, erect, dumpy lady who would end each sentence with an 'urring' sound which the dog echoed. Or was it the other way round?

I was taken aback when she said, "I need to talk to you about last night, you didn't go to the nurses' dance." "No," I replied. I wondered what was coming. "So I take it you think it beneath you. You think you are better than everyone else?"

I didn't know what to say, but tried to explain that I had never been to a dance before and didn't know what I was supposed to do. She glared at me over her glasses and said, "From now on you will join in with your colleagues, do you understand"? "Yes Matron". I was dismissed and beat a hasty retreat. She was a strange character, but Matron's word was law.

From time to time if the hospital was busy she would deliver an edict, "No day off this week". The order was accepted with only a few grumbles. No unions at this hospital. A few weeks later, great news, two days off next week.

On another occasion my parents were summoned. I had developed dermatitis on my hands and the doctors were concerned that they might have become infected. I was admitted to one of the wards. She marched them across to the ward and then pronounced, "There are no germs in this hospital, your daughter must have picked them up outside." My father looked totally nonplussed. A fever hospital with no germs?
We worked long hours and at times I would feel tired and long to be at home. One January evening as I sat by my window a dreadful sense of loneliness engulfed me. Christmas was over and

I was desperately missing my family and friends. I looked out at the bare branches of a tree illuminated by the streetlight. The light shimmered on the branches in the damp evening air. It was strangely comforting. I still find trees oddly inspiring at times. The hospital was aptly named Cherry Tree Hospital. As spring came, the sight of those trees in bloom raised my spirits as I wearily made my way across to the ward.

Social life mainly centred around days off. Meadows and I decided to check out the local churches, where the youth clubs and social events were great fun and provided welcome relief. Our one big argument came when deciding which one we would go to. Basically it came down to which boys we found most attractive.

The year spent at Cherry Tree was such a mixture. It was great to have my independence. The work, though often mundane, was also interesting and challenging. I did not realise the huge responsibility that was at times thrust on my shoulders. I was given the minimal amount of training, which basically consisted of how to wash my hands properly. It is interesting to recall that cross-infection was never a problem.

So why did I want to be a nurse? I am still not certain I can answer that question. I only know I am glad I did.

The Camping Cough Cure:
Heavyweight Camping In The 1950s
Christine Riley
(Rydal)

Formerly a chartered librarian, working in nuclear
information retrieval, I joined Rydal Women's
Institute after I retired. My success in a WI writing
competition encouraged me to try writing my
memoir. Married with two sons, we all still camp,
although not for five weeks and with a lot less gear!

The Doctor snapped shut his case. "It's bronchitis," he said, looking down at his tiny wheezing patient. "The fog doesn't suit her. What she really needs is plenty of fresh sea air."
My baby sister, Charlotte, nearly died after the notorious 1952 London smog - that pernicious mixture of smoke and fog that settled like a shroud, blind-folding and suffocating our cities before the 1956 Clean Air Act. Moving to Manchester had helped, but not much.

Mum closed the door, looking worried.
"How on earth can we afford that?"
Dad, looking up from the pile of exercise books he was marking, smiled.
"Wait for the summer holidays and we'll go camping! She can live in the fresh air for the whole five weeks 'till autumn term. Shouldn't break the bank. We've most of the kit already!"
WW2 army surplus was cheap and Dad, a scoutmaster and

ex 'Green Howard', had always camped.

By the time summer came I had forgotten all about the mysterious 'camping' but, three weeks before the schools broke up, strange things happened. On the floor of the living room appeared two enormous khaki canvas envelopes which Mum said were 'bedrolls'. "Pass me your dresses." (Little girls never wore trousers). She laid them flat on the bedding. I passed blanket pins to fasten the bedding around most of our wardrobe. The canvas top was laced across, the whole rolled up and secured with leather straps buckled around the bulging canvas.

"Girls! Climb on top to keep it rolled whilst I fasten it."

Giggles.

Thump!

"Oh NO!!! It's unrolled AGAIN!"

Eventually, panting, the job was done.

We had an enormous and very heavy khaki canvas ridge tent, originally intended to sleep 20 soldiers. The thick wooden tent poles were in four or five foot long sections, roped together for transit. There were several large canvas bags, tea chests and a tin trunk into which were packed the rest of the equipment. An enormous Primus stove, originally found on a rubbish tip and mended with solder, accompanying prickers, bottles of meths, and paraffin, saucepans and frying pans, cutlery, enamel plates and mugs, an entrenching tool, trowel, and two folding pale green canvas officers' chairs were packed. Also a square enamel table top with curved rim, a small square canvas wash basin and larger canvas bath each with corner loops. The rim and the loops fitted over a set of collapsible wood and metal X legs, constraining them to the correct height. The shallow bath could be used by small girls as a paddling pool.

In short, in bulk and in weight, our luggage and equipment was as different from modern camping as a 10 ton truck is from a Formula 1 racing car. It needed a lorry to shift it. A few days later the 'Luggage in advance' lorry would turn up, load and away it went. We children weren't sure why the lorry took all the stuff and had forgotten about it when schools broke up.

120

The following morning we got up and had breakfast. "Here's your luggage," said Dad, passing me a small picnic bag. We set off for the two mile walk to Didsbury railway station, my parents carrying suitcases and holding Charlotte firmly by the hand, I following grumpily behind. Charlotte didn't have to carry anything.

At the station, we crossed the bridge to reach our platform. Clutching my bag I inched forward, feet firmly in the centre of the planks, stomach knotted, convinced I would fall through the cracks to the gleaming lines below. The train arrived in a confusion of noise and steam. Our carriage smelled of damp coal with a taint of something sulphurous.
"Any more luggage?"
Mock horror!
"Oops! that's not luggage! It's Charlotte!"
The baby squealed and giggled as she was lifted back from the knotted string luggage rack above our heads. With billows of steam, a lurch and loud puffing, off we went.
The train travelled along the North Wales coastline.
"Are we nearly there yet?"
"No, but if you like I will read 'Noddy' to you."
Mum told stories and sang. Dad would play 'I spy' or tell 'weak jokes'.
"Why did the chicken cross Didsbury railway bridge?"
"Don't know."
"Because the train was de-layed."
"Is that a weak joke?"
Obligatory loud groans, with suppressed giggles, followed the explanation.

Those first two summers on Anglesey melt together in my memory. I would have been just six and Charlotte, a November baby, three. The journey by train, local bus, then walking, carrying those bags, seemed tedious and long but could only have taken a few hours. Reaching the strange farmhouse, we waited nervously in the sunshine as Dad knocked. Then all round to the old barn. The farmer unlocked the door and there, wonder of wonders, were the bedrolls and baggage last seen in Didsbury disappearing in that lorry. Magic!

Out came the farm tractor, the bulky camping gear loaded onto the trailer. The farmer turned to me.

"Up you come!"

Delight! Charlotte and I sat regally on top of the baggage. Then the highlight, the glorious ride to the camping field. I remember the hot sun on my face, the smells of the dusty canvas, the grass and hay mixed with the odd whiff of exhaust from the tractor, the green hedges and always the yellow dandelions and buttercups along the hedgerows.

Once we reached the camping field all was action. As the older sister, it was my privilege to help Dad with the tent, leaving the domestic arrangements, including erecting the high bed frames and bedding, to the others. Assembling the tent was certainly a job for two. The long ridge poles were slotted together on the ground and the three uprights put together with the spikes through holes in the ridge-pole. Then the heavy canvas tent was unrolled and spread out like an open book on the grass. Mum and Charlotte were sometimes allowed to help push the frame so that the ridge poles lay along the ridge, the holes in the canvas over the spikes. The canvas folded over, all was ready for the exciting lift.

Charlotte was given a rope and told to hold it tightly (to keep her well out of the way). We others grabbed a main guy, my parents at each end, me in the middle. Feet were placed on the base of each pole, the main guy ropes pulled taut.

"One, two, three. Pull!"

Up came the tent.

Dad, with home-whittled wooden tent pegs and heavy wooden mallet, secured the guy ropes, whilst I proudly steadied the outer poles until all the pegs were hammered in.

The beds were lined up across the tent behind the mid pole, screened somewhat by Mum's dresses hanging from looped ropes. The bulky trunk and packing cases were reorganised to act as storage nearer the entrance, the groundsheet supplemented by Dad's gas-cape. The tables and chairs erected, Dad retrieved the Primus and kettle. I was dispatched with a large canvas bucket to look for a tap. By the time I found it, half filled the bucket and staggered back, slopping water despite my best efforts, all but my chores would be done. (As well as water-girl, I was tinned food-store quartermaster and deputy dishwasher.)

Meanwhile, Dad, with his trusty entrenching tool, would have found a bush some way from the tent and dug a deepish trench behind it to do duty as an earth closet. We soon learned to do our business and wield the trowel to cover our efforts without thinking twice about it. If it rained we had a large enamel chamber pot, but I don't remember using it much.

The tent was always in a sheltered spot, with the entrance facing the view. That first year, we were alone but, by the second trip, smaller tents would arrive and stay for a few days. Every day we would pack our swimming things, collect our buckets and spades and walk to the beach to dig, climb the rocks, paddle and watch the sea. Mum often made tomato sandwiches for lunch, sometimes sprinkled with a little sugar for us children, or salt for the adults. No fridges, even in the houses, so eating what was in season was obligatory. The juice often made the bread soggy, and by the end of the season I remember getting very tired of tomatoes.

We would go for long walks in the country, hunt for crabs in the rock pools, pop seaweed, build sandcastles and dig canals, living outside in the fresh air. If it rained we would put on plastic macs and wellingtons and go out anyway. In severe downpours I remember sitting in the tent and learning to play whist. There is nothing quite so cosy as lying snug in a warm bed, listening to the sound of the rain on a tent roof.

There was a terrific storm in the small hours during the second summer. The other tents in the field, smaller and lighter, blew down, so the refugees came into our tent and sheltered until daylight, drinking tea and exclaiming over the weather. Most went home the next day but we didn't. It rained heavily for about three days. The water table rose after the storm and on day three we awoke to find ourselves almost a foot deep in mud, with more rain falling outside. That day we children stayed in bed, sang songs, played card and word games and kept ourselves amused for the whole day, whilst Dad, his wellingtons ankle-deep in mud, fed us and kept an eye on the tent. Fortunately the ground dried out quickly.

On Saturday nights we often took the bus into the nearest town to go to the pictures. Afterwards Dad sometimes bought chips from a fish and chip shop which we ate from newspaper in the street, much to Mum's disapproval. She came from a working class Methodist household and considered being an officer's wife, now a teacher's wife, a step up the social scale. She was wary of any behaviour likely to let the side down, but Dad could do no wrong.

"How do you expect me to bring up our girls as ladies if they eat CHIPS in the STREET! It is COMMON! Come into the snicket in case someone sees you!"

We enjoyed the treat and the sense of wickedness, but she made sure we finished them before we ventured where we were likely to meet anyone. Back at camp, we drank our cocoa and slept like logs.

After a week or so, the grass between the guy ropes, which supported the skirts of the tent, had grown long and juicy. One morning the steady chomping of grazing cows, a canvas thickness away, woke us. Mum sat bolt upright in terror!
"John, John, Get rid of them!!! "
Dad evicted them, laughing.

Her sisters thought Mum must love Dad very much to go camping with him, as she didn't like creepy crawlies either. One year we inadvertently put her through torture, as we had an earwigs nest in the ridge pole. Mum could not understand where all the earwigs came from and Dad was kept very busy evicting them. The nest was eventually tracked down when I mentioned that an earwig had fallen on my cheek, waking me up, and Charlotte, rolling fast asleep, flung out an arm, swatting it.

Some of the locals, like Charlotte, assumed that we had moved there permanently. Charlotte was very surprised when we went

124

home. She had her last bout of fog induced bronchitis aged five. Our solitary tent by the sheltering hedge was soon surrounded by others and purpose built camp-sites with toilet blocks replaced our field and homely 'trench'.

Tomorrow my son is going camping for five weeks, carrying his tent and all his gear in his backpack.

Boarding Woes
Anne Orr
(Crathorne)

I was brought up in Ireland but sent to boarding school in England. After marrying a doctor, and bringing up three children, I trained in psychology and worked in the NHS. I have recently retired and joined the WI mainly for the walks. I also enjoy writing based on experience.

I had always known I would go to boarding school when I reached the age of 13, but had not been looking forward to it. My mother had found another girl due to start at the same time, even though the school was in Bath, while we both lived in Ireland. We had met a couple of months earlier, when her mother invited me to lunch. We were initially wary of each other until the pudding when Jenny passed me the cream for the fruit salad. As I helped myself her mother came in, and was horrified to see that my fruit salad was covered in salad cream. This broke the ice and made the occasion memorable. The next time we met was to travel by overnight ferry, train and taxi to the school, accompanied by my mother.

The small whisper of excitement I felt was rapidly swallowed by foreboding as we went up the lime-tree lined avenue. I could see bits of an imposing-looking building between the branches, but as we drew nearer, the size gradually became apparent. As my eyes travelled slowly upwards, I could feel a tremor move down through my body right into my toes. There were stone steps up to the front door, which looked as if it had been made for giants. The edifice was four storeys of yellow Bath stone with Gothic style windows. Although it looked like a stately home, it immediately put me in mind of a prison. My legs shook as I went up the stone steps. I could see a gaping hall with grey stone flags, polished by generations of feet, and a massive red-carpeted staircase. The hall was cold and dark and seemed to stretch into the far distance.

At this point a fierce, grey-haired woman said in a forbidding voice "Welcome to the Royal School. We expect you to work hard, be guided by God and we will turn you into young ladies. This is Isla and she will take you up to your dormitory." She was the headmistress, who then beckoned to my mother, who looked as scared as I felt, while Jenny and I followed Isla up endless staircases and gloomy corridors to a long, high room, so dark that the lights were on in the middle of the day. Along each side were a series of dismal curtains separated by partitions. She approached one of these, slightly wider than the rest, pulled it back and inside were four narrow beds covered with identical flowery bedspreads. My immediate impression was that the flowers on these covers were dead as they were all yellowish-brown. We were each allocated a bed, and Isla then left us and said she would be back later to take us to the dining room for tea.

We looked round the dormitory, and I spotted an inventory of the necessities we had to bring with us. My mother and I had been through our copy with a fine toothcomb, and had even brought the 12 vests deemed necessary. As a family we never wore vests, but my mother had found a tubular roll of soft woollen material, like tubigrip only bigger, and had made me vests of this, with blue ribbons as shoulder straps. I was quite proud of them, but was teased for wearing such weird garments. First on this new inventory was ST's, which were not on the one we had worked from. I thought, "I'm not sure I have any of those. I wonder what they are – small towels; short trousers?" As I was very law abiding I was terrified I would get into trouble, so didn't dare ask, becoming increasingly worried. After several weeks I eventually asked another girl who responded at the top of her voice, "You don't know what they are, stupid? Sanitary towels of course!"

The school was divided into four 'Houses', each with a common room for girls across the age span. Any spare time was spent in the allocated common room where there was a definite hierarchy, the girls with the most dominating characters ruling the roost regardless of age. It was also the place where bullies were able to enjoy complete freedom. Despite spending three years at the school, I never really fitted in. It didn't help that I was Irish, and spoke with a 'funny' accent, but it went deeper than that. I was too naïve (or perhaps stupid?) to pretend interest I didn't have in pop groups or film stars, which in the 60's were all the rage. I was once challenged to name a "Beatle". Even I could manage this but was met with mockery when I proudly named all four. The only film stars I knew - Audrey Hepburn and Hayley Mills - the rest of the girls had long since left behind. Everyone else swapped teenage comics and magazines, while my interest was in animals.

I subscribed to a monthly animal magazine with beautiful photographs, which I treasured, but was met with mockery by others. My mother, inadvertently, did not help. Concerned by my weight loss each term, she sent parcels of dried fruit and nuts as 'tuck' rather than sweets, and this also underlined my difference. However, when my cupboard was occasionally raided, the disdain of the perpetrators temporarily disappeared as everything was eaten with relish, and my magazine photographs were seen on walls around other desks.

Once I received a circular parcel wrapped in brown paper and lots of sellotape, with a large, sticky pink patch. A crowd soon gathered, and watched by several pairs of eyes, I removed the sellotape and tore off the paper. Suddenly the lid blew off and sprayed pink liquid in every direction – it was full of fizzing raspberries. I carefully removed a stained letter from my mother explaining that there was a bumper crop and she felt I should share them. Everyone had a small spoonful and I have never forgotten the deliciously sweet, but slightly alcoholic, taste.

I suppose the worst 'sin' was my complete lack of interest in boys. There was a 'twinned' boys school across the road from us, and this lent itself to endless speculation and spying. Four girls in my class broke out of our school one night and were found in one of the boys' dormitories. Needless to say they were suspended for the rest of term, but the punishment backfired as their fathers, impressed by their escapade, rewarded their bravado. We also treated them as heroines and it certainly raised our spirits.

Clearly there was little in common between the other girls and me, but I did make several attempts to be liked. These were rather awkward as I had no idea how to fit in. We were only allowed two baths a week, and there was pressure to be quick so that others could slip in an extra one. Thus I became adept at a quick scrub down and out of the bath in record time. It rapidly spread that if I was on the rota at least one extra bath was likely. However, rather than gain in popularity, it was assumed I was dirty, although this was not true.

Another attempt was more desperate. Whenever it was her birthday, each girl was allowed to choose a cake, to be delivered by the bakery. A table was set at tea for her party and she could choose 11 guests. Needless to say I was rarely chosen. In my second year I persuaded my mother to finance a birthday cake in the July, and as word spread that I was having a party, I suddenly became popular. I invited several of my class group and enjoyed the experience, although I was under no illusions that it would last. It didn't. No sooner had the cake been eaten, questioning revealed that my birthday was in August, and I was accused of cheating.

My love of animals meant that I hated leaving my pets each term. I was particularly fond of my cat, who came when I was seven. She was Siamese, at the time very rare in Ireland, with dark brown ears, legs and tail, a little blunt brown nose in a creamy-white face, and brown back shading to a light cream tummy. She also had remarkably blue eyes that changed with her mood. She would stand on the table and put her paws around my neck, butting my face gently with her own while purring loudly. She slept in my bed,

130

stretched alongside my body with her head on the pillow beside mine. On arriving home after my first term, I reached to pick her up, but her look of utter disdain stopped me in my tracks. She walked off stiff legged with her tail erect and I was devastated, unable to understand her standoffish behaviour. However, two days later, she took a running leap up my chest, butting and rubbing my face and purring her loudest. This was to be the pattern every time I returned from school – first the sulking and then the joyful reunion.

Fitting back in with my family was also problematic, as my sister and I, who had always enjoyed a relatively easy relationship, grew apart due to our very different experiences. I was jealous of her as she was allowed to stay at home, and she was jealous of me when I was treated as the "Prodigal Daughter" by our parents. There was a history behind this. Older than I was, she had refused to go to the school, causing a real rift between our parents. Thus I was left with no choice but to go. The fact that I went, and she did not, complicated the way we felt about each other, and our father's treatment of us. I was rewarded for cooperating and she was punished for defying him.

Over the three years I spent at the school, I changed in many ways. Part of this was normal growing up, but the very different influences, and the necessity to fit in as best I could, meant that I grew away from my family. Even the way I spoke, both my accent and many of the words I used, lost their Irish idiom, and my sister, an excellent mimic, would imitate me. This was amusing at first, but then became irritating. My changed accent also had long-term results as I was assumed to be Irish when in England and English when in Ireland, so that I felt I did not belong anywhere.

Towards the end of my final term, my excitement was hard to contain. Although I had managed to adapt to some extent, I couldn't wait to leave and was looking forward to ending my 'split personality' existence. There was a definite line between those who were leaving and those who were staying on for the sixth form, with a jostling of friendships and loyalties between the two. Some really close relationships were ruthlessly and hurtfully cut off, so that emotions were running high. It was also the school's Centenary year so the end of year celebrations, culminating in an elaborate pageant mapping the 100 years of the school's history, lent a bustling, upbeat atmosphere to the place.

All this barely touched me as I was totally focused on counting down the hours, and even minutes, until I left. Eventually the day came. Our parents had been invited and I waited impatiently for mine to arrive. My welcoming hug knocked my mother's breath from her prompting my father to ask "Don't you have any regrets about leaving school?" The answer was an emphatic "no".

What was my legacy from those three years? A heightened tolerance of the foibles of my fellow man, a stark awareness of my own insignificance coupled with an ability to 'disappear into the woodwork', and a lasting inability to enjoy a long soak in a hot bath.

Sibford School Days

Anne Brooker

(Brightwell cum Sotwell)

After a nomadic childhood following my restless parents, I have found an ideal place to set down roots and raise a family. Brightwell-cum-Sotwell is where my husband was born and grew up, so moving into his family home has given me the stability lacking in my early years.

It was January 1956 and I was not yet 11 when I arrived at Sibford Quaker boarding school. My father had gone to take up a post as Administrative Officer in Kano Hospital, Nigeria, and my mother and my two younger brothers joined him there later that year.

The small Cotswold village of Sibford Ferris was quite a shock after Seymour Road in Gloucester with its lines of Victorian semis. The school occupied two main sites: the Manor House, a lovely old 17th century Cotswold stone building with a Victorian extension, was the setting for the girls' dormitories, kitchens and dining room, while "The Hill" housing the boys' dormitories and classrooms, was built in the 1930's. There was also "The Ark" which held the sanatorium and Matron's rooms.

My dorm – Stansfield - was long, with beds either side. Twenty three girls had already had a term at the school and were intolerant of homesickness. I cried myself to sleep for many nights. Slippers were the usual missiles to silence snoring or weeping. Our lives were governed by bells, a hand bell rung by prefects to wake us, another to announce breakfast, and so on. Each morning the mattress had to be folded over on the bed during breakfast but once I managed to curl up inside to snatch a few more minutes sleep. Downstairs in the bathroom, baths lined one side of the large room each with its own curtain and wooden duck board opposite a line of basins. The wooden stairs creaked and groaned as we dashed down to breakfast. Long tables were laid out, each with a teacher at the head and boys and girls all chattering ten to the dozen either side. We soon learned to grab what we wanted to eat. When I went home my mother was horrified by my table manners.

After breakfast we dashed to the dormitory to make our beds and then headed to the Hill for lessons. Up the steps, past the tennis courts, then the sloping drive past hockey and football pitches and the rounders field, to the classrooms. Lunch bell rang to signal the return trip to the Manor for lunch and the whole process was repeated for afternoon lessons. No wonder we seemed always hungry and always on the move. After supper we trooped up to the Hill again for homework session, no excuse for forgetting to do it. Finally time for bed.

Sunday regime was different. In winter we wore our dark green wool Sunday best dresses, which made us itch, and in summer we had a freshly laundered green and white check dress starched to within an inch of its life. Breakfast was a bit less rushed and followed by the crocodile to Meeting. Two hundred and fifty of us set off through the gate, down the field path and up the other side to Sibford Gower Meeting House. There we would file in with the older ones grabbing the back seats away from prying teachers' eyes. Like all Quaker Meeting Houses, the benches were set out in a square and Meeting began when the two elders sitting on one side of the square settled down. This was all familiar to me, coming as I did from a Quaker family. The silence was broken by readings from the Bible or "Advices and Queries" and spontaneous contributions from members. The end was signalled by the two elders shaking hands. After lunch the school doors were locked and we were sent on a compulsory walk or, when we had reached the magic age of 13, bike ride. Our destination was duly noted but we thought it fun to put in the wrong direction (with no thought as to the consequences in the event of an accident). We returned at five o'clock for tea.

Occasionally as a treat I would be invited for Sunday tea at a friend's house. The two homes I remember were Sheila's in Sibford Gower, and the farm house in Hook Norton. Sheila lived in the Manor House, a rather rambling thatched building and her mother was famous for her chocolate biscuits which she baked specially. As they were slightly rough shapes we joked they looked like cow pats much to Mrs K's pretended annoyance, which only led to more giggles. We had to cycle to the farm house in Hooky, past the cross roads with the "Gate Hangs High" pub. The tea was memorable for the ample spread and my first taste of Ovaltine. There was freshly baked bread cut into doorsteps, proper butter and home made jam as well as the rich fruit cake.

One hot summer morning after leaving Meeting, having heard that the pub opposite would serve cider from the back door, we decided to test this out. We were successful and having consumed our half pint and feeling decidedly merry we stumbled across a dead fox in the road. I had the bright idea that this would make a change from the usual frog for dissection in Science class. So we dragged the carcase back to the school. Imagine our disappointment when on presenting the prize we were told in no uncertain terms to "take it away and bury it".

School life settled down to a mundane routine, but there were were exciting moments. "There's been a fire at The Hill. Someone has set fire to the piano in the Senior Boys' Common Room!"
"Gosh! That'll cause a stink."
"One of the boys set fire to a piano and then used a fire extinguisher to put it out."
"What will the Headmaster say about that?"

Eventually the whole story emerged. In an unguarded moment the Music Master had uttered the fateful words "that piano is only fit for burning". So a small group of senior boys had taken him at his word and done just that, then, panicking, had used an extinguisher. We were aghast, but also secretly impressed, and waited for the inevitable reaction from the Headmaster who was not known for his forbearance. It came at Assembly the next morning. As the culprits had not owned up, he gated all the boys until some one came forward with names. The reaction from the boys was immediate. They refused to sing in Assembly. The stand-off escalated. All the boys were put in detention the following Saturday. The senior boys organised silence at meal times. It was very effective with the teachers at the head of each table trying in vain to initiate conversation – not even the usual "please pass the bread" to break the quiet. Any sign of speech was met with a sharp kick under the table. The end of the impasse came with the summer holidays. When we returned next term all was forgotten.

For a child whose parents were abroad the holidays were not necessarily something to be looked forward to. My father's tour of duty was for 2 years and at the end of this he had 2 months leave that could be taken in Nigeria or England. The dates of the leave did not always coincide with my school holidays.

My first long holiday, in Summer 1956, was spent with friends of my parents from Gloucester. The Ruddles had two children, Malcolm, my own age and Graham, who was away at University. I was not looking forward to it. The family were vegetarian, a slightly alien concept to me, and had an odd, to my mind, idea that drinking anything with a meal was not good. At one memorable meal Mrs R served up a plate of spinach, a vegetable not familiar to me but one taste of the soppy gritty strong tasting greenery was enough to put me off. Mrs R was not pleased and sent me to bed. Next day the plate was there again, still with the revolting green slime, this time cold. I held out and eventually it was taken away and no more was said. Suffice it to say that Malcolm and I did not get on and spent as much time as possible as far away from each other as possible. I took to roaming the house and surrounding

area on my own. Once I almost severed my finger with a chisel
in Mr R's workshop. The highlight of the holiday as far as I was
concerned was the visit from Graham the older son, tall, dark and
handsome, who rode a motor bike and played pop records. He
gallantly invited me to listen with him and so became my hero.

For the shorter Christmas holiday it was arranged that I spend half
with my friend Barbara and her family in Pinner. Her grandma
lived with them and I had the thorny problem of presents on a
strict budget. I need not have worried about Grandma as she
would only accept useful presents such as string or brown paper.
After Christmas I was taken to the station for the train journey to a
Prep School near Bideford, Devon. This school stayed open in the
holidays to cater for ex-pat children and we were left to have fun
exploring the grounds and watching the New Year's day hunt.

When I was 12 I finally got to join my brothers and parents in
Ibadan, Nigeria, for the summer holiday. The school bus took
us to Banbury station and then I joined the group going to
Paddington, where I was met by a "Universal Aunt" who guided
me to the Victoria offices of BOAC. Here she accompanied me
to lunch in the dining room upstairs. This was my first experience
of a restaurant and I was quite overwhelmed. At that time the
Victoria offices acted as a booking-in desk and when the time for
the flight approached the little group of unaccompanied children
were ushered on a coach for the trip to Heathrow Airport. Here
we formed a crocodile and marched to the plane. As children of
government staff we were seated in first class and given boiled
sweets to suck as the plane took off. I was entranced by the sight
of roads with tiny cars, and fields with hedgerows, then the sea,
which filled the window for what seemed like ages. Across France
to Frankfurt – where we landed for refuelling. Back on the plane
dinner was served with a starter of smoked salmon. How I wished
for bangers and mash! Finally the long journey was over and we
approached Lagos airport. This in itself was terrifying – the plane
flew away from the coast, lost height and then flew back towards
land at a frighteningly low level, seeming just to skim the palm
trees. The heat hit me as the door opened and we climbed down

the stairs to the runway. But my journey was not yet over as I had
to take the twin-engine 'Dove' plane to Ibadan. I was settling down
after take-off when the sky ahead lit up – we were flying through
the regular afternoon thunderstorm. I shrank down in the seat,
squeezed my eyes shut and put my hands over my ears. However,
we landed safely and Mum and the boys were there to meet me.

1960 dawned to the knowledge that my father was returning
to England as, now that Nigeria was independent, posts in
Government Service were to be given to Nigerian nationals. He
began work for the hospital service in Aberdeen. As I was in my
final year and taking 'O' levels in the summer I stayed on at school.
After the exams I packed my trunk and it was despatched for the
last time by Carter Paterson while I made the long train journey to
Aberdeen and a whole new period of my life.

The Bentong To Bangkok

Jean Clarke

(Steeple Ashton)

I am now an octogenarian. I had a happy childhood despite being an evacuee. After school, I joined a Government Department and in 1953 went to Singapore on a two year posting. While there I met Iain Clarke and we married in 1957. He was the love of my life but that is another story.

I was a happy, 23 year old girl, working for a British Government department in Singapore and looking forward to travelling by myself to Bangkok for a holiday. After work on 24th August 1954, my friend, Gilly and I, fortified by tea at the Cricket Club, went to Clifford Pier at 5.30pm. There were quite a number of people around, the usual loiterers and a group of missionaries- my fellow passengers - who entertained the crowd with hymns of a jovial kind accompanied by a banjo. Mr. Yo, the Straits Steamship Agent, and Iain Clarke of Mansfield and Co., who had organised my journey, arrived. We all waited and waited for the 'Bentong' to come round from the wharf, where it had been loading cargo. It was a good psychological move to take us in a very small launch to meet the 'Bentong', as she was no cruise liner. The cargo had priority and there was only a small section amidships for passengers. I had a cabin to myself with a bunk, a comfortable chintz-covered couch and a table, everything ship-shape with storage for clothes, a light above my bunk and a bell-push for service. Mr.Yo, Gilly and Iain talked for a while, my passport and ticket were collected and then they left. I waved them off, feeling slightly lost but very excited.

I was interested to meet my fellow passengers from the China Inland Mission, three girls and two men. At dinner, served by three Chinese, I sat beside the Chief Engineer, a Scot, who had a chip on his shoulder about missionaries, which was unfortunate considering the majority of the passengers were in that category. Immediately, an argument started with Kathie from Glasgow, a rather naïve nurse who had very firm convictions about her Christian mission but left herself open to criticism. Gerry, another nurse, from University College, London, had enough commonsense for ten people. The third girl, Carmen, an American from Tennessee, had fair hair, blue eyes, was considerate and, surprisingly, hated coffee. The two men were going to live on a 20 foot launch, plying up and down the rivers of Thailand preaching the Gospel. Eric, a jovial chap who had played the banjo, was fair, slightly bald and had been engaged to a girl for six years but had to wait two more before marrying. Roy was a dour, good-looking Scot, ex RAF. All five were firm believers in Christianity. They were worried that in Singapore they had been learning the Royal Thai language instead of Market Thai, which would limit their effectiveness.

We left Singapore Harbour at 8pm, watching the lights disappear in the distance. I talked to the three girls until it was time for bed at 9.15pm, unbelievably early for me, as the night before, I had been Scottish dancing and then onto the 7th Storey Nightclub with Iain. The next day we rigged up a deck tennis net and a quoit out of rope and had energetic games. I shocked them all by smoking, and wearing lipstick and nail varnish.

The first port of call, to unload some cargo, was Tumpat in Kelantan on the north east coast of Malaya. When we approached the coast, a member of the crew was on the bow taking findings, passing close to the sunken hulk of a boat, which had been torpedoed by the Japanese during the war. We anchored in two fathoms of water at least one and a half miles from land. The

Agent came alongside in a launch, 'Lonestar', protected by a
Malay bodyguard, complete with gun and spotted bandana.
Carmen, Katy, Gerry, Roy, Eric and I were soon in the launch,
butting our way to shore.

There was only one street, which could have come straight out
of an American Western film, single storey wooden houses, and
a covered sidewalk plus rail. I expected to see horses galloping
up with handsome men in ten gallon hats. Strangely, there was a
properly built bamboo theatre, a roof thatched with atap leaves
and a ticket office - an ideal setting for a Shakespearean play in the
Elizabethan style, complete with bugs and smell. A friendly man
from Ceylon, who worked on the railway and wanted to practice
his English, told us the history of the area and gave directions to
Kota Bahru.

It was extremely hot and we were pleased to pile into a bus to
take a 35 cent ride as far as a ferry, bumping along the dusty road
through paddy fields being ploughed by water buffalo (which
Carmen thought were found in the sea). We boarded the ferry, a
second cousin to the one in "The African Queen". The passengers
were loaded with all sorts of parcels, including Durian fruit, which
give off a ghastly pong but taste delicious.

We walked into Kota Bahru and reached the welcoming
Government Rest House, sank into chairs, ordered some non-
alcoholic drinks, ate our sandwiches and I then lay on a couch and
had forty winks. On our return journey, we walked and walked
along the shore, threading our way though kampongs (villages),
much to the amusement of the inhabitants. Some of the Malay
women were very beautiful in their colourful sarongs and gold
jewellery. Thankfully, a bus came along and we scrambled in
amongst the baskets of vegetables and live chickens in wicker
containers. It was standing room only with 45 in the bus - plus
one boy on the roof - instead of the official 21! We were all in
high spirits, laughed a great deal and then decided to get off the
bus and have a swim in the sea, which was splendid. Afterwards as
we walked along the beach, we were horrified by the putrid stench
from primitive sanitation and I was glad to be wearing shoes.

While the 'Bentong' was delayed in discharging cargo, we took
other local bus journeys along the coast, but it was dangerous
because of the fighting in the jungle with the communist
bandits in the Malayan Emergency. There could have been dire
consequences if we had been kidnapped.

Back on board, Dave, the First Officer invited us to go for a swim.
We set off in the ship's lifeboat with a number of crew for the
one and half miles run ashore, landing at a lovely beach and had
a glorious swim. However, the return journey was fraught as the
lifeboat's engine seized up. The oars had to be used (the passengers
proved better than the crew at rowing) and it was difficult to
keep the lifeboat from being swept sideways towards the beach.
However, the clever crew tinkered with the engine, it came to life
and we arrived back safely.

The view from the top deck of the 'Bentong' was wonderful, with
a cool breeze, seeing the blue sea, glistening sands, palm fringed
shore and high mountains beyond jutting out of the jungle.
Occasionally, one or more fishing boats came past with sail full
spread, the prows coloured and carved in the shape of a bird.

The 'Bentong' arrived at the mouth of the Bangkok river on 30th
August, took on a pilot and immigration officials and zig-zagged
through sandbanks, past mangrove swamps and eventually tied up
at a wharf a long way from the city. I said a sad goodbye to
the missionaries who had been good fun. Captain Phillips took
me to the Borneo Company office. I contacted the British
Embassy as previously arranged in Singapore, and saw something
of the city. There seemed to be no drains, no road mending, no
traffic regulations, chaotic with buses, trams, cars and trishaws, so
unlike Singapore.

Captain Phillips and his lawyer had to attend a Court in Pak Nam
at the mouth of the river, because of a previous accident, and I was
invited for the ride. We travelled there and back in a Chevrolet
driven sometimes at 80 mph on poor roads. I was pleased to return
alive to Bangkok, changed travellers' cheques into ticals (58 = £1)

at a bank, and lunched in the cool air-conditioned Trocadero Hotel
with Captain Phillips.

That evening, one of the crew managed to find a sampan for
15 ticals to take me up river to a wharf where a taxi was said to
be waiting to drive me to the house of Robert, who was Third
Secretary at the British Embassy and had invited me to a dinner
party. I sat down in the sampan unsteadily, with a smiling woman,
who paddled at the front and a man standing behind me, with an
oar. We set off upstream for 25 minutes. They didn't understand
English and I didn't know where we were going. The woman was
shouting to all the passing sampans and riverside homes; maybe
about me and my pearl necklace. I had visions of robbery or worse
in some sordid backwater. However, they were good people and
took me to the correct wharf and the waiting taxi.

After dinner there was a diplomatic flap, so Robert had to see the
Ambassador. His Excellency, imposing Berkeley Gage, invited us all
up to his apartment; we chatted to the other guests, had drinks and
listened to gramophone records instead of going to dance at one
of the nightspots. Robert and Mike, a "Sunday Times" journalist,
took me back by car and sampan to the 'Bentong'. The river
looked more glamorous at night, the smell less obnoxious, though I
was grateful to be chaperoned.

The next night, I was invited by three Embassy girls to stay in
their house. Mike collected me from the boat after breakfast
and we went to the enormous Sports Club, for lunch, a swim and
in the evening to see a Danny Kaye film, "Knock on Wood". In
the house, if you wanted a shower in the primitive wet room,
very necessary in the humid heat, you had to shout down to the
servant, "Plong, pump, please". Robert was able to arrange a visit
to the Grand Palace and Temple of the Emerald Buddha, I was
bedazzled with the bright colours and unusual architecture. Before
I returned to the 'Bentong' to sail for Singapore at 5pm on Friday,
3rd September. I bought a Thai straw hat for a lampshade, a silver
compact for my mother, a bronze paper knife for my father, and
another for Iain as a thank you for arranging the voyage.

The return journey to Singapore was dull, no stops en route, only one other passenger, Margaret, a teacher who was moving the school for missionaries' children from the intense heat of Bangkok to the cool Cameron Highlands in Malaya. There were no children on board, just boxes of books and equipment. I had been seasick on the voyage up but had now found my sea legs; but Margaret succumbed during the heavy seas. One night was quite frightening when the high stacked deck cargo of teak started slipping, the crew frantically hammering to secure it until it was safe. Thankfully, a capsize was averted.

Way out to sea, with no land in sight, the 'Bentong' picked up three dishevelled men in two very small fishing boats. These men may have been the reason for the delay when we arrived in Singapore harbour as customs officials searched the ship, possibly looking for drugs. When we were returning to Singapore, Dave, the First Officer showed me the charts and explained about the working of the ship. I invited him, when he was in port, to join our group going Scottish dancing, but he only came once as it may have been obvious that I was falling in love with Iain.

I was delighted to be back in Singapore on Tuesday, 7th September 1954, having had a wonderful holiday with many adventures. There were no e-mails or affordable telephone calls in 1954, so I quickly posted an airmail letter, which usually took three days, to my parents to reassure them that I was safe, very well and back at work.

Life After

Kate Mosley

(Loddington)

I am a quietly determined individual whose attitude reflects the era of my youth and northern roots. Born in Cheshire, I now live in the Leicestershire countryside. A B.A. (hons.) graduate, I trained in Silversmithing/Jewellery, ran a business, took on freelance work and exhibited – then lectured in Art / Design. I am now retired and disabled.

"I hate that thing!" I cried, pointing at my wheelchair. It was not sitting in it that I objected to, but the problems and the prejudice.

It all started in hospital. I was born with a condition that I only knew about when it started to cause problems late in life. At 40 I had a stroke. Once survival was certain (Dad always called me his 'little fighter'), I determined to make the most of my life and not be a burden. I was transferred to another hospital for rehabilitation (hard work and a positive outlook were said to aid recovery), but I was still grieving for the life lost.

Craft workshops, speech therapy, physiotherapy twice a day, walking practice and writing exercises were now my world. At first I hated the rehabilitation ward - surrounded by sickness and death, some things that I witnessed shocked me. Then familiarity cushioned and resignation came. Allowed home for weekends (my respite), then returning for 5 industrious days, I aimed to be discharged as soon as possible. Yet this was my abode for the next 6 months.

Both those on rehab and people there for respite care taught me a great deal. Sadly, it is still assumed that a wheelchair user is stupid – not true. Even those who are severely disabled can be intelligent. We seem to have lost the ability to 'read' expression or body language (the only way that some can communicate). Not all disabled people use a wheelchair, it is only a mobility aid, and yet this has become a 'badge of office' for the disabled.

Wheelchairs are a nightmare on rough ground, and impossible on gravel, as Prince Andrew can confirm. If unable to self-propel, a manual wheelchair-user must rely on others. They cannot hear you speak and so lean forward - not good for backs. At their mercy, and with no control, you are spun around to look at something; sometimes it's helpful; often you end up dizzy and confused. A frustrating experience for both.

Access has improved but will always be a problem: steps to the disabled toilet and lift - we have all been there. We are not at other people's eye-level, and they fall into our lap, kick our stick or bump into us. Some do not know how to react or are just plain ignorant. Preferential treatment and a convenient seat are advantages, but don't get me started on the parking pass.

Not permanently in a wheelchair, I am able to walk short distances with a stick while hanging on to someone. People often think that I am drunk, since my balance and eyesight are affected, and even my speech is slurred. "Walk properly and bend your knees!" I can hear the physio cry, as I waddle along, feet wide for balance. Preferring no aids indoors, I stagger between solid, immovable objects, while a mobility scooter has given me some independence outside.

My G.P. didn't think that I qualified for free NHS prescriptions (tick box criteria) though later this was altered by a social worker.

The incident influenced my attitude. I could not rely on others. When a doctor told me that a Tenotomy was needed, (an operation to lengthen the tendons in my calves), I was unsure. Though not unduly concerned about having an operation; I did not think that it was needed.

My physiotherapist agreed with the doctor. After arguments, I gave in. Admission to another hospital and examination by the surgeon did not remove the doubts. He agreed with me. The operation was cancelled after conversation by telephone between surgeon and therapist. I was later informed that the procedure could have permanently weakened my legs. "A lucky escape, I must believe in myself."

I recall a memorable occasion whilst ski-ing in France. Cold and tired, I was heading towards a chalet looking forward to a seat and a warm drink. Traversing a steep and rocky slope, I picked my way down carefully - thank goodness it was wide. I was experienced, but few people were around. The tricky section loomed towards me – I WAS SCARED. If I did not turn soon the consequences could be dire, and the same were true if I fell. Steeling myself to point skis down the slope, weight forward, the turn was executed. With new confidence and adrenalin flowing, I picked up speed and soon descended.

Many times there was a need to be brave and face things. Treatment required that emotions were checked, keeping blood pressure low. Heavily sedated, but conscious, I had to 'listen' to my body and communicate with the surgeon whilst he undertook the procedure. I got through it. "No point in getting emotional, only you suffer. There is an end to this." Sent home to recover fully, then back to face it all again.

This lasted for three years. The worst experience was undergoing laser surgery. When farriers are at the stables, the smell of burning hoof reminds me of the smell as they drilled into my skull to fit a 'crown' of metal. Eventually leaving hospital, the hard work had paid off; I was more capable and looking forward to going home, determined to face the challenges ahead.

I am not sporty but like to be active. A sedentary life is not for me. Being positive and making quick decisions were not alien, nor were exercise and keeping fit. After all, if you wanted a good life, a strong body and mind were essential. What was I capable of now? I tired easily, (two or three hours was all that I could sustain) and was unreliable: a job was out of the question. Voluntary work seemed the perfect answer. I joined a local organisation that housed several charities. I enjoy being there, need their help, and the benefits have been huge, including a garden party at Buckingham Palace and presentations to Royalty.

First up and the routine is almost complete. The early morning chill makes me sit by the Aga with a mug of coffee. Only the dogs and a ticking clock are my company. Under the amber glow of electric light I unscramble my waking thoughts, plan for the day ahead, and do my exercises. A favourite time of day – I'm definitely a morning person.

As the dawn light becomes brighter, thoughts are broken and priorities change to the needs of others. If I fail to rise early, before anyone else, or do not plan, the day descends into chaos. Lurching around like the proverbial 'headless chicken', hoping to remember what I could and should do.

All activity now requires absolute concentration, switching off to any insistent interruptions - blaring radios, conversations on telephones and the dreaded open plan office. In preparation I rest for up to two hours and am not available for the whole day.

Many activities can still be done. The intrepid gardener crawls around in kneepads, relying on others for heavy work. Clay pigeon shooting, falconry, horse riding, gardening, voluntary office work, WI and their trips, outings to shows, theatres, game fairs and horse trials – all since the stroke.

"No pain – no gain", "use it or lose it", cheesy but annoyingly true.

We once picked up an Aussie hitchhiker. "Been surfing mate, ski-bum for the winter then off to the Caribbean."

"Lucky you!"

"Luck's got nothing to do with it, if you want it - go and get it!"

I totally agree. You can't spend your life hoping that things will come your way - they don't.

A student once said, "You can be a bitch sometimes, but at least you're fair". The barb sank deep, it was meant to hurt. Now her words remind me that as a northerner with considerable 'baggage' - I can be blunt. Experiences have instilled in me the need to be firm and a little selfish at times.

Constant worry that my tone and sharpness have offended stops me from becoming hard. I am - and always have been - somewhat 'matter of fact', but in need of reassurance: answering the door and going outside without mascara are unthinkable. Sometimes, included in an outing, I've felt like 'the token cripple' and anger boiled. I now accept that I need help, and mellowness has come with age. Please, no sympathy - just patience and understanding.

Most activity causes pain. Unable to stomach anything stronger than paracetamol, I have regular acupuncture. Always careful, I heed the advice of consultants; determine whether the pain is a warning or my body saying I'm not fit/strong enough. A pain management course taught me about pain and how to control it. Some things didn't work, but most did.

Today, years on, I still exercise and listen to their relaxation CD. The knowledge that I will suffer the next day does not always prevent me doing things, but I learned to limit or give up some activities.

We had to decide on goals to achieve. Mine was to ride a horse again. A lady in our village with links to RDA (riding for the disabled) arranged a session. Not expecting much and armed with written permission from my GP, I went, rode, loved it, and never looked back. This knowledgeable friend still takes me riding, and encouraged me to join the WI. "Thank you".

Authorities proved to be a bit like most animals, the more you went against them, the more they resisted. I learned to be subtle and 'play their game'. I recall a time when they tried to reduce my benefit. I needed that money - transport and cleaning were costly. Examined by a doctor, I was told "Nothing's changed - but the forms have". My benefit was cut. I had been here before – forms. Determined to fight their decision, I gathered all the documentary evidence possible, told them to contact anyone mentioned, and with nothing to hide I was prepared for court. Success!

I am my own worst enemy -"Come on Kate you can do this". In order to join in, the full extent of my disadvantage is not shown. I have always been independent, not one for following blindly. I AM ME!

The insurance issue prevented involvement. Ten years on I desperately wanted to do something, was well practised at avoiding the problem and had to choose my words carefully. I understood their reasons but thought that caution was unnecessary in my case, after all I was no stranger to risks– accidents were my fault.

Once my ability was seen (despite knowing more) the instructors let me continue. My riding partner and I are well matched, and had been working on a drill to music. It was not easy to be together and in time. When one of the horses was quite forward, whilst the other had to be urged on. The music helped both horse and rider to keep the pace constant.

Dressage is now my thing. It was considered boring when I was young, but now the trained eye can see the subtle commands. The discipline involves precision, control and accuracy.

Let's face it I can't exactly show jump or play polo. I can barely trot and hold onto a strap whilst I am led and someone runs alongside.

"THE PRINCESS ROYAL FEELS RIGHT AT HOME."

Treated to a presidential opening, excited youngsters were to welcome Princess Anne with a posy. Dignitaries had to be presented, then HRH would watch riding displays. All co-ordinated – even the rosettes matched. Mounted, we warmed up and waited nervously, rehearsing in our heads. A helicopter droned above – she had arrived.

The children finished their riding routine – it was our turn. Led in, we gave beaming smiles and began. No problems, it was soon over and everyone waited in line. Rosettes and awards were presented, a plaque was unveiled and she was shown round, then left - phew! The media pounced on the only understandable adult rider - me. Local newspapers, radio and TV - all wanted interviews. My work wasn't over.

This is my story. We are all different. Others will have another tale to tell. Words alone cannot teach. We need to get out, join in, and be seen doing.

Too Far From Tipperary

Therese Charnock

(Pontyclun)

I qualified as a State Registered Nurse in 1966 and State Certified Midwife in 1968. I held a variety of positions, as a nursing sister, in anaesthetics, theatre and midwifery nursing. I am married with two grown-up children, and I finally retired after 40 years in 2003.

There was a lot of things I did not know when I took my first faltering, trembling steps into a nursing career in 1963. For instance, that nursing as I was to know it, had been established only within the last 90 years, and its founder, Florence Nightingale, had died only 53 years ago. Nor was I aware that my hospital had been an old Dickensian Workhouse, and that the National Health Service had only been established fifteen years earlier. Catapulted from a tiny rural village in Ireland, into a busy industrial town, a northern dialect I could not understand, and the rapidly changing world of the sixties, with no money to speak of and very few clothes, I was much too busy trying to survive to worry about the wider issues involved.

Although very homesick, I was not alone, as I had two other sisters already living in the town. On arrival at the hospital I was met by a friendly matronly woman in her late forties, dressed in maroon, with a white frilly cap. She introduced herself as Miss Black, the

Home Sister, who would be our point of contact in the event of any queries or problems. She seemed kind and friendly, showing me to my room and presenting me with my uniform.

"Welcome to the hospital Nurse Carroll. PTS (Preliminary Training School) starts in two weeks time. Prior to that you will be working on a male medical ward. I'll take you to the canteen, linen room and general office, and then the ward where you start at 8am tomorrow, working three early shifts and two late shifts for the next two weeks. The other students start then and you'll share your room with Pauline. The night nurse will call you at 7am. I hope you settle in quickly and I'm always here to deal with any problems."

The check list I had been advised to bring with me included:
Good walking shoes
Two pairs of black stockings
A nurse's watch with second hands
A pair of scissors
Black and red pens and safety pins

My laundry consisted of:
A long navy wool cloak with red lining
Two blue short sleeved dresses with a single stripe to show I was a first year student
Six starched aprons
Two petersham belts
Two starched white round collars
Two caps starched and ironed out

The dresses contained multiple pockets and the skill of making up my caps took some time to conquer.

Filled with trepidation I reported on duty the following morning to be met by a man in a white coat, navy trousers, and navy lapels on his sleeves.
"I've been told to report to the sister," I stammered.
"I'm Mr Libby, the Charge Nurse."

154

"Yes, sister," I said, trying to suppress a giggle.
He looked me up and down and gave a resigned sigh.
"You call me Mr Libby, at all times. Now I'll get Staff Nurse
Chapman to show you around. You call him Staff, by the way."

The male Staff Nurse talked very fast with a strong Northern
accent. We gave up the ghost of trying to understand each other
in a matter of minutes, as with mutual relief he handed me over to
the supervision of a cadet nurse whom I will call Rebecca.

She took her responsibility very seriously and introduced me to
the mysteries of bed making and the general ward routine. The
breakfast arrived in a large metal trolley and was dished out by
Mr Libby. My first task as a nurse was to help to feed an old man.
Next was the bedpan round, and I was introduced to the mystery
of the bedpan sterilizer, after all the contents had been washed
away in the sluice with gloves and a mop. This was a task I would
become very familiar with in the next few months. Bad as they
were, the bedpans paled into significance, when confronted with the
task of emptying and cleaning the metal sputum mugs, a task that
never got any easier.

"We have to do the bed baths now," Rebecca said. "Fetch the linen
skip."
"What's a linen skip?"
"That tall round thing on wheels with a canvas bag in it," Rose the
cleaner told me kindly.

Rebecca seemed very worldly wise as she started the first bed
bath. Shy, inhibited, giving to blushing at the least thing, I helped
anxiously as she washed with expert ease the upper part of the
first patient's body. Then when she handed him the flannel to
wash his private parts, making sure of his privacy, I visibly relaxed.
Everything seemed to be going well until we came to the last
patient. Without any warning, she pulled the bedclothes back to
reveal a bilateral amputee. I gasped in horror and almost fainted
on the spot.

I felt extremely proud and self important in my new uniform. It took me some time before I realised the dress and aprons were far too long, and the, "sensible," shoes caused many a good-natured giggle until I could afford to replace them. No one warned me about the male urinals until I managed to give myself a cold shower trying to use one. My starched hat and apron collapsed, along with my hair, and in this sorry state I was called to the Matron's office. She was a tall intimidating woman whose bark, I was to find out, was generally worse than her bite.

"You've had an encounter with the male urinal washer?" she said trying to suppress a smile. "It happens to most student nurses, they never warn you."

The men made me blush and sang, "It's a Long Way to Tipperary" as soon as I appeared on duty.
"How do I look Nurse Carroll?" A plump man with receding curly hair in his early forties enquired.
"You look disgustingly healthy to me," I replied honestly. "I don't know what you're doing in here."
"Did you all hear that lads," he said and they all had a good laugh.

The following morning his bed was empty. Rebecca told me that he had died in the night. He was suffering from Coronary Thrombosis, invariably fatal at that time, yet one more fact I was blissfully unaware of.

Our PTS had been a lovely old stately home and still retained many features of its affluent past. At meals we had waitress service and the food was very good. Our tutors sat with us, unlike the main hospital dining room where there was a strict segregation of staff. In the main dining room, the matron, consultants and senior administrative staff all sat at the top. All qualified staff sat on the next levels, and students were at the bottom of the dining room. We had three main tutors. The Principal, Miss Salt, dressed in grey, with frilly hat and cuffs. She was a cold woman who appeared to dislike us all and loved to humiliate us. She may have had a good side but I never discovered it. The other tutors, both married,

were dressed in maroon, with frilly caps, and kind generous
personalities.

A large room was set up to resemble a ward. Two beds had
dummies resting in them. Here we were introduced to the skill of
proper bed-making, minus creases and with tidy envelope corners.
Taking temperatures, pulses, respirations, and blood pressure was
explained to us.

"Don't let the patient know you're counting respirations," the tutor
advised, "because they will stop breathing."

Other subjects introduced included, Anatomy and Physiology,
Bacteriology, basic hygiene, protecting patient dignity at all
times, Intake and Output Charts, and observing the colour and
appearance of urine. The equipment necessary for testing included
some of the following,
Specimen tubes and containers,
Albumen,
Litmus paper,
Tincture of Guaiacum,
Specific gravity measure
Bunsen burner
The large cupboard also contained bandages, splints, and red
rubber tubes and funnels for giving enemas and colon lavages.
Anatomy and Physiology charts lined the walls, and a skeleton
leered at us from the corner of the room.

We were also taken on to the ward for ward experience and there
it was explained to us that we must never show our feelings in front
of the patients. This was easier said than done as I rushed into
the sluice to hide my feelings when confronted with my first dying
patient, a pretty woman in her forties dying from cancer.

We also went on field trips to various places such as a school for
children with learning difficulties which I found very intimidating.
My homesickness and naivety was too obvious at times, and I
probably bored the girls talking about the lovely country and

mountains I had left behind. One of the girls informed me we were going on a lovely trip into the country, with scenes comparable to what I had eagerly described. We ended up in a built up area exploring the delights of the local sewage works.

Moorgate Hospital, situated in the mining town of Rotherham, now long replaced by a new District Hospital, had been a Workhouse. This stigma still lingered in the minds of some older people. It was a large, spread-out building, with several different blocks, covered in soot, dark, Dickensian and sinister at night. There was a little building at the top of long metal stairs leading to the dining room.

"That's Rose Cottage," one of the girls said.

"Rose Cottage?"

"The Morgue, beware when you're on night duty. It's a favourite trick for someone to be dressed in a shroud, waiting for you on the top of the stairs."

"And," she continued, "There's Mr Squibb, the night auxiliary on Ward Two. He's a real dirty old man. First year students get sent there on night duty, because it's mainly elderly patients."

"You mean he doesn't wash often?" I asked, and she collapsed with laughter.

In general, staff were kind and friendly and the South Yorkshire sense of humour and generosity prevailed. But I was especially lucky with Pauline, Susan, and Eileen, who befriended me from the start and invited me into their homes where I seemed to become part of other people's families. There was a sense of camaraderie, and people helping each other, and, compared to bigger hospitals I was to work in, more "laid back," and tolerant.

Other issues in my new life included food and clothes. Food was very different as I was introduced to pickled onions and gherkins, pork pies, various steamed puddings with custard, meat and potato pies, and strangest of all beef dripping on toast. Nor had I ever tasted a hamburger or fish and chips. We were well fed, but the kindly night cook still gave us chip butties before going to bed. The ward cleaners also fed us scones and jam behind the kitchen door when the sister was not looking.

Clothes were another issue as I had so few, with the sum of £10 when I arrived and a payment of £12 a month. I was very proud of my pure wool green coat with the huge collar and pink high heeled shoes, until the girls kindly advised me to get rid of both, and buy some trainers and an Army Stores duffle coat. This was the accepted off-duty gear.

I learned quickly that the order of importance on the wards was the Sister (godlike, invincible), the Staff Nurse, and the ward cleaner. Ward cleaners seemed to hold a certain intangible, invisible power. They had no compunction about warning the consultants (of whom the rest of us were terrified) off their newly washed floor. But for students a ward round meant having everything spick and span, including the patients, before the omnipotent consultant's round.

Three months later, my proper training began and I still had a very long way to go. Yet, despite my appalling inexperience, lack of clothes and money I survived. I found true friendship, and my love of nursing lasted me for the next 40 years.

The Letter

June Welham

(Yockleton)

I am a retired Business Process Analyst who's worked in the UK and the USA for a number of years. Throughout my working life colleagues have commented that I have a way with words. If ever I gave up my day job perhaps I should write – here it is.

"Oh this is a much better sample. The first was stilted, stifled and forced. This is more natural and free flowing. See how the left margin is narrow at the top and widens at the bottom. Look at the alignment; it's mostly vertical, occasionally slanting to the left but more often to the right. Oh my goodness, look at the d's! See how they differ depending on whether they're at the beginning, middle or end of words. I've never seen a 'd' written like that before, you definitely have issues."

I wonder what the handwriting expert would make of this example. Each letter perfectly formed the tops and tails reaching precisely the invisible guide lines. No sloping in any direction, each letter absolutely perpendicular, every word evenly spaced and no expanding margins. "Just like a child's hand," Granny remarked.

The envelope was yellow (an odd choice I thought under the circumstances) and heavy. It must have weighed at least two ounces, confirmed by the row of stamps squashed beside the airmail sticker across the top. Granny would never have been that extravagant: prepaid aerogrammes were her staple, every inch utilized, the blue paper so thin the Biro indentations competed with new words on the reversed page.

How I used to long to receive letters in that childish hand. I'd be so excited when they dropped through the letter box which they rarely did. They closed the distance between us and I knew he was thinking of me: he'd taken the time to write. As the years went on, the letters became more depressing and less frequent. He would rail about subjects I knew nothing of and I didn't understand the point he was trying to make. Receiving a letter became a trial, since I never what they would contain. Instead of tearing them open, I'd procrastinate: I'll open it after breakfast; I'll read it when I get home tonight, when I've more time. And then the following day I'd have to force myself to open it. Tears. "How could he say these things? Why does he do it, what does it mean?" Ultimately the letter I always knew would arrive, the one telling me there would be no further communication, landed on the mat. The letter was short, two dark lavender, 5 ½" by 7 ½" pages containing the final words:

"I still love you but I'm tired of trying to live two lives, mine here in Canada and yours in Europe. I'm not tired of the people just tired of trying to be interested in places and events that have no meaning for me. You're my only daughter and you'll always be 'Daddy's girl'.
As always
All my love
Your loving Dad."

Almost 22 years to the day separate this short letter from the yellow envelope. 13 years have passed and the yellow envelope remains unopened, the letter unread. I see now in my carefully written name and address, the characteristics that were to reveal themselves over the years, control, rigidity and an utter conviction to be right no matter what the cost. I couldn't see it then, much less understand it. I made endless excuses for his unpredictable behaviour, often blaming myself. I see the pattern emerging and realize it had nothing to do with me; it was all there before I was born.

Granny told stories of how he would corner his sisters with his fists up, urging them to fight whilst they cowered. He'd pick fights with older boys and say "I'll bring my brother to sort you out." He'd return with my uncle who was big for his age. The boys fled, leaving my father laughing and my uncle bewildered. The same uncle told me that when my father would enter the Mess, the room would fall silent. Men would turn their backs or walk away from the bar. At 5' 8¾" he was of average height and build but his pure belligerence ensured people avoided him. No army buddy, friend or colleague ever visited our house, and I assumed this was because we were a single parent household. It never occurred to me that people didn't want to be in his company.

Circumstances varied but the pattern was the same. At any occasion involving fun and gaiety, perhaps my Father was taking part or he'd arrive later. At some point for reasons known only to him, he would decide the fun had to stop and some ploy would be devised. When this occurred the associated company would meekly submit and at that moment, a smile of satisfaction would appear. Now that he had made everyone miserable he was happy.

My earliest memory was also my first experience. Grey army-issue, woollen blanket spread out on the grass; toys abandoned, we'd grown tired of the game and wanted our own tea party. In the distance a man, with a kit bag on his shoulder was walking towards us.

"It's Daddy," I cried, leaping up, running to meet him. He looked like he was in a good mood so I swung on his free arm and bombarded him with questions, "Are you home for good? Will you be staying long? Can I have tea with you tonight? Can I stay up late? Will you come and play with us?"

"Maybe," was his nonchalant reply. Why did a cup of tea and a cigarette take so long? We crowded round him, jumping up and down excited, at the prospect of games.

"What do you want to play?"

"Aeroplanes!" we cried in unison.

"Me first, me first," I shrieked, but to my surprise and disappointment, he gestured to Jane first. "Me next, me next," but Hazel was chosen. I jumped up and down, hopping from one foot to the other, with my hand between my legs. I knew the toilet beckoned but I couldn't miss the fun. He grasped my right foot and hand in both his hands and now at last I was in the air, girls' faces, houses and trees spinning by, squealing, letting myself go in sheer pleasure. Unfortunately at the same moment, I let go of my bladder. All laughter stopped and I was sent straight to bed without any tea.

"In the morning," he said with an expression I didn't recognise, "You'll go to the Children's Home. We don't want dirty, naughty, little girls, who wet their knickers in this house." My five year old brain couldn't comprehend the last statement. All I could think of was going to the Children's Home. Getting ready for bed I cried, as Maria retrieved a valise from the top of the wardrobe carefully packing the necessary items.

"It's too much Bill, far too cruel, she's very upset." Maria's voice was trembling.

"All the better, she needs to learn a lesson. Besides you're paid to keep house, not to give advice."

Hope faded that the incident had been forgotten and forgiven when I saw the valise, as I entered the lounge. Daddy was in his 'Do Not Disturb' position, lying on his back, full length on the couch, feet crossed at the ankles, his head cradled in his hands and a cigarette in his mouth. An old Glen Miller standard 'In the Mood' was playing on the gramophone. Without turning his head, he said:

"Sit down. Just let me know when you're ready to go." When the cigarette was finished I took this to be my cue. Somewhere deep inside came the strength to utter

"I'm ready now."

Leaning against the front doorframe, with a vague gesture he pointed down the road adding "On you go then". Case in hand, my gaze followed the direction he was pointing.

"But I don't know where the Children's Home is," panic and realisation rising inside me.

"That's easy, just ask anyone you meet and they'll tell you where to go."

Bewilderment and fear gripped me. My bottom lip began to tremble, and through tears I sobbed "I'm sorry Daddy for what I did. I don't want to go to the Children's Home."
"Well you better come in and we'll forget all about it." And there was that expression again. He picked up the valise and walked down the hall. I stepped inside closing the front door behind me.

Through the years there are countless episodes, being subjected to fear, the key turning in the lock, what mood would he be in, would we have to scuttle to our bedroom not making a peep or would there be a 'normal' meal? Terror, returning from boarding school, through the Black Forest, stopping the car, being left in the middle of the road, in pitch darkness, watching the red tail lights disappear from view - the reason, squabbling with my sister in the back of the car. Abandonment: day turning into night whilst he 'went to see a man about a dog'. We'd missed the ferry. He whiled away the hours in a bar, leaving us, without food or drink, to amuse ourselves. Rejection - he refused delivery of his seventieth birthday present, a midi system to replace his faulty stereo system, because he wouldn't pay the import duty. I didn't know until days later when the shipment arrived back. He didn't call me to clarify, which would have revealed that the freight company had made an error, and the duty had been prepaid.

Happily married to a supportive and caring husband and enjoying a successful career, I grew more bold and would stand up for myself against his manipulations, always knowing that if I over stepped the mark, ties would be severed. That time arrived at Christmas.

When I was 2 and a half, my Mother hanging decorations alone, fell off the ladder, had a miscarriage and died on Christmas Eve.

Consequently my Father didn't celebrate Christmas. In 47 years we'd only had two or three Christmases together. To remedy this I invited him to stay in our new home. At the dinner table on Christmas Eve, small talk evolved into a discussion, developed into an argument and progressed to a full blown row, my Father banging his fists on the table to bring his point home. He could never agree to disagree, he had to win. When we refused to argue anymore, he sulked and retired to his room. A morning cup of tea in his room was refused and I busied myself with Christmas dinner. My husband answered telephone calls from far-flung relatives and at this moment my Father descended the stairs with his suitcase and that expression on his face that I recognised and knew. It means "I know what's coming next and you'll be sorry," the triumphal "I've won". He must have seen the horror on my face.

"Order me a taxi," he demanded. My heart was pounding and my mind racing, the same old thoughts. What's he doing and why? I flung the telephone book at him.

"You want the taxi, order it yourself. This is the last time I'm putting up with your crap. I'm warning you, if you walk out of my house now, you walk out of my life. I will never, ever, have anything to do with you again". The taxi arrived and he left. Six months later a huge floral display arrived for my birthday and I asked who'd sent them. Since they were from him, I refused acceptance. Several months later the yellow envelope arrived.

They say time heals all wounds. If you confront the issue, forgive and let go you can move on. But after all these years the hurt, anger and recriminations are still too deep to expunge. Some relationships are poison, too toxic to heal, and this was one of them. I no longer have to worry about when the next row will erupt, or when I'll be rejected or receive a letter in that childish hand.

I thought I'd finally won. But does this unopened letter, which I can't bring myself to read or throw away, mean he's still in control?

Part 4

Passions and Aspirations

Vintage Days

Sue Wissgott

(Leverstock Green)

My only published work prior to this was a poem in a school yearbook. This experience has been totally different. Once you start the words flow and it turns out you do have a lot to write about after all.

"Should we meet up at the Grappenhall Steam Fair?" My husband's cousin did not realise what he was starting. That day was to shape our weekends and holidays for years to come. I don't remember much detail about the day, other than that we all enjoyed it. Afterwards our four year old eldest lad wanted to know if he could have 'one of those machines'. My husband had some knowledge of agricultural machinery and we thought 'why not?' Soon we were the proud owners of a 1952 Lister D type. These were often used on farms to power an elevator, for lifting hay bales up into the barn, pumping water or milling corn. My husband knew about engines from working on a friend's farm at weekends, so felt able to do any necessary repairs and maintenance. I never thought it would be such a major influence in our family life. It didn't seem to be such a significant purchase at the time.

The 'machine', is a stationary engine, so it doesn't move, unlike its counterpart the traction engine. Most people think of a steaming and puffing traction engine rolling along the roads, as they have seen these on television.

Our first outing was the 1000 Engine Rally, held in the rolling grounds of Tatton Park, Cheshire in June 1993. Here the engines are all lined up in enclosed pens, as if they might escape at any moment and go rolling away. They would be chugging and puffing clouds of blue-grey smoke, which was trapped by the surrounding majestic trees and low lying ground. You could taste the fumes and would be glad to walk up out of the dip, to the gaily displayed stalls with all manner of tempting goods.

People were all relaxed, happy to stand around whiling the time away. Owners of engines chat to visitors about what they were used for and how they have been restored. At first you feel like you are also on display sitting on a deck chair behind your exhibit. But you soon get used to it, forgetting the curious faces passing by.

Visitors to the show want to know everything they can about these lumps of metal, all sitting in a row whirring, popping, belching steam from their hoppers and puffing smoke from their exhausts, wheels spinning and arms moving. What was it used for, how old is it, how does it work and what does it run on?

A young man strolls up inside the pen introducing himself as Chris. We invite him to sit with us and start chatting about how we came to be there. He would like to know if we are interested in going to a small village gathering in Antrobus and we are delighted to accept. We found that we enjoyed the small familiar gatherings, just as much as the grand sprawling events hosted at places like Welland and Billericay.

A few years later we returned to Grappenhall where this all began. This time, I remember meeting Fred Dibnah (an icon in the steam world), who signed postcards for our children and let them look at his traction engine like a kindly grandfather might.

Our hobby has taken us to widespread places, such as Llandudno, to a Victorian Extravaganza weekend. People dressed up in traditional costume, ladies in long skirts, white blouses and large feathered hats and the men in narrow black trousers, collarless shirts with waistcoats, bright red neckerchiefs and either black bowlers or flat caps. In the town centre the gaily painted fair is powered by steaming traction engines, the drivers with blackened faces and gleaming polished brass.

We also visited Bodelwyddan Castle in Wales for rallies and fondly remember our younger son, who would be around five, asking if we were going to 'Boddelwiddling' this year? The grey castle walls would contrast starkly with brightly coloured swing boats. At the centre of the fairground a large galloper ride would whizz round. Horses going ever faster and faster, their nostrils flared and eyes wide open.

In 1999 a Grand Millennium Festival was held at Old Warden in Bedfordshire. We set up our tent and soon got in the swing of things. All the exhibitors had agreed to dress in period costume; mine was a long skirt, which swished as I walked, and a lace edged blouse. The rest of the family was suitably attired in dark trousers, white shirts, brightly coloured neckerchiefs and patterned waistcoats (sourced from charity shops).

Our exhibit was a butter churn loaned by friends (whom we met through joining the local stationary engine club) and our own dark green Fairbanks Morse "Headless" engine running it. We shared the area with friends and they had a large bright blue mill for grinding corn to make flour. Having a mill makes you appreciate supermarket shopping, as it constantly requires your attention filling the hopper and removing the sacks when they are full. It is also very dusty work, especially as it was a blazing hot weekend. The smell of bread baking drifted from the baker round the corner. He had a large metal drum, which mixed the dough, powered by a small engine whirring away in the corner.

We also camped at Welland by the Malvern Hills for several years. A three day event spread across large hilly fields, filled with a vast array of vehicles and displays including army tanks, fire engines, vintage cars, motorcycles, bicycles, horse drawn ploughing on the hillside, dry stone walling, cider making, thatching and so much more.

Each morning you could hear rumbling and thundering as the tanks went into the main arena, kicking up dust, or mud, depending on the weather, as they rolled down the bank between the traders' stands. At night time they had fireworks filling the black sky with bright splashes of colour. Then the tractors would start 'tractor pulling' which consists of tractors linking up to a large heavy block and pulling as hard as they can. You could hear the revving engines for miles. By day, noises came from fairground rides and organs, with little soldiers standing to attention beating a drum, or ringing a cymbal in time with the music.

Some years have been badly affected by the weather, like in 2000 when there was severe flooding in Welland and the rally had to be cancelled until autumn. In 2001 foot and mouth led to the cancellation of some county shows. For those which went ahead there was a strange lack of animals bellowing and bleating.

When our eldest son turned 18, we asked how he would like to mark the occasion and he said 'Go camping in France'. This sounds simple enough, but of course we had to include some kind of 'vintage experience' to make his day special. This turned out to be more than one trip to view machinery, the first being Monsieur Du Fresney's museum of everything you could imagine, including the cart and guillotine used to behead people.

Our second day out was a challenge for my grasp of French, as we only had a map drawn on a coffee filter paper with a name, phone number and place - Giverny. This is mostly famous for Monet and his paintings, but we were not there to admire his lilies, which confused the residents greatly when we were asking in broken French where the private engine collection was housed. There was much shoulder shrugging and pointing to the Monet centre and I suspect a lot of head-scratching after we left. A young lady sent us in the direction of the Monet centre, so we decided to ask a lady in the garden opposite the centre, who pointed us back to the house next door to where we had spoken to the young lady.

As we approached, two dogs looked up at us with little interest. I was a bit nervous as we rang the bell and asked for the owner. We had the right place, but the owner who spoke English was away. His son, who answered the door, did not. However, he was happy for us to look around and we did manage some communication via exclamations of awe and amazement. The small frontage gave way to a cavernous whitewashed area holding all manner of mechanical wonders. They even had a full size vertical saw which went deep into the foundations of the building and would take a whole tree. This explained why it was a private collection, even in France, Health & Safety would have a field day.

Our third French experience of vintage machinery also involved a lot of driving backwards and forwards trying to decipher the novel French road directions where destinations are measured in minutes, not miles and you find the names of places only on one side of the signpost, so you can only see it when you have passed it. This was an old farm set out as a museum, so you wandered at will amongst the old rusty farm implements. It had a bakery complete with brick oven and inside the farmhouse, an old knitting machine, which I found extremely interesting, because I own a modern machine. By this time our younger son (14) had tired of the vintage experience and had to be placated with visits to the indoor BMX parks.

The Mini plant at Cowley is another type of event, where the main attraction is the model aeroplanes and vehicles, which are lined up along the edge of a flying area. These models include tanks, small planes about 30cm long, and a half sized Red Bull display plane. The highlight of the day is the re-enactment of a battle in both the sky and on the ground. The brightly coloured planes dip and swoop, with the wing tips reflecting in the sunlight and smoke streaming out behind them, simulating dog-fights. On the ground, tanks move into the cardboard village firing flashes of bright light causing the buildings to light up with clever pyrotechnics and explode out to collapse in a heap.

There are so many different memories of this period of time. Over the years we have built the engine collection and added a collection of brass oil and grease guns. We have also made boards to show the brass plaques and explain about the engine we are showing. Although our younger son (now 20) no longer comes to all the rallies as he has different interests, he is still friendly with the people and probably his bike interest has in some way come from being outside every weekend tinkering with machinery. The older lad (23) has completed a mechanical engineering apprenticeship, so his interest has never waned. Indeed, if anything it is greater than ever. We have gained so many good friends, which are more than weekend acquaintances. This in turn, has given us a variety of different experiences. It has greatly influenced our family life in a way we could not have anticipated when we first started.

So the pattern of our lives has been shaped by this all-pervading interest in all things vintage. Each year we rush out and buy the events guide and start planning the summer outings with a sense of anticipation. Hoping the weather will be kind and we will have one of those long enjoyable summers relaxing with friends and meeting new people with interesting tales to tell. Both keeping the past alive and looking to the future.

The Tale Of A Would-Be Star

Lily Emmerson

(Marlow Bottom)

Born in 1928 in Ardwick, Manchester, in a row of two-bedroomed terraced houses, where coal fires were burning in everybody's grate, I moved to Marlow Bottom in 1980 and joined the W.I. in 1988. Well known for my stage talents, this is my first attempt at writing.

It was 1935 and I was seven years old. How I longed to be part of the "Pinks and Blacks". This was a dancing class, not far from where I lived, where only "posh" kids went. The Mums wanted their little darling daughters to be another "Shirley Temple". She was a famous child star and was seven years old, as I was, and I used to go to the picture house (cinema) on a Saturday afternoon to watch her films. It was a penny to go in and you got a bag of sweets on the way out. You never saw the Pinks and Blacks there, they were too "posh". On the way home I would sit on a swing in the local park and look up at the sky and pretend I was a star, sitting on my very own swing. We only had a back yard, so swings were out of the question.

My Mother had given me three pence to go to the shops to get some bread. I then did the most awful thing. Instead of going to the shops for some bread, I went round to the dancing school, knocked on the door, and it was opened by a lady who looked me up and down. Imagine the look on her face when she was confronted by a "little urchin", wearing a tatty old frock, laced up boots and cropped hair (no curls for me). I held out my hand with the three pence in it and asked if I might have a tap dancing lesson. She must have taken pity on me as she let me in, and told me to keep my three pence and stand in line with the others. And there I tapped and shuffled my way through the next hour, in my scruffy old boots. The other girls had beautiful curls and ribbons in their hair and tap dancing shoes, but I didn't care, I'd danced with the Pinks and Blacks and went home with stars in my eyes. I told my Mother that I'd had to wait for fresh bread being baked.

I knew that I could never be a child star, though I longed with all my heart to be on the stage, and maybe famous one day. But for now I would settle for a Shirley Temple doll. I asked Father Christmas to bring me one (we believed in him in those days) and if he couldn't, I'd mention her in my prayers.

It's Christmas Eve, I can't go to sleep, I'm so excited. I have asked Father Christmas for a Shirley Temple doll. Me Mam is turning the gas light on, very low, and I can hear footsteps on the stairs. I think I'm going to die with excitement.

It's him, he's standing by my bed, I've just got to open my eyes. Mam is standing over me and Father Christmas is taking a box out of his sack. Mam says "Are you awake love ?" Oh, I am I am. He gives me the box, he's stumbling slightly. He must be feeling very tired with all the children he has to visit. I take off the lid and – Oh, there she is, my Shirley Temple doll, with beautiful golden ringlets, pink dress and white boots.

I can't remember much after that wonderful moment. Thank you, Thank you, Thank you, Father Christmas. I must have fallen asleep then, clutching my beautiful doll. Many years later my Mam told me that the lady she cleaned for at the time, had bought me my precious doll.

At 15 years old I was working as a "runner" in the Mill. I fix the broken cotton reels so that the machine will start up again. "Sing for us Lily". And so I did, above the noise of the machines in the Mill. I would sing my heart out like Deanna Durbin and Jeanette McDonald, who were famous at that time. When the Manager came up to me (to shut me up as I thought would happen) he asked if I would sing for the workers in the canteen at break time. I was thrilled and scared at the same time.

I never needed accompaniment to sing, but there was a piano in the canteen and someone would get on it and play along with me. I would start and he would follow. I didn't know a note of music, I just used to go for it, and the poor pianist would have to try and get into the key I was singing in. This was the start of my singing career, which was to end when everything should have been beginning. Fate took a hand and sent me down a different road, but enough of that, the journey towards that end was very exciting.

I went on to sing with big bands at the American Air Base in Liverpool. Then my mother decided to move back to Manchester (she was always on the move) where I started to sing with the "Ted Astley" band as their regular vocalist. I would sit on the side of the stage next to the band, in my prettiest dress and my blonde hair long and flowing. I always sang the romantic waltzes. The lights would be dimmed and I would sing while watching the couples dance very closely together.

I would feel a little envious. One night the trumpet player fell ill and a replacement came in. That's when fate stepped in and sent me down the other road. I had been for an audition with the band to broadcast for the BBC. I always remember the number. It was called "Summertime". We were all assembled in the recording studio in Manchester. "Quiet now everyone." (Oh please God, don't let me sneeze.) They played, I sang. We made a record, the BBC liked it and accepted us fit for broadcasting time.

Time has passed now. My dreams all changed, but that's another story. I never got to go to London and sing with the band on the wireless.

Years later, my family (two boys) have grown up, one married. I'm living in Marlow Bottom and have joined the local W.I. How exciting to be singing again in their little concert group. Now and again I am given a solo spot. Magic. We did concerts for charities. One night we were part of a group of W.I. concert parties putting on a big show in Aylesbury Civic Centre, the theme being World War II. Ration books and paraphernalia were on tables for the audience. Waitresses (W.I. ladies) were serving food, dressed in Lyons Tea Shop uniforms. Aeroplanes on film were the back drop to the stage. Everyone was dressed in wartime style. Wonderful atmosphere. It was our turn, our W.I. to shine. We took to the stage to sing "Pack Up Your Troubles" and "White Cliffs of Dover". Then it happened. My voice went. I opened my mouth and nothing came out. That was the beginning of the end for me. I could sing no more.

Moving on. It's Christmas and I've been asked to do a monologue as part of the W.I. entertainment to be presented at the Wycombe Swan Theatre. I am standing in the wings, I'm scared, my hands are sweating. A voice behind me says "Alright Lily, you're on, good luck." My feet won't move, so someone gives me a gentle push. A thousand faces are looking at me (go for it Lil). "On the first day of Christmas my true love said to me". I've started, I'm away, I've done it without singing (Halleluiah). From that performance I've been asked to do two more monologues at different venues. I can't believe it, they want to pay me – so it's going to Charity.

I'm getting old now, too late for a new career, but I will continue enjoying it, till the voice packs in, along with the singing voice I used to love.

Signs Of The Times

Sherrian Guest

(Hassocks)

A member of Hassocks WI in West Sussex, I'm enjoying its Book Group, Singing Group and especially the Creative Writing Group which gives me the incentive to write regularly. I enjoy writing short stories (often semi-autobiographical) and poetry. I also help publicise community events through articles and press releases and have written, compiled and edited copy for two websites.

"What's an autograph?" The street was full of talking, laughing girls, spilling off the pavements, all clutching little books.

"It's when someone famous writes their name in a special book," mum explained.

According to her, these girls were waiting to see the pop star Adam Faith who was coming to open a new shop: DER television rentals. They were his fans - another new word - and they were hoping to get his autograph. I couldn't understand why anyone would want to collect famous peoples' names and even have to have a special book for doing so.

I was six years old and I'd been fascinated by my view of the world

from this first floor window since moving in above Smeeds Wine
Merchants, (or "Smee Wily Merch" as I often announced on my
toy telephone) which my father managed, when I was two and
three quarters. With the dusty net curtain behind my head like a
veil I spent much of my free time watching what happened on my
street: The Quadrant, Richmond, Surrey, England, The World,
The Universe.

Today, the street looked even more interesting than usual so I
stretched as far out of the window as mum's hand on the back of
my coat would allow. Normally Saturday morning was my time to
ride on Stardust, the grey horse in *Wrights* department store.
I couldn't wait to get up the stairs then run towards him, hoping
no-one was already having a ride, climb up and slip my threepence
into the slot by his head. To me he was a real horse, my horse and
the ride always ended too quickly.

But today we couldn't have got to Wrights. Traffic was virtually at
a standstill and the policemen were having trouble keeping the fans
on the crowded pavements. Outside DER, the staff tied a ribbon
across the door for Adam Faith to cut.

It was a long wait for a six year old but eventually a vintage car
came over the railway bridge and he was here. I didn't really know
who he was but the fans certainly did. They screamed, they pushed
towards the car, they waved their books frantically. It seemed
unbelievable, (if this Adam Faith was as important as these girls
seemed to think), that he'd come to the street I lived in.

I could just see his blond hair. I wished he'd come closer. Even if I
didn't recognise him, I'd have liked him to smile up at me. But he
couldn't get out of the car. There was no way through the crowd.

Somehow the police cleared the road and the car drove off, round to
the shop's rear entrance. The screams died down then some of the
fans started to run in the opposite direction to the car, still waving
their books, to meet it at the back door. Now, collecting autographs
didn't just seem pointless to me, it also looked like hard work.

Most of the fans stayed around the entrance where a few minutes later Adam Faith appeared and cut the ribbon on his way out of the shop. He smiled, posed for photos, scribbled his name in a few of the books then went back inside with the manager, followed by as many of the girls as could squeeze through the door.

I didn't see him leave. My brother Nigel and I went back to our toys, mum to her Saturday chores. Below us, dad served customers in the off licence and outside in the street the traffic moved again. My first sight of the tide of pop culture that was to sweep all before it had been exciting but didn't leave much of an impression at the time, though I had missed my ride on Stardust.

That afternoon Mum took Nigel and me over to the new shop. I walked through the same door as Adam Faith had done. I got a quick impression of shelves and shelves of television sets, all showing the same pictures: picture after picture after picture. Each was better than the one on our tiny screen at home. Wide-eyed, I stuck close to mum as we looked into the future but our glimpse of things to come was cut short.

"Hello, young man. How are you?" A clown approached Nigel and stuck out his hand. The screams and tears caused by the hidden squeaker in his glove meant we were soon on our way home. The perils of having a younger brother!

Two years later, at my eighth birthday party in the tearoom of the local theatre, I offered pieces of birthday cake to the pantomime cast. As I did so I shyly asked each of them to sign my new autograph book, a present from my grandmother.

The book had been a surprise and I still wasn't very excited about autograph hunting as a hobby. I didn't recognise any of these actors' names and I wasn't convinced anyone really famous would ever write in my book. Also, I'd been told that an autograph only counted if you had met the person and were there when they'd signed. My dad's pride at getting my TV favourite *Mr Pastry's* autograph at a Round Table meeting shortly afterwards was met with dismay as I felt it was cheating.

Meanwhile, the temperature on the music scene was rising. In winter, my bedroom was too cold. The sash window wouldn't close completely and there was a permanent draught. I'd leave tomorrow's clothes on the cover the night before and then try and dress under the sheets.

In summer, it was too hot. Dropping the top sash didn't let in any cool air, just the accumulated heat and dust of the day from the street. It let in the noise of traffic and of aeroplanes making their way to London Airport. During my eighth summer, it began to let in the music.

"Mum, go and tell them to stop."

"Please make them stop."

"Tell them I can't sleep."

Mum spent her evenings patiently trailing up and down stairs, opening the window because the heat stopped me sleeping; closing it again because the heat seemed preferable to the music.

But she couldn't stop the music. No-one could. It was 1963. Although I never missed *Thank Your Lucky Stars, Juke Box Jury* or *Ready Steady Go* on television, I was only eight years old so bedtime was early. My nights were long yet I wasn't sleeping. Night after night, the drums kept up their insistent 'thump', 'thump' backing for the guitars and the rough voices that kept me awake.

I was too hot and fretful and, unfortunately, too young to realise that I was being sung and played to sleep by Mick Jagger, Keith Richards, Bill Wyman and Eric Clapton. Less than a quarter of a mile away from where I lay grumbling myself to sleep, The Station Hotel rocked to debut performances by The Rolling Stones and The Yardbirds.

To me, it was just a jumble of noise but years later, hearing The Stones *Little Red Rooster* on the radio, I recognised it instantly as one of my much resented lullabies from that time. How I wished then that I could have realised at the time what the noise was and oh

182

how I wished I'd been ten years older and part of the audience.

Despite my lack of sleep, by the following year I couldn't get enough of pop music and my autograph book reached the dizzy heights of the London Palladium's roof in search of a star. For my friend Alison's ninth birthday treat I joined an excited group of school friends and parents for the matineé of a show starring Frank Ifield. He'd been at the top of the hit parade and his unique yodeling style had been the soundtrack to my family's holiday the previous summer.

As we stood outside afterwards, the stage door manager collected autograph books and took them up to the roof where Frank signed them then came to the parapet and waved down to everyone. I didn't feel I'd cheated this time: I had *almost* met him. And, unlike Adam Faith a few years earlier, I did know who he was.

The next summer I watched from my window half fascinated, half shocked as crowds of young people with long hair, colourful (if scruffy) clothes, sandals and, in some cases, bare feet carried their tents and rucksacks towards the Athletic Ground. This was the annual invasion of Richmond for the National Jazz & Blues Festival. It had been happening each year since 1961, about the time I'd seen Adam Faith, but, typically, I'd been too young to be interested until now, its final year.

Dad wasn't too keen on serving those who called into the off licence on their way past. Mum called them 'beatniks' and clearly didn't approve but I thought they were wonderful. I decided then that I going to be a beatnik when I grew up. I demanded to know why we couldn't get tickets for the festival and see The Yardbirds, The Moody Blues and Manfred Mann. It was only just down the road but I was only nine years old so another piece of rock history rolled on without me. Once again it was a case of being so near and yet so far.

In 1967 though, I finally managed to be in the right place at the right time. I was almost in my teens; my head full of pop music, the inside of my school desk lid covered in pictures of The Monkees and, for once, I was about to be where it was happening.

I had no fashionable clothes and I'd never met a pop star so Cathy McGowan (the Cheryl Cole of her day) was way ahead of me on both counts.

I wanted her long, straight, silky hair instead of the short, tangly natural perm nature had given me. I wanted her fashionable clothes. Most of all, I wanted her job. She'd presented *Ready Steady Go* on television each Friday. She'd stood next to, talked to and even touched John Lennon, Paul McCartney, Mick Jagger and so many more of my favourite pop stars.

Now she was coming to open a 'boutique' department, squeezed next to Accounts on the top floor of *Wrights*. I was determined to get a good view but by the time I arrived with my best friend Peggy, the place was packed. We'd be lucky to see the top of her head. Suddenly the staff moved the tiny stage to the other end of the boutique. We turned round and found ourselves on the front row.

There I was, looking up at Cathy McGowan. At her straight, shiny hair, at her heavily made up eyes and at her trendy trouser suit. My curls were scraped back under a pink cotton hair band, I wore no makeup behind my spectacles and my school-made shift dress (the one with the bow on the front covering the hole which had appeared during my impatient cutting out!) was accessorised with a home knitted cardigan. I was hardly one of the people the boutique was aimed at.

But I was there and I did get Cathy's autograph. She scribbled her name without looking at me yet I felt that at last I'd made a real connection with this famous decade that I'd spent most of my childhood in. Plus my picture was in the local paper to prove it. The cutting still survives, though sadly the autograph book doesn't.

The Sixties are long gone now and I'm nearer to *my* sixties. They say that if you can remember the 1960s then you weren't there. That's not true. I was there and I remember it so clearly: that decade when to be young was everything, but to be too young was torture.

It's Never Too Late
Andrea Bowra
(Rufford)

I have been married for 39 years and raised three children. When the opportunity came to create a memoir for this book I wanted to produce something that might inspire others and so decided to write about my return to education at the age of 43. That changed my life and hopefully my story may spur others on!

In my youth it was easy to obtain employment and I had a variety of jobs after leaving school. My teachers had wanted me to stay on and train to be a teacher but I wanted to get out into the world of work and earn some money. In those days money was tight and my parents would have had quite a struggle to send me away to college.

My first job was as an office junior and I progressed on from there. I was never really a 'wild child' and although I was a teenager in the 1960s I didn't see much free love or drugs going on in Bournemouth where I lived. I was rather middle of the road, considering myself not to be a mod or a rocker but somewhere in-between – we called ourselves midi's. Later on I went through a 'hippy' phase and attended the Isle of Wight Pop Festival with my husband to be, we camping in a tent and enjoying the whole experience. I smoked very little and occasionally drank CherryB's, but nothing too wild.

When I was expecting my first baby I gave up my office job and became a full-time wife and mother, the same as most people did in the 1970/80's. Over a period of years I had three children and stayed at home to look after them. When my youngest child was small the headteacher of our local village school asked me if I would consider supervising the children in the playground at lunchtime, as they couldn't find anyone and were rather desperate. I agreed to do it for a short time until they could find someone, but in the interim I found that I enjoyed working with the children very much. This fostered an interest in working with children and as soon as my youngest child was old enough to start school I applied to a local further education college to train as a Nursery Nurse. The course was part-time and I was thrilled to be accepted. But also I suddenly realised that, now in my early 40s, I actually had to do it.

I didn't have any unhappy memories of the education system. In fact I quite enjoyed my time at school and left with a reasonable array of qualifications. However, I was never really all that interested, just doing the bare minimum required to do reasonably well. I was a bit of a joker and I went to a single-sex school and really liked the social side of life with my peers. Even though my memories were quite good it still took a great deal of courage to actually enrol and start my first class at college. I worried about being the oldest at 43 and that all the others would be young. The fear that I would make a fool of myself was also at the forefront of my mind. I had not been in the education system for over 25 years, so it was very daunting.

I find it hard to describe what a joy it was to find that education had changed dramatically from when I was young. I was used to putting my hand up and only speaking when I had been spoken to. Yet here in the classroom the tutor and students really seemed to want to hear each others' opinions. The atmosphere was very supportive and, despite my initial fear of appearing foolish if I answered a question wrongly, I found that all ideas were valued. After a while I really got into the student life and loved the feeling – even got myself a pair of Doc Martens to look the part. I was still a bit of a joker, but I was interested in what I was being taught and always got my work in on time. We were on first name terms with our lecturers, something unheard of when I was at school. The whole atmosphere was relaxed, making the learning enjoyable and fun.

I still remember the first assignment that I got back. It was in a Psychology lesson (a subject I had never taken before) and the tutor gave prizes for the best assignments at the start. I was so afraid that my assignment would be no good, she handed it to me and I shakily looked, it had a *D*. "Oh I thought, a D" – I was still thinking in the old way of the marking being a,b,c and then d. But then I noticed that the tutor had written 'prize' on it and to my great surprise I read the marking criteria and I had a Distinction. I couldn't believe it and the feeling of euphoria was brilliant. I wasn't a fool after all, and from that moment on I was totally hooked.

I actually gained distinctions on all my assignments for the whole course, and can honestly say that I loved every minute of being at college. Having been at home bringing up my children for a number of years, my self-confidence was really low and I didn't feel like I could do anything. When I went to college it was as if a door into the future opened up and I could see that there were endless possibilities.

After my course I gained employment in a primary school supporting a junior child with special educational needs. I enjoyed my time there but after a while I missed being part of college life, despite all the late nights trying to finish assignments on time. I missed the banter and the atmosphere of learning, and so I enrolled on a Higher National Certificate in Early Childhood Studies course, which was part-time in the evenings and so didn't interfere with my job. In fact you had to be working a substantial number of hours with children, to do the course. It was great to be back at college and I found that I had some of the same tutors on this course as I did on the previous BTEC National course.

I thoroughly enjoyed the new course and again achieved distinctions in the same way as I had before. Of course both

courses were hard going at times, and I felt as though my home-life
suffered a bit because I was always working on assignments. All
the tutors were again friendly, helpful and supportive. I was almost
sad to finish after the two years were up but I was relieved that the
pressure was off. At the end of the course the college put on a
presentation evening and our small group wore caps and gowns. It
was brilliant and we all felt so proud – it had all been worthwhile.

I was still working at the primary school but the child I supported
had moved on up to High School. I was happy there but one day I
saw that the college was advertising for part-time lecturing staff and
when I expressed an interest, I was encouraged to apply. I got the
job provided that alongside teaching I completed a City and Guilds
Further and Adult Education Teachers Certificate.

Originally I started teaching just one class a week and continued
working at the primary school. However, soon I was asked to
teach more and so eventually I worked at the college as my main
employment. I remember so well the first class I taught. The
students were a mixture of ages but mostly 17 and upwards. I
didn't tell them that I was new to teaching and after a short while
I found that they were responding well. I felt almost immediately
that I loved teaching and that this is what I had been waiting to
do all my life. I was very nervous that first lesson, my knees were
knocking and my palms were sweaty, but I was determined not to
show it. The students were very varied academically and 'very
lively'. However, about half-way through the lesson I thought to
myself 'I love this' and I have felt the same way ever since, come
what may. That first class that I took will always have a special
place in my heart and I know that they enjoyed my teaching
because they told me so, and also gave me a great big bouquet of
flowers and lots of cards when they left.

Sometimes I wish that I had taken opportunities when I was
young, but then I realise that without all my life experiences I don't
think that I would be able to teach adults as I do now. Somehow
all the patterns and threads of my life including bringing up my
own children, have matured me and enabled me to bring my
experiences to bear to help my students.

I think that one of the main advantages that I have is that I can empathise with the students because I have been a mature student myself, and I understand the pressures that they are under. I understand how difficult it is for mature students to make that first move and come into our college, especially if they are juggling home and family as well. I also know how low their self-esteem may be and how easily it can be shattered. I have had three teenage children myself and this also helps me to relate to where the younger students are coming from.

I have gained further qualifications along the way including my Certificate in Education, again a ceremony with a cap and gown on achieving the qualification. This was a very proud moment for me and my family. I often wish that my parents were still alive and could see what I have achieved. It is typical of me that I did everything back to front, qualifying in my forties rather than at school, but it just proves that "it's never too late". I have been employed by the college for nearly 13 years and having reached 60 last year I am due to retire shortly. I will remember my time as a teacher with great fondness and have happy memories of all the students that I have taught. I don't regret a single minute and am so glad that I took the plunge and went back into education as a mature student. Being 'student turned teacher' is a wonderful feeling – sometimes I have to pinch myself to believe it.

A Chance Taken

Denise Ziman

(Peckforton and Beeston)

A qualified social worker, I believed in unstinting mothering, so when I had three children in five years I gave up my career. When my husband faced redundancy or relocation, we switched to working together in the interests of family stability. Now happily retired, we pursue artistic interests with the U3A.

It was in 1976 that my husband came home one evening saying his firm was planning to relocate to the south coast. We were dismayed. Where? When? What about my job which paid our mortgage? What about education? Our eldest would soon be ready for secondary school, a decisive and important step for him. We had struggled for years to establish ourselves, had put off starting our family until Robert had qualified and settled into an appropriate job. We had adjusted to his long journey to work and had three children in five years. The idea of unsettling us all was appalling. Which was worse, relocation or find another job? If only we could be independent, work for ourselves. Nothing was ever perfect but at least then we'd have control over our lives. Tired of fretting over things we seemed to be able to do nothing about, we escaped to our old caravan for a relaxing weekend. We found the familiar site, complete with its house and out-buildings, was up for sale! For two days we played with the idea of owning it, living there, running it and making it pay year round by hosting study groups, painting holidays, providing workshops for craftsmen, a locality for film-making. Life would be ideal for the children, living in the country, with both of us at home for them. Robert could manage the site, I could do the admin. We could offer meals, sell home made jams, pickles, cakes. We went home totally in love with the idea of working for ourselves.

A couple of phone calls on Monday shattered our dreams. The price was far too high; the caravan site lettings would be our only immediate source of income; and we would need a big mortgage. We would need capital to develop other aspects of the business. It would take time, a couple of years at least. The whole venture was far too risky. We had to wait for Robert's firm to determine our future.

But we could not quite give up the dream. Since upheaval was inevitable, why not look for a more realistic alternative? There was that little village shop the caravaners depended on. It had been on the market, so what about running that? It had a Post Office, the only one for miles around, which would provide a basic salary. Neither of us had any knowledge of running a shop but so what? We knew from experience what shoppers wanted. It couldn't be that difficult. And the Post Office would train Robert to run that side of the business. The lure of independence was too strong. The shop was still for sale; we could just afford it without a mortgage. We went for it.

Some hectic four months later, one Saturday in June, we moved to start our new life. The shop was attached to the house and there were shacks at the back for storage, and two small fields. We made plans for a garden, maybe a pony for the children. We would put off rebuilding the greenhouse until the spring. There were more urgent things to do, like getting to grips with the business. Our predecessors' part-time assistant had agreed to 'see us in' by working until the end of the month, but after that we would be on our own.

That Saturday morning our vendors continued to run the shop while we moved our furniture in as theirs was taken out. The day's takings would be theirs and we had yet to pay for what would remain of their stock. Robert observed what went on in the shop and I tried to make a home for us in rooms which seemed large, dark and inhospitable. After the shop closed at lunchtime we all set about stock-taking, snatching something to eat from the left-overs in the cool cabinet. I was introduced to the routine of cleaning the various machines. A tour of the out-buildings to survey the stock - paraffin, firelighters, turps, crates of bottles, some empty for return, some full - made me realise how complex the whole enterprise was. Figures were agreed, papers signed, hands shaken all round and we were on our own.

We had until Monday morning to get straight indoors. The survey had warned that the place was in need of repair and redecoration. Top priority would be to make the roof watertight. The windows had nearly all been nailed shut. The bare wooden floors were dirty, inclined to splinter. The kitchen was best described as inadequate, and I was apprehensive. I had never cooked on an oil-fired range. There was a washing machine in one of the outhouses but the whole place needed cleaning before I could use it.

We established bedrooms, used our few rugs beside each bed, and put our chairs into the sitting room. The range grudgingly yielded us only basic meals, but no one complained. The children helped or hindered, and explored. Much too soon Monday morning dawned and around 5.30am the daily newspapers arrived. Robert sorted them as he had been shown on Saturday, and before breakfast took off on his first delivery round. We were shop-keepers now. At 8.30am sharp we opened for our first customer who was already waiting at the door, as she was to be every morning thereafter. We speculated that living alone she was desperate for human contact.
Each day brought new things to learn, more mistakes to rectify. We struggled and, exhausted each evening, we complained. But hadn't we known this whole adventure would be a challenge? The important thing was to secure a living and provide the children

with a settled background. It would take time but we would get there. So as a family we settled down to keeping shop in a small village where strangers - in-comers - were politely accepted, but watched. Our invaluable assistant took pity on us and stayed on working mornings. She it was who must have told people we were OK, because within a couple of weeks the shop was taking about the same amount daily as before our takeover. A relief Post Master trained Robert on the job for the first week. Our assistant advised Robert what to order each week and served in the shop in the morning. Robert and I coped with the afternoon trade.

My daily routine consisted of cleaning the house and the shop. I cleaned the shop floor, the windows, the steps, the out-the-back area where the dustbins overflowed and the crates accumulated. I learned to take in goods on delivery, price them up, stack them in the stock room. We knew it was vital for a village shop to present only really fresh food, so I learned to monitor the vegetable rack and the chiller cabinet, to remove each day's left-overs. Rather than throw anything away, we ate the perfectly good rejects ourselves. I devised fail-safe methods for preparing orders, and ensured the shelves were well-filled. I did serve customers but I left the post office strictly alone. Never confident with figures, I was afraid of adding by my mistakes to the headache of the weekly reconciliation which Robert had to face on Friday nights. I concentrated on presenting a clean and welcoming shop and trying to run the house.

The reps from the wholesalers who visited regularly took pity on us greenhorns and taught us a lot. One of them showed us how to bone sides of bacon which he said were a much better buy for us than the pre-packed stuff. Better as it turned out for the customers too. They began coming from neighbouring villages to buy their bacon; some even took supplies away on holiday, because 'it tastes like it used to, no water weeping into the frying pan'. We had yet to make friends in the village, but our tally of regular customers went up every month. The weekly takings continued to rise and the shop, instead of going downhill, which many had predicted, seemed to be modestly thriving.

Our first winter was going to be hard, we knew that. The urgent thing was to repair the roof. It was old, very steep, consisting of two inverted Vees with a gulley between. Originally intended for thatch but now clad in slate, it leaked so badly we had to put buckets out whenever it rained. We were told it was too far gone, the only thing to do was to re-roof the whole place. So we were relieved when, just before Christmas, we found builders who could tackle the job. They worked fast. To harmonise with the nearby properties, pantiles had been chosen - heavy, shapely and a warm red - to replace the old slates. The weather forecast was threatening and the Christmas weekend was upon us. The roofers reckoned pinning the tiles was unnecessary and made an extra effort to finish the job on the Friday evening. After the shop closed on the Saturday we engaged in an orgy of cleaning and that night, in bed early for once, exhausted by the most hectic week of the year, we lay listening to the wind and the rain and rejoiced. No more buckets. We congratulated each other on having had the roof done just in time.

Later that night the sound of the storm woke us up. The house shook, the windows rattled as never before. We got up to reassure the children and suddenly there were crashing noises, things falling. We heard glass shattering. The shop windows were intact so that must have been the old greenhouse. The whole building began seriously to vibrate. Our daughter's bed travelled across her uncarpeted floor. We all met on the landing, faces white in the torchlight since the electricity had failed. With a roar the nightmare came to a climax as the newly laid pantiles cascaded off the roof and smashed into the gulley and in front of the house. In the relative silence that followed we stood clinging to each other. Then Robert declared he must go outside to assess the damage. We were terrified. All those tiles and that glass flying about. He would be hurt. Seizing a torch and with a futile balaclava helmet, which I hastily produced to protect his head, he went out. Lacking anything better to do I put the kettle on.

The storm passed and in daylight we saw the damage it had done. Not just to us. Fences everywhere were flattened, people had lost tiles, lines were down. It was Christmas Eve so there was no one to call. We would just have to wait till after the holiday for help. Luckily we were insured, but did storm damage count as an act of God? There was nothing we could do except worry and cope somehow.

We had underestimated our neighbours. For a couple of hours no one in the village stirred. Then two men, farmers we rarely saw in the shop, arrived carrying big tarpaulins, with which they contrived to cover and secure the two slopes of the roof that had been stripped. A neighbour brought us a jug of hot soup. Another sent over extra blankets in case the children were cold. Someone else brought us a heater, in case our paraffin stocks out the back were not intact.

People did not say much. Most of them had suffered storm damage of some sort. But their actions were eloquent. They valued their shop, approved of our efforts. Our first self-employed Christmas, disastrous as it seemed, cheered us greatly. Independence was only relative, Fate always had a card to play. We were touched that people had been there for us when we needed them. We resolved to see to it that theirs was a good village shop.

Playgroups, Jumble Sales And
Lonely Young Mothers
Meg Burford
(Ambleside)

I was born in Scotland and am now happily settled in Cumbria with my husband of 52 years. I have had an eclectic career including playgroups, health services and charity administration. My interests include family and local history, walking, reading and being involved with my three daughters and eight grandchildren.

"Thank goodness it's not raining," I thought, as I fastened Sarah into the big pram, settled Jane on the apron, checked the shopping tray was empty and set out with Alison holding on to the pram handle. We were off to collect jumble – an entirely new venture for all four of us. There had been so many new experiences and challenges in the last two years that another seemed quite normal. How life had changed since I first arrived in Lancashire as a very lonely young mother.

"We're going to collect jumble."

"What's jumble? Why are we collecting it?" asked Alison. Explaining this took some time so we soon reached the first street which I had leafleted one evening two days before.

I took a deep breath and knocked on the first door which was abruptly answered by a very grumpy man, "No, no, I haven't anything for you." And he banged the door shut in our faces.

The next knock was much more productive, a charming old lady, obviously desperate to talk, came to the door. She was highly organised and produced two bags of jumble. She then disappeared and returned with biscuits for the girls which went down very well.

"What's the sale for, love?" she asked.

"We're planning to start a playgroup in the village."

"How nice, and what plays will the children be doing?"

I seized the opportunity to explain what we were planning and how hard life could be for lonely young mothers. She listened very patiently and would have loved to tell me her life story had the girls not become fidgety.

We carried on and made good progress. The shopping tray filled up and I had a few bags tied to the handles. Another lady obviously expecting me greeted me with great enthusiasm until she saw my laden state.

"I'm so glad you've come but I've got three large boxes for you."

I arranged to go back in the evening when I could borrow my husband's car. By then we were all ready for home and tea. Soon after I got home the phone started ringing. All my friends who had spent the afternoon as I had, reported similar success. We were going to have a large storage problem as the date for the sale was still two weeks away.

Later that evening, after collecting the outstanding jumble, I was enjoying a quiet cup of coffee when I reminded my husband how grim things had been when we first moved to Lancashire two years ago in a cold wet January in 1966. It was our fifth move in six years.

We left friends and family to move two hundred miles to Lancashire where we moved into one of the few occupied houses on a new and very muddy estate. We had two daughters, aged one and three, and another baby due in June.

I felt very isolated and lonely, until one day I spotted another mother with a pram and rushed out and dragged her into the house with her two little girls. We became the best of friends and remain so to this day.

Our children often played together and we made many other friends as other families moved in. There were no facilities for under-fives in the village other than the monthly baby clinic. This led to Mary and me running a small playgroup in our own homes, one morning a week each. We kept the numbers to eight and soon we had many more requests than we could cope with, so after chatting to friends we decided to try and start a community playgroup in the village.

We had soon identified a strong group of committed mothers and we worked through the challenges together. It was all tremendously exciting and many cups of coffee were drunk after the children were in bed and we squeezed into someone's lounge.

We found a disused class room and were given permission to use it. There were no toilets or running water but someone knew a plumber who would put in a sink and water. As for toilets, the Headmaster in the adjacent school was persuaded that the playgroup could use the outdoor toilets in the school playground, as long as we did not use them during playtime. In practice it worked beautifully and the little boys had many weeing competitions on the pitch-painted outside wall – very educational to those of us who only had daughters.

We set our sights high when it came to play provision. We wanted to provide experiences that children could not easily enjoy at home such as sand, water, paint and other messy play. But there were many things we needed to buy before we could start. That was when a jumble sale was suggested. It proved to be a scary experience. None of us had any experience of jumble sales but we had lots of energy and enthusiasm. We also got some useful tips from a grandmother, who was a jumble sale veteran.

"You need to put the tables into a hollow square and all stand inside it. Don't forget aprons with pockets and keep all the money in them or your profits will disappear. When you get a note, stuff it in your bra. Oh, and you need lots of small change and a strong lady on the door."

There had obviously not been a jumble sale for years so we did very well. The collection process also proved to be a good publicity exercise as we often had to explain why we were fundraising. Of course we also got more children's names for the playgroup, a volunteer – a bored childless middle-aged lady and a Nursery Nurse, who would be our play-leader.

When we stopped collecting we had mountains of clothes, masses of bric-a-brac and hundreds of shoes. It took us two whole days working in turns to arrange it on borrowed tables in some semblance of order. The massed jumble had a distinctive musty smell and we worked with the windows open. We plundered the goods for dressing up clothes, and we took anything that might be useful in the home corner and a pile of men's shirts to be converted into painting overalls. We put posters round the village and put a small ad in the local paper "Thursday's the day for Jumble Sales," our mentor had said.

We were nearly ready to open the doors when suddenly someone said "There's a queue."

We rushed to the windows and saw lots of tough-looking women in sensible shoes with large bags and hordes of children, plus a few weaselly-looking men lurking at the back.

Our hearts sank. Could we really cope with this? When they saw us they started banging on the windows and shouting at us,

"Open up, it's past 4 o'clock, and stop picking the best for yourselves."

Collectively we braced ourselves, took up our positions behind the tables which were piled high and nodded to Iris, the tallest of our number, who had been delegated to man the door. Cautiously she opened one side of the door, struggling to control the heaving mass of determined women, and managed to extract sixpence from most of them.

They rushed to the crowded tables and started rooting in the piles of clothes while shouting to know where the children's clothes were and commenting loudly that it was all rubbish. At the same time they were piling huge numbers of garments over their substantial left arms and then eyeballing one of us and offering 5 shillings for the lot. When we quaveringly agreed they would stuff it into a large bag and start again. While this was going on their children were crawling under the tables and collecting the many items which finished up on the floor. These were then either passed to their mothers or stuffed into the poachers' pockets in their or their mothers' clothing. Gradually we got the hang of it and started facing the women down and limiting sales to 10 garments for 5 shillings, which was still remarkable value.

The men, in the meantime, had made a beeline for the bric-a-brac which was also piled high. They turned it over disparagingly while making rude remarks about the quality, then offering derisory sums for the goods on show. By this time, some of us were getting a bit braver and refused the offers, until they crept up a bit.

As the rush died down, the women set up camp in the tea corner to recover from their efforts while consuming huge quantities of biscuits and numerous cups of tea. It now became apparent that they all knew each-other and were expecting to make huge profits on their market stalls from their purchases.

Mums from the village who had come to pick up clothes for their children huddled in another corner and eyed the dealers resentfully, while muttering to each-other. We surveyed the mountains of stuff that remained – what were we going to do with it all? Now we knew what it was like we were so grateful for the advice given to us.

While we were still drawing breath one of the shifty men sidled up to me and said "You'll never get rid of that lot" indicating the still piled tables with his thumb. "I'll take it off your hands for £5." Drawing breath I looked him in the eye and said "Let me talk to my committee………" We had a quick huddle and decided that we would keep 'that lot' and have another jumble sale in a week or two. So I declined his offer and he went off muttering "You'll be sorry."

But we never were, when we counted all the copper, silver and grubby notes, we had taken over £50, a huge sum which would go a long way to paying for all the equipment we needed to start the playgroup.

We had another Jumble Sale three weeks later and were much better at facing down the tough women and yanking their children from under the table and frisking them. We also learnt that the way to get rid of the final debris was to book a ragman to come and take it all away and give us a reasonable price. His only stipulation was that it should be in black bags and "no shoes." Strange to relate, some shoes were hidden in the middle of some of the bags. We again made an excellent profit and reached our target.

Jumble sales became a regular feature in our fundraising programme for many years. As well as raising valuable income for the playgroup they provided an opportunity for mothers to buy clothes for their children and themselves. Forty years on I have a long skirt which I still wear occasionally.

I am delighted to say that the playgroup is still flourishing. It was great for children in the village but also for the once lonely and isolated mothers. Many of us developed skills we didn't know we had. We were a disparate group of women from different backgrounds and different parts of the country drawn together by a common aim: to improve life for our children. In so doing, we improved life for ourselves and developed new skills. As our children grew older we were able to take the experience and skills we gained into other settings. From the founder members, two became magistrates, two trained as teachers, one founded a local charity, one trained as an accountancy technician. Other later volunteers became school governors, hospital volunteers or became involved with Guides, Scouts, and St John Ambulance cadets and so on. The volunteering habit lived on.

Wembley Two

Gill Irwin

(Coniston)

A sporty memoir telling of an exciting family trip to a Wembley football final, which stirred poignant recollections of a similar historic event twenty years earlier. So many emotions in one day.

"We've done it Rob! We're off to Wembley!"

"Another once in a lifetime event I suppose," teases my non-footie fan husband.

"That's right love, but this time I'm going to take our grandsons."

It is not often that the team, supported through thick and a lot of thin for over 60 years by your family, grandparents to grandsons, gets to play at Wembley. The FA Trophy, our non-league cup final, has been won once before by Barrow AFC. For the first trip, 20 years ago, I was a wife, mother and daughter. This time I am also a grandmother, but four years without Mum. She'll be badly missed today.

It doesn't seem five minutes since I was telling the lads, 14 year old Ben and 11 year old Morgan, to try and get some sleep, but now it's time we were stirring.

205

The blue and white jester hats and T-shirts urging "COME ON BARROW" look unsuitable for the cold dark morning. But layers will be topped by club scarves, old and new. I wear Mum's and remember her smiling and jumping up and down as she waved it on that very hot day in May.

No one is very interested in breakfast, but a large picnic bag is ready. We just want to be off and let the adventure begin. Rob takes me and the boys while Kerry, our youngest daughter, takes Dad, my sister Sue and brother-in-law Adrian to Barrow station. Even in the dark the town feels blue and white. Vehicles we meet heading out bear club stickers, scarves and banners. Many of the houses and businesses along our way show colourful support, adding to that tingly, slightly unreal feeling.

"Have a great time."

"Don't forget to watch and record it on the TV."

"If we wake up, Kerry and I are off back to bed!"

As we head to the platform where the chartered train is due, Adrian nips off for a newspaper.

"Would you say a few words?" a smiling young woman asks holding out a microphone and beckoning to her cameraman. Four of us huddle round a proud Dad as we declare our team the winners "just like last time."

"Will we be on the telly?"

"Could be, but they are talking to quite a lot of fans. Better tell Mum and Grandad to watch the local news just in case."

"Here comes the train."

"Which coach are we?"

"First class coach A."

The picnic bag takes centre stage as we settle round two tables amid the faded grandeur of privileged travel. Adrian settles to his Guardian crossword, the lads huddle together over Ben's I-Touch, Dad sits smiling at them, while Sue and I breathe a sigh of relief. All preparation and plans are over, anything forgotten is too late, time to sit back and enjoy. Excitement and anticipation has not dented the young male appetite as they eat their way to the capital.

"Let's pack the bag away, we're nearly there."

"Any Monster Munch left?" from tall, slim, dark Morgan.

"One more pork pie please," from cool, stocky, redhead Ben.

"Don't know where you put it all," laughs Dad.

"I can't remember a train journey with grandchildren where I haven't had to fund a trip to the buffet car! We'll take that as a compliment Sue." Good-humoured banter, big smiles and the odd rendition or chant have punctuated the six hour spell with now familiar fellow passengers.
"Look out for Aunty Kay, she's here somewhere!"

 I remember that first low key trip down on a service train, when we were greeted with the excited faces of Mum, already South on a visit, Kay, my youngest sister, and Nicky a cousin, who both live in Essex. That walk down Wembley Way to the twin towers was all blue and white as the opposition's colours matched ours.

Today our opponents, league winners plus last year's Trophy winners, play in red, easy to see in the cold grey around the modern frame of the new stadium.

"There she is." Kay's only small but her smile is always large.

"I'm not sure if they've opened the gates yet, but its blooming cold, should we find a café?"

"It might be an idea to have something hot," I smile as Morgan holds his tummy. Something and chips are ordered by all as Kay is told of early rising, possible TV fame and which players to look out for.

"Pass it here Nanna, what do you want to say?" Ben laughs as he can't bear to see me struggle any longer to send a text.

"Just letting them know we've arrived."

"I can't eat anymore."

"Not really surprised, Morgan," we all grin and secretly vow to remind him of this next time he's starving.

We find the right gate and make our way to our seats, looking out for familiar faces of the usual 1,000 strong Barrow crowd amongst today's 20,000. The lads flank Dad, who last time gave up his seat for Nicky. I sit between sisters with Adrian in the middle and we all strain our eyes to the pitch. Directors, managers and players filter out to wave and acknowledge our cheers. Photos are taken before the teams leave to change. The cameras pan round the ground as the atmosphere builds and we sisters hold up a piece of card saying "Hello Coniston". The boys declined to perform such an "uncool" gesture. Instead they listen to Dad's account of our last trip, when he'd sat separately and in all the excitement left behind his jacket. It had been purchased by Mum but never really liked, and sure enough someone picked it up and it was kindly returned to him.

"Nice try Grandad."

"I don't think you'll leave it today, it's too cold to strip off."

"Wait till our lads start scoring, that'll warm us up."

"Here they come."

"I've got butterflies in my tummy."

"Why does the other team look so big?"

"I'm sure they've got more than eleven players."

Barrow battle hard but Stevenage play with confidence and control and take the lead. It is 1-0 at half time when the family inquest begins.

"They need to make a change, bring on at least one sub."

"We're not doing so badly against such a strong team."

"I thought Edwards was great though there was that dubious tackle."

"If we can just get an early goal, it'll be a tester."

"It only takes a second to score a goal, there's plenty of time."

Sue twirls her clapper, much to the annoyance of the little lad sitting in front, who rolls his eyes at this funny woman with sore hands. Ben leans forward, quietly willing Barrow to score. Morgan is finding it hard to keep still as he plays each ball with them. Dad and Adrian look more serious as the time ticks by. Kay and I try to reassure each other.

"We're bringing on a sub."

"Who is it?"

"Oh no, I don't believe it!"

Our managers put on an unpopular, unfit player who has rarely played in the team.

"Oh Kay that's it we've no chance, he's hopeless, too fat, too sloooooow ......it's a GOAL. HE'S SCORED."

I leap out of my seat forgetting Dad's usual instruction to "sit down" when all around him jump up. He's no chance of being heard let alone heeded today. The dent in the ground is probably still there as our unlikely hero celebrates with a belly flop.

"What were you saying Gill?" Kay laughs as we jump up and down and hug each other. Big beams and thumbs up from the lads as I look along the row. There's not long to go and if the score remains level there will be extra time; another half an hour of play. Our train will just have to wait. No one considers leaving before the end whatever arrangements they may have made.

3-0 up 20 years ago was so much easier to enjoy. This time it's a real battle as players begin to tire and voices sound more desperate to be heard. Jason, our only true 'local' player, has the ball, looks up and fires it – hold your breath – it's in the back of the net. Morgan can't defer to Dad's age and Ben's cool any longer and comes to jump, hug, laugh, cry, cheer and scream with his grandmother and great aunts.

"I didn't know I could jump so high," Kay declares as we try to settle down for the next 12 minutes.

"Steady lads, keep the ball."

"I can't look, get it away."

"Phew that was close."

"Has that clock stopped, how much longer?"

"Blow your whistle, PLEASE."

Finally the whistle goes and Barrow players, fans, managers and directors are ecstatic. It's a fairytale we could never have dreamt. As the players collect the coveted trophy amid a cacophony of

cheers, songs, hooters and drums we feel the happiest family ever –
again. Mum's shining blue eyes are in my mind as I wave her scarf.

"Can you believe it?"

"They did us proud against such a strong team."

"Now have we got everything? We have to hurry back to the train."

We walk out of the ground together before big hugs and kisses for
Kay as she heads home alone. Wembley One we all went with her
to celebrate, but work, school and transport issues dictate this time.

The big smiles at the start of the day have grown and become
fixed on the face of every Barrow fan as we gather on the platform,
tiredness forgotten. We drop into our seats and look at each
other with incredulity. More food is eaten as we trundle along
in the dark, trying to keep awake but ignore the illicit alcohol
consumption around us. Adrian reminds one group that there
are youngsters present as their celebrations become rather bawdy.
Good spirits prevail and they continue with less noise and tempered
language. Morgan has lost his battle against sleep and feels very
heavy next to me as I try to keep him comfortable. Ben smiles from
his paler but still cheeky, freckled face as he plugs himself into his
music. The rhythm of the train soothes away the miles and our
over-active brains.

"How are we going to get this boy off?"

"When he goes, he goes."

"Come on Morgan."

Ben and I support him off as the others gather our bits and bags.

There are lots of police at the station, I see one bottle quietly but
efficiently confiscated but otherwise fans dance and sing their way off.

Rob smiles as he listens to us all, and Kerry looks for someone to unlock a loo, Morgan's desperate now he's awake.

"I think they should've had a penalty you know."

"Hey you did watch the game."

"Yeah I thought it was a game of rugby when that sub came on!"

"He scored a priceless goal but Jason's still our hero."

Ben sits in the front to laugh at Grandad's version of the game and add some of his own. Emma our eldest daughter is waiting half way to collect her son.

"You were on the telly."

"Really? Wow."

"Thanks Nanna, it was great."

"Thanks for coming Ben; you made it even more special."

The bear hug I get is brief but meant. My eyes fill as they head home to Windermere. Was it only this morning we left Coniston?

"Can we watch the video?"

"Tomorrow Morgan." Kerry and I laugh as we pile into the house.

"Does anyone want anything to eat?" Rob asks.

"Why are you groaning?"

I go upstairs to say goodnight to a wobbly Morgan, flopping into bed with his Mum's help, just in time to hear him declare, "That was the best experience of my life."

It is one I will always remember.

A Year In Savile Row
Marion Dangerfield
(Stock Harvard)

I was born on the Essex/London border. After leaving school I pursued my interest in dress design then worked in a London office. I am married with two sons and grandchildren. Now retired, I live in a rural Essex village and enjoy green bowls, horticulture, bridge and photography.

As I awoke, I didn't know why this Monday morning felt different from every other Monday. Then I remembered. Today would be the beginning of my working life, however long or short this would prove to be.

The school where I had spent many happy years was almost useless when it came to careers advice. My parents advocated that I follow a trade and hoped I would take up an apprenticeship. Needle or comb? That was the question. I chose the sewing needle over standing all day learning the art of hairdressing.

So here I was, in 1960, outside Number 14 Savile Row, checking the highly polished nameplate. Hardy Amies, Haute Couture Establishment shone back at me.

Yes, I was ready to enter the world of fashion design, beautiful materials, hand-made gowns and luxurious surroundings.

Well some of that was true, but our workroom was anything but luxury. My first impression of the dressmaking workroom was how huge and imposing it was. I felt very insignificant in my new tweed coat and highly polished black court shoes bought especially for my first day at work. I was introduced to Miss Brand and her second-in-command assistant, then I was taken on a tour of the building to familiarise myself with the layout and meet the other employees.

Down in the basement there was the haberdashery stockroom, about the size of a walk-in cupboard and packed tightly with all the sundries and items needed to complete any garment. This was expertly managed by Milly and Dorothy and was where the initiation for every new apprentice took place. In my case, two weeks into my employment, I was asked to "pop down" to see the girls in the stockroom and ask for a long weight.

"What's it for?" I asked.

"It goes into the hem of a dress to make the skirt hang evenly."

"Do I need a docket for the dress?"

"Not on this occasion," I was informed.

Obediently I went into the stockroom and announced that I had come for a long weight. After ten minutes or so, I was told, "You can go back now, was that a long enough WAIT?"

On the same level as our workroom, but separated by a short corridor, was the luxurious showroom where the season's collection of new designs was paraded by the Amies models before the rich and famous clientele. In the adjoining corridor was the workroom staff's lavatory, serving approximately twenty of us. It was very basic, as were most of the conveniences post-war. There wasn't much incentive to while away more than a few minutes there.

The workroom itself was large and high-ceilinged with tall unadorned Regency windows, basic gas fires for heating, and worn brown linoleum underfoot. At one end of this room was the pattern cutting table, large enough to hold a reception of 30 or 40 people upon it. On either side of this monster, on high stools, perched Miss Brand, the Queen's fitter, and Miss Little. Miss Brand was a gruff middle-aged lady who dressed mainly in black and wore red heavy framed glasses pushed towards the end of her nose so she could peer over the top when speaking to you. The tell-tale streak of yellow through the front of her grey hair was probably the result of years of hot smoke curling up from the cigarette that often dangled from her mouth as she worked.

I would spend nine long hours a day, five days a week, learning how to construct dresses from scratch – a very different job from a dress machinist, who can put a dress together in an hour or two. A Haute Couture design would take from six to eight weeks and possibly longer from design to finish, and the price tag then for a simple little black dress was 99 guineas. The price comparison today would be £4500.

There were a lot of mundane jobs to be completed in the sewing room. One such concerned one of Queen Elizabeth's gowns. The design was a beautiful full length multi-layered chiffon creation in soft powder blue. As silk chiffon is so very fine, it takes yards and yards to make up the skirt and the hem has to be hand-rolled and sewn with minute stitches. Consequently, the gown was placed on the customer's personal dummy and up to six hands sat in a circle round the dress and sewed the hem until they all caught up with their neighbour's starting point.

Another job which all Haute Couture dresses, tailored coats and suits require is hand tacking from the pattern on to the material. This is initially done using white tacking cotton, unless the material is white. When the garment has the first fitting the dress fitter makes any alteration in a different colour. There was a court dressmakers' saying which went, 'Go home with a tack – sure to be back'. Therefore we all did our best to remove any stray thread.

I remember feeling very nervous when I was allowed to work on the wonderful satins and brocades in fashion at the time. The exquisite hand beading was breathtaking and the apprentice just looked, never touched. This was something you aspired to and would take a few more years to learn.

We were taught to change our needles frequently if working on fine silk and crepe and always to use a thimble, and to wash our hands frequently and dust them with fine powder or 'pounce,' we were expected to supply our own tools of the trade, such as scissors, thimbles and tape.

Towards the end of the working day, part of my duty as the apprentice was to tidy the floor of the workroom. This meant taking a magnet on a string and collecting the steel dressmaking pins from around each hand's table and carefully extracting the pins to leave with the dressmaker. Each table consisted of the senior hand, in charge of the garment currently being made, and two junior hands. The apprentice worked alongside any of these court dressmakers. As I went from table to table, swinging my trusty magnet, I was aware of eyes upon me, and woe betide me if I left a few pins on the magnet to take to the next table and their area of floor. Such was the thriftiness of the time.

One of the highlights of my time working for the house of Hardy Amies was when Hardy himself flounced through from the showroom with a request for Maude B to send someone to help dress the models for a fashion show.

"Marion," came the command, "You go – and make it snappy."

I scurried through to the sacred changing room, where all hell seemed to be let loose. I was in an alien place of frantic, hectic glamour. The models were in various states of undress, shouting for different gowns, shoes, wraps and coats to make up the particular ensembles. So I ran about zipping up dresses, finding the matching shoes and changing their jewellery ready for them to go on stage, where they would emerge looking serene, haughty and oh so confident.
Apart from my basic training, I had the important role of

organising the items needed when Miss B was going to Buckingham Palace for the fitting of H M Queen Elizabeth's gowns. Carefully wrapped in tissue paper was a special belted needlework pouch, and into this went the scissors, chalk and tape – everything, right down to the pins, was brand new each time.

On one occasion the Queen came to our address in Savile Row. As our workroom overlooked the front of the street, the sash windows were opened and we craned our necks to catch a glimpse of our important visitor.

My education was not confined to the workroom. One lunch time my work colleagues and I decided to go along to Soho and Berwick Street market. This area was completely new to me. The market was noisy and vibrant with the traders shouting their wares from the stalls down the middle of the street, while amongst the shops on each side were a few Chinese ones selling items with unusual names like Tiger Balm and Ginseng.

June, who was keen to show me everything, pointed to two women standing across from us.
"See those two girls?"
"Where?"
"Over there, in the doorway. They're on the game."
"What sort of game?" I asked.
"You really don't know, do you?" answered June in astonishment.

I was soon given a quick but very explicit explanation, and proceeded to follow my friends on a tour of Soho. Strip clubs were everywhere, as were sex shops with photo displays of models and strippers, along with tattooists and massage parlours offering weird and wonderful treatments. Small groups of prostitutes seemed to be out on the streets looking very smart and stylish in good tailored clothes. Who knows, a few of them could have attended our fashion shows and been our customers.

Another afternoon during the summer of 1960 when we were all busy sewing, the door to the workroom opened to reveal a very handsome young naval officer resplendent in his No 1 uniform with his white cap under his arm. He strode up to Miss Brand and announced that he had come to request that his girlfriend, Pat, be permitted to have the rest of the afternoon off as he was being drafted overseas the next day because of a crisis abroad. The whole of the workroom, including Miss B, had a lump in their throats as Pat collected her belongings and disappeared with her sailor into the sunshine. An Officer and a Gentleman comes to mind every time I remember that day.

I look back on my time at Hardy Amies and question how you cope with all the things which made up your transformation almost overnight from a child to an adult. For example, I had travelled to London on the underground numerous times with my parents, but nothing had prepared me for the early morning rush hour. Crushed together with strangers, breathing each other's stale breath and trying desperately to avoid each other's eyes, while swaying rhythmically together. How does a 15 year old girl cope with being goosed by a bowler-hatted city gent looking the epitome of respectability?

After almost two years in the trade and being offered the chance of promotion to Junior Hand, I decided to make my own choice of career and train for a better-paid job in the City. I took my highly skilled dressmaking training with me, enabling me to enjoy design, colour and fashion for the rest of my life. I appreciated having been given the opportunity to be apprenticed to Haute Couture dressmaking, which was a privilege and highly sought after. But it was very poorly paid, and this was a new era. Carnaby Street, The Beatles, the swinging sixties and package holidays were calling. I was young and they were all there for the taking - and life felt good.

Memories Of My Life

Anne Shave

(Marlow Bottom)

I am a Member/Secretary of our W.I., having moved from Northolt, Middlesex to Marlow Bottom in 1988. I have been on my own since 2009. I am involved in several organizations and enjoy walking and getting together with friends.

I was an only child and was born in Kilburn in 1930, but we soon moved to Clapham Park, South London. Until September 1939 I went to the local school and did the things that youngsters in that era did. My maiden name was Kerton, and I was usually referred to as 'Blackout' during my evacuation days. (Say my name aloud and you will see why).

In September 1939, it was decided that rather than be evacuated by the Local Authority and School, I would be taken to Cherry Hinton, Near Cambridge, to stay with my Great Aunt and Uncle. My mother was born there and my Grandad lived nearby in a house owned by the local cement company for whom he had worked. Other relatives of my mother's were also in the area. My mother stayed there with me until December. Then, on coming home from school one day, I found that she had returned to Clapham Park.

My Great Aunt's house, did not have a bathroom. We had a bath every Monday in the washhouse, following the weekly washing of clothes, when the boiler had been replenished. A tin bath was taken down from the wall and filled with warm water. The toilet was outside as well so we had potties under the bed to use at night.

I didn't really know that there was a war on, although we lived quite near an airfield and did spend some time in the newly constructed air raid shelter in the back garden. My Great Aunt used to keep a University Lodging House in Cambridge before the war and her daughter had continued running it. She therefore had good relations with the local shops (getting a bit of extra rations here and there) and with produce from the garden we ate quite well.

Next door was a small general shop and I was friendly with the daughter so we were able to "get" some extra sweets. My father also sent me some of his sweet rations each week, together with the issues of Rupert Bear. My Mum and Dad used to come by train once a month to get some respite from the air raids. It took them about half a day to get there and they stayed over the weekend.

During the war we had double summer time so it kept quite light until about 9.30 - 10.00 pm and my new friends and I spent the summer school holidays playing in the fields and "cooking". We took an old tin, some carrots, potatoes, etc. and water and made a fire and cooked the vegetables. I can't remember how long it took, but probably now hands would be held up in horror at eating out of a tin.

I attended the local school which had evacuees and a headmaster from a school in Islington. Two boys from this school were also billeted with my Great Aunt and family.

At the age of 11, I changed school and went into the Secondary School in Cambridge. We used to cycle to and fro every day through "the tins" a footpath with cycle access enclosed by metal fencing. The journey took us about 45 minutes each way. I stayed there until Christmas 1943 when I went home to London, as things had quietened down. Unfortunately, we then had the "doodlebugs"

- the V1s - so spent time in the cellar many nights. We didn't know where these "flying bombs" were going to land so it was quite scary.

I wanted to go to the Secretarial College, but this was closed due to the war, so a friend and I used to go to a Secondary School in Balham, South London, which taught secretarial subjects. We would often get to the bus stop and the siren would sound. We would then go down the Underground and spend time at Balham Station waiting for the all clear so that we could continue to school. Looking back it sounds frightening, but in those days it was just a way of life, and we had to get on with it.

In school, reinforcements were made to one of the class rooms so if the siren went we would all huddle in this room until the all clear.

In 1945, when the War ended, our school was merged with a Secondary School in Battersea. I was keen on shorthand and typing so decided I wanted to be a secretary. In September 1946, three others and I went for interviews at Imperial Chemical Insurance (a subsidiary of ICI) in Victoria. I actually wore a pair of silk stockings belonging to my mother. Fortunately, all of us were offered jobs and I went to one of their offices in Victoria. Two other friends worked in Victoria so we used to meet up for lunch at the ABC and the lady behind the counter used to save us the Apple Pie and Cream if it was running low.

I started in the typing pool and then graduated to a secretarial position. It was very well-placed as our office was opposite the side of Buckingham Palace, so had a good view for any processions or occasions involving the Royal Family.

In the summer I used to go on cycling holidays in the Lake District, Devon and the Isle of Wight, staying at Youth Hostels. We started the trip to the Lake District from Leeds (having caught the milk train from London). After touring round the Lakes we stopped at Penrith. And, after talking to a driver in a transport café, my two friends and I "obtained" a lift home to Kew Bridge on the back of a lorry, thereby getting a refund on our rail tickets.

In 1947, three of us went very early to Green Park to get a good view of the processions for the wedding of the Queen and Prince Phillip. We did the same in 1953 for the Coronation procession.

By this time I had met my boyfriend who later became my husband in 1955. We lived with my mother at Clapham until 1960 when we bought our first house in Southall (£1,350). I worked at the local Launderette and my husband was a conductor on London Transport buses.

In 1967 it was nearing change of school for my son and Southall was a fast-changing community. We moved to Northolt so that my son could be eligible for the Secondary School. I decided that I wanted to go back to secretarial work, and went to work at Gallaher Ltd. in Northolt in the typing pool, graduating to Supervisor. Following this I worked in an Estate Agents in Hillingdon and in 1984 I transferred to a Solicitors in Uxbridge. On moving to Marlow Bottom in 1988, I travelled to and from Uxbridge until I retired in 1990 .

The Power of Music

Anne Massey

(North and South Clifton)

I am fascinated by my love of music. Why did I ask for Tchaikovsky's first piano concerto as a gift at 11? I bring you from my earliest performance, to my most recent, discovering just how influential my teachers were. If only I'd realised this while still a teacher myself.

I hated the visit to the aquarium! OK, so it was in Genoa and I should be impressed by the size of the collection and variety of creatures, but after strolling past one or two 'windows on the deep', I just longed to be elsewhere. Why were my husband and younger daughter so content to stare at these animals and discuss them at such length?

I'm like this with a zoo. Recently the same daughter, we have two, opted for a visit to the zoo on the Isle of Wight for her birthday treat. This might seem a strange request for a person turning 26, but let me explain. We were on the Isle of Wight, my two daughters and one son-in-law, to attend a Music Festival. We'd had a great weekend, bopping to a variety of bands, and I'd acquired a henna 'tattoo' of a dragon "for Wales" at the top of my right arm, and a pretty garland of tiny multi-coloured flowers and pearls, twisted to fit neatly onto my hair.

I was integrated beautifully, or so I thought, and with no need for alcohol. My daughters feared I would hate the loos, the crowds, the noise, the smells, the drinking (by them as much as by anyone else) the mud (there wasn't any while we were there). But I loved it all. Well, I don't mean I loved the drugs, the drink and the loos, but they didn't bother me. I loved the whole festival. The atmosphere was amazing and the accessibility and range of music brilliant. In fact, when it rained continuously like stair rods on the last day, I was the only one of our party who wanted to go.

I was disappointed that the joint decision was not to go, but didn't fancy the bus ride home alone after midnight. So we stayed in our static caravan all day on Sunday, with the gas fire blazing, reading papers, watching motorsport, doing crosswords, eating, drinking and chatting. I loved it.

Come Monday the forecast was bright, it was Heather's birthday and her choice of activities, and our ferry wasn't until late evening. She chose the zoo, and my heart sank. What is it I hate? Is it the smells? Questions concerning animal welfare? It was a glorious sunny day, with hardly a cloud in the bright blue sky, a complete contrast with the day before. As we looked at each inmate I couldn't wait to make my escape.

So I hate visiting zoos and aquaria, but I love visiting museums and art galleries, attending concerts and theatre. Why? Why, when asked what I would like for passing the 11+ exam did I say "Tchaikovsky's first piano concerto, please." Where had I ever heard the music to know that I would like it, at 11 years old?

Perhaps my piano teacher, Mrs Willis, had played some of it to me. She not only played through my pieces, but excerpts from musicals, classics and opera. I loved to listen and to watch her play, sitting bolt upright in her front room, her magical fingers hitting all the right notes.

How thrilled I had been when my dream to have piano lessons had become a reality. I had begged my poor mother for years. I think she might have even taken a second job to pay, and I actually started lessons without having a piano at home, until Mrs Willis got a new one and I was able to have her old one. Fantastic, I loved it and practised every day for many years, much to the annoyance of my older brother who would shout "Has she GOT to practise NOW?!" from his bedroom, especially when I was at High School and he worked shifts or had been out late the previous night.

But where did this great interest in music come from?

My father played the mouth organ and the accordion occasionally. Maybe that's where I get my love of music from. He seemed to work full time, have no holidays and spend any spare time working in the garden, growing fruit and vegetables for us to eat. But when he was indoors he loved to listen to the radio. We had no television until I was in my teens, so the 'wireless' was good company. It brought us the news, quiz and comedy programmes, and on a Friday night 'Sing Something Simple'.

Dad loved the voices of Maria Callas and Paul Robeson, and I distinctly remember admiring the rich, deep tones of Kathleen Ferrier, hoping to follow in her footsteps one day. Maybe the radio introduced me to that Tchaikovsky piano concerto?

One of my earliest memories is playing the triangle as an infant on a huge stage in Sofia Gardens, Cardiff. I remember anxiously waiting at the side of the stage to climb the steep steps, triangle in hand. The music was 'In the Hall of the Mountain King' by Grieg, and I loved the way it got faster and faster, louder and louder, as more instruments were added in and then the final clash of the cymbals.

Miss Brewer, the Headmistress of Rumney Infant School, was a tiny lady with a huge personality and rasping voice. Wearing her hair short and curly, serious glasses, smart suit and high heels, she was in complete control of the many children taking part. This must have been my stage debut.

During my time at the Junior School I joined the recorder group and became part of the school choir. Our Headmaster, 'Billy' Williams, was quite short and rather plump, with greying hair and a ruddy complexion. He too always wore smart suits, but removed his jacket to teach us to play the recorder in the lunch hour. He conducted both the choir and the recorder group at concerts, and ruled with a rod of iron.

Sometimes our Welsh teacher, Miss Thomas, taught us Welsh songs too. They were passionate about music and the Welsh language, but taught in very different ways. Miss Thomas was gentle and quiet, she was tall, slim and wore pretty clothes. Her dark brown, curly hair was almost shoulder length and she wore fashionably large and angular glasses which she frequently moved up her nose. She smiled a lot and, with a smile in her voice, called us 'Cariad' (love).

Miss Thomas chose a small group of us to take part in a choral speaking competition at the Urdd (Youth) National Eisteddfod. For two years running we won each round, getting through to the final, and, after performing on a huge stage in front of a packed marquee, won again. I said to my mother "When I grow up, I want to be like Miss Thomas."

"What do you mean?" my mother asked. "I want my cardigans to go in and out at the waist like hers and I want to be a teacher like her," was my reply, and that's what I became: a Primary School teacher. I'm not sure about the cardigans.

My mother was a go getter. She hadn't had the best start in life and wanted the best for us. Our education was very important to her and she worked hard for us to have all the opportunities we could. When I was about seven, she took me to join the 'Ladybird Choir', which had mostly old ladies, a few younger girls, and then me. We wore beautiful, long royal blue shiny skirts, which I loved. We entered talent competitions and gave concerts and I was soon given a solo. I enjoyed being part of the choir and my mother travelled with us, wherever we went. On the way home from rehearsals

on a Monday night I had money for chips. One night I must
have had some change and bought a penny liquorice. I found the
combination of chips and liquorice rather good. I haven't tried it
recently though.

I don't remember whether I left because of pressure of homework
at Grammar School, but my mother who had scrimped and saved
for my piano lessons managed to pay for singing lessons at Cardiff
Castle for a while. How amazing is that? I didn't realise at the
time how privileged I was, attending there, but I knew it was very
difficult for my mother to pay. She had taken the advice of ' Billy'
Williams, who said I had talent, and we were told there that I had
an unusually low voice for someone so young - thus the interest in
Kathleen Ferrier. I went for a few years, until I preferred gospel
singing at my local Chapel.

At High School I joined the choir and the orchestra as soon as
I could and learned the viola as well as the violin but not to any
great standard. Imagine the fuss when I practised those at home.
I loved music lessons and liked the strict Miss Llewelyn. Another
Welsh heroine. Blonde and bespectacled, wearing sensible shoes
and tweed skirts, she ruled supreme in all things musical. I used to
enter the solo competition at our school Eisteddfod, which was held
on the morning of St David's Day, March 1st, and I also remember
singing beautiful mediaeval songs unaccompanied as part of a
quartet. I enjoyed the sensation of holding my own part whilst
listening to the harmonies of the others.

During my teens, I acquired a 'tranny' (transistor radio) which I
could play upstairs, while doing my homework. It had no plug,
just small batteries. Radio Luxemburg was the order of the day,
but I watched Acker Bilk, Chris Barber and Kenny Ball and His
Jazzmen on the television and bought their records. Years later I
went to see them all perform at the O2 with our youngest – the one
who inflicted the zoo visit upon me. She was dreading it, and only
came because I couldn't get a contemporary to travel midweek to
London. But she loved them. They were amazing.

I continued to learn about and experience music whilst at College, becoming a Primary Teacher. There I played piano and sang in three choirs, including one which was formed for special events, such as the performance of Handel's Messiah, which I was thrilled to take part in. I was an alto – still am.

Once qualified, my music became teaching children to play the recorder, playing the piano for assemblies, and preparing the children for Christmas, Easter and summer productions. I found myself teaching drama as well as music and loved it, sometimes writing songs too, as I'm sure many Primary teachers do.

Along came marriage and children. I switched Radio Four off and, as they grew up, tuned in to Radio One, not always through choice, but over the years I have become quite a fan. Our children were encouraged to play instruments, our youngest had singing lessons for a while, and our eldest played the leading role in an amateur production of Aladdin, in Sevenoaks, in her twenties. She was brilliant. None of them now play, but they all enjoy music in different ways. Why? Because I encouraged them?

After taking early retirement I found my nearest Women's Institute and was thrilled that each autumn a group of ladies start rehearsals for a County Federation Carol Service in early December. Count me in. We learn new and unusual carols. I like the discipline and the harmonies.

This summer we also took part in a Gilbert and Sullivan Concert, which was a new departure for me. Wearing our black skirts and white tops we gave it our all, thoroughly enjoyed ourselves and entertained the audience at the same time.

I love all kinds of music and I love singing. But I still ask myself - why?

Part 5

We Did It Our Way

Not Doing Things By Halves

Liz Howard

(Hawkesbury & Horton)

Until I was in my late 20s, I had lived in 14 different places and been to 7 schools plus two colleges. Since 1987 I have lived in one place – a lovely village in the Cotswolds. Having family in Australia and America means travelling is one of my pastimes.

I have always been accident-prone. Mishaps constantly seemed to come my way. These were partly due to my tendency to rush headlong into everything without stopping to think first, but more, I believe, because I was in the wrong place at the wrong time. This is rather like our cat Sheba, who, when a kitten, decided at the moment of the Queen's Coronation on the television, when the lounge was full of neighbours, to climb up the chimney and come down covered in soot.

I was a very active child. Relatives raise their eyes when I ask them now about what I was like, and say, "You never stopped...you were always on the go...always into mischief."

A good place to relieve me of some of my energy was our local park. When I was very small we lived in West Kirby in the Wirral. My favourite place was the swings and the climbing bars – too high to reach so I would shin up the poles to get to the bars. I can remember the elation of being able to reach the first bar while standing on the ground, pulling myself up to turn somersaults. I could also shimmy up the swings to the top and turn somersaults, giving my granny near heart attacks in the process. Then there was the see-saw, bouncing up and down with a friend at the other end, until the friend (aged about 3) jumped off while I was at the top. Down I came, onto the hard concrete (none of this soft rubber / tree bark to cushion my fall). A severe case of concussion resulted, when I was very sick and had to be kept in a darkened room for several days.

Even my first year of life was entertaining. Perhaps entertaining is the wrong expression. My mother would call it: "never being able to take my eyes off you for a minute." She would tell the story of my first birthday: while waiting for all the dear friends and relatives to arrive for the party, I was left in my pram looking beautiful and in my new white dress - but not for long. Whilst I was left alone, I tipped up the end of the pram, crawled out into the garage and got myself covered in oil and blood - oil from the car and blood from a knocked-off scab. It was something of a shock for my aunt to find, not her dear little niece Elizabeth in the pram, but a black, oily, bloody thing sitting contentedly on the garage floor. I have a photograph, taken on the day, of me cleaned up - with a plaster on my finger.

In the early 1950s, we were fortunate to have a car – a black Austin 7. To get me to go to sleep, and to give the family a bit of peace, my father would drive around the block a few times. But having a car had other advantages – it enabled us to get out and about a bit.

My memory of one of the places we visited is hazy but it was where I gained the scar on my knee. If I close my eyes I can see a large mansion house and grounds with a long drive down which I was running at full pelt (having been told by my parents not to run so fast). It was that feeling of one's feet and legs going so quickly that you lose control, and your legs get tangled up, and down you fall – onto the hard asphalt. I must have landed on a stone because it wasn't just a graze but a hole in my knee, something to be really proud of. I then made absolutely sure that the scar would be a good one because, just as it was healing, I fell on the knee again –

running too fast down a hill – déjà vu or what?

My Junior School was in a rough area of Birkenhead. I went to this school because it was "attached" (by religion not by distance) to the church where my father was the curate. It was considered the done thing for the clergy children to attend the church school, even though it was about a mile walk (or run) away from where we lived.

One incident at school could be played like this:
Scene: Lunchtime playtime – girls only yard.
Me: (to friend) I'm going to get the netball base out.
Friend: Let me help, it's heavy.
Me: No, I'll be OK I can just roll it along on its side (proceeds to do so).
Friend: Put it over here.
Me: OK (drops base down on ground) OOWW it's dropped on my toe!
Friend: Oh no! I'll get Miss. Miss! Miss! Elizabeth has dropped the netball base on her toe!

Two weeks later, after turning black, the toenail came off.

Accidents continued to pursue me as I grew up. From the age of 13 I went to a boarding school in North Wales. I was sent there by my parents with the idea that it would calm me down, and make me more like a young lady than the a little ruffian that I was.

It took some time for the boarding school effect to happen. In my first term I had to stand up in front of the whole school while the headmistress told me I was too 'cock-a hoop'. I think I had been flicking wet tissues at a teacher's legs while she sat at her desk taking our evening prep lesson.

Yes, it was really stupid, but I was obviously bored. This wasn't so much of an accident, but more about doing things before thinking of the consequences.

In the 1960s you could get all the way from North Wales to London on the train without having to change. So when I was in the sixth form, getting to London for an interview was easy – or should have been. I can remember the shoes I was wearing. They were brown leather moccasin-type slip-ons. Very trendy I thought, but unfortunately they were rather loose. So when I stepped from the platform onto the train one of them fell off between the carriage and the platform. Panic!

Fortunately the guard realised my plight before blowing his whistle and found a long pole and fished the shoe up from under the train. I made it to London but cannot remember the results of the interview.

After leaving school I spent a few months in Bermuda, where my father was a parish priest in one of the eight parishes on the island. I was in between school and starting at Occupational Therapy College in Oxford. One of the things I had to complete was a first aid course.

Everyone in Bermuda rode mopeds, particularly those old French machines called a 'velosolex' that had an engine in the front basket. They would also grind to a halt if it rained. I was coming home on my moped from a first aid lesson on, 'How to treat fractures in accidents'. To get the mopeds off the road, where they were a hazard to all other road users, the old Bermuda railway track had been converted into a cycle path. The houses alongside the cycle path had to drive across it in their cars to reach the road. I was driving along the cycle path when a car came out of a drive... the driver didn't look - and drove straight into me. I can remember saying to the lady driver that I had just been to a first aid lesson and this is what she had to do – not knowing that she was a nurse. I ended up with a broken femur and an extended stay in Bermuda of five months.

While on my extended stay, swimming was part of the physiotherapy for my broken leg – no problem there with ocean everywhere. You had to beware of dangerous things in the sea. One of them was a creature similar to a jellyfish called a Portuguese Man-of-War. Meeting one with 20 metre-long tentacles in the Atlantic could be deadly. Closer to land, they were smaller, but still dangerous. On the surface of the sea they looked like beautiful turquoise balloons floating harmlessly around. There were two problems however. You couldn't see them approaching if you were swimming in rough weather when the waves were higher than usual; and their tentacles, still full of venom, could break off and be floating around anywhere. It was this latter problem that I ran, or rather, swam, into. The loose tentacles, rather like sticky string, wrapped themselves round my arms. It felt 100 times worse than a nettle sting. Various remedies, such as vinegar and ammonia, gave minor relief, but for months afterwards, if I rubbed my arms, the marks of the whip-like tentacles would show up.

As I grew older, the scrapes I got into were fewer but still dramatic, like breaking nine ribs in a car accident in my mid-20s. My memory of recovering from this is of trying not to sneeze or cough for a month. My friends delighted in making me laugh, which in turn would make me cry because it was so painful.

Then there was my ruptured Achilles tendon. This was at a college reunion about 12 years ago. My main subject at college had been dance/drama and we were reliving the folk dances that our tutor taught us, supposedly to improve our rhythm. It was a very simple Israeli dance involving slow twisting and turning. I thought someone had hit me on the back of the ankle with a cricket bat and even turned round to look. It sounded like a twig snapping. There was no acute pain but my foot wouldn't work properly. I managed to drive home and then went out again in the evening for a reunion meal. It was the next day that I decided something serious must have happened because my foot was still behaving most oddly. At A&E they confirmed a ruptured Achilles tendon, so it was key-hole surgery and a month in plaster and on crutches.

Should I be touching wood now when I say that nothing dramatic has happened since then?

Maybe I have slowed a little, but there is still the tendency not to do things by halves and to run full tilt at life. Perhaps, instead of being in the wrong place at the wrong time, I am in the right place at last. I hope so.

Under The Influence

Clare Marsh

(Horsmonden)

I live and work in Kent where I am currently studying creative writing with the Open University and love the writing process, from first idea through to final editing. Working on these memoirs has enabled me both to make new friends and get to know old friends (including myself) better.

'Give me a child until he is seven and I will give you the man,' Jesuit saying

My school career started inauspiciously in September 1962 when I discovered on the first day that I was too small to reach the door handle of Miss Sayers' classroom. Fortunately it was soon lowered and I could get in unaided.

The previous day Dad had photographed me with his Box Brownie camera. The print shows an elfin face (with unfortunate matching pixie ears) squinting into the sunlight from under an ill-fitting navy beret. The cross on the badge singles me out as a Catholic. The dark gabardine coat swamps my tiny frame, allowing for never achievable growth. The leather satchel slung across my body was the envy of my younger sister Mary. Sadly, this is the only photo of me with my fair wispy hair braided in 'platters'. The pink satin

ribbons constantly fell out of my unravelling plaits. Within weeks
my appearance changed forever when the doom of the pudding-
basin haircut fell upon me. Mum no longer had time to do my hair,
being preoccupied with Baby Frances, whose birth coincided with
me starting school.

My school was attached to St Mary's Catholic Church in Croydon,
Surrey. This wasn't our parish church, but had the only Catholic
school in the area. I'd already uniquely disgraced myself by
running away from St Andrew's Sunday school a few months
earlier. My quiet rebellion had started.

Mum had to stay at home with my younger sisters so I travelled
to school from Thornton Heath with older girls. Dad would leave
me with them at the bus stop before he headed off to the City. I
realise now that my parents intended me only to mix with Catholic
children, effectively segregating me until I was 18. I learnt that the
world, and indeed eternity, was divided into 'Catholics' and 'Non-
Catholics'.

I'd never encountered a nun before so I was curious when a portly
penguin with a white wimple, long black veil and habit came into
my classroom on the first day. Nothing was visible of Sister Mary
Theresa's face apart from a few fascinating whiskers and wire
framed glasses reflecting inscrutable circles of light. From my low
vantage point our headmistress looked as wide as she was short and
loomed over us bristling, the large wooden crucifix on her chest
heaving with each angry breath. She thumped the desk to drive
home her message of absolute obedience. A black rosary jangled
from her thick brown leather belt. I suppose her aim was to inspire
awe. She certainly put the fear of God into me, but not in the way
she intended.

Surprisingly, some of my Irish friends shared Mum's romantic view
of nuns. Some even prayed for vocations as they grew older. Not
me, because when I was six I decided to become a Go Go dancer. I
watched all the pop music programmes and was star-struck by the
glamorous dancers and glitzy costumes. I didn't change my career

choice even when the Singing Nun and Julie Andrews made nuns positively fashionable.

Morning break was blissful, with its pre-Thatcher miniature bottles of free milk. Whether the milk was too warm or frozen solid with the foil cap sitting jauntily on a column of ice I attacked the cream with a blue and white striped drinking straw. I spent 2d every day for a shiny currant bun. No wonder I had no room for the disgusting school dinners.

The canteen was my torture chamber. I'd always been a fussy eater but leaving food was no longer an option. Shortly after starting school I ran away, back to the safety of my classroom to avoid eating 'bacon and egg pie'. Although warned that my grandmother would be told when she collected me, I flatly refused to return to the canteen and pie. I was now a 'marked' child and my daily battle of wits with Mrs Gravy, the Head Dinner Lady, began. I'd sit alone in the canteen staring stubbornly at my plate until the end of lunchtime after which, I soon worked out, she could no longer detain me. Passive resistance definitely worked for me. I also became adept at hiding food in pockets and hankies, concealing grey lumps of mashed potato and loathsome butter beans. I surreptitiously emptied these into the bushes outside the canteen. Mrs Gravy was ancient and stern. She'd lean over me, roughly pushing food around the plate. My little face, brimming with tears, was lost in her scratchy brown tweed coat. Her influence has lasted longer than that of many teachers, hardening my food dislikes, especially of nuts, into life long aversions.

Anyway, forget school dinners, I was saving my appetite for home time. Mum always gave me a few extra pennies to spend in the Catholic Repository near the bus stop. Whilst the shop was crammed full of prayer cards, crucifixes and other religious artefacts, it was the sweet counter that lured children in. I never, ever bought any devotional objects, but by the time I left infant school I'd suffered five agonizing fillings. Love Hearts, chewy Black Jacks and Fruit Salads, cheek-stretching gobstoppers and liquorice Sherbet Fountains all took their toll. My favourites were the 'Thunderbirds' sweet cigarettes, as they came with picture cards which could be swapped. I knew for certain I was destined to become Lady Penelope. Her ladyship's motto, 'Elegance, Charm and Deadly Danger,' was vastly more inspirational than the school's 'Fidem Serva' or 'Keep the Faith'. I would soon be chauffeured in my pink Rolls Royce FAB 1, cigarette holder in hand, by my safe-cracking butler, Parker. It was a miracle I didn't become a toothless, hardened smoker.

Miss Sayers, my first teacher, was a gentle, elderly lady who dashingly rode a motor scooter. She was very tolerant when I brought my pet snail 'Janet' into school. Janet occupied pole position on the nature table, sometimes wandering around on black paper leaving her silvery trail. Eventually Miss Sayers suggested freeing Janet 'to find a husband, dear'. We released her among the long grass and apple trees of the overgrown Presbytery garden. Miss Sayers can't have known of the snail's un-Catholic hermaphroditic sex life or we couldn't have liberated her/him on such hallowed ground. Miss Sayers was responsible for my belief in fairies. She took the class on nature walks around the back of the hated canteen to a magical wild area she called 'Fairyland', where almost invisible thistledown floated around us.

Realistically I can't have spent much time in her classroom as I contracted not one but two notifiable diseases from school. Shortly after my fifth birthday in November, I was struck down by Sonne Dysentery, caught from the gruesome outside toilets. I sobbed with abject disappointment when I missed my first school Christmas party. To console me Mum gave me a set of card dressing-up dolls to play with on my paisley patterned eiderdown. Whilst recuperating I was reading *'Larry the Lamb in Toytown'* in Dad's armchair by the hissing gas fire. There was a knock at the front door and Mum ushered in a big man from the Public Health Department. With gloved hands he removed my beautiful library book to be burnt.

Just after Christmas I caught measles from school and passed them on to Mary, who became seriously ill. Fortunately she

recovered, but gave our parents a worrying time. Early in the
New Year the 'Big Freeze of 1963' descended in one of the worst
winters for a century. Thick snow lay on the ground for weeks so
there was no chance of getting to school: the lethal toilets would
have been frozen anyway. Icicles like swords hung from our roof
and permanent swirling ice patterns feathered the inside of my
bedroom window.

When I was seven I was taught by the elegant Miss Strawson,
who came from Nice. Tanned and well dressed, she stood out like
an exotic bird from the other teachers. She spoke English with
a marked accent and taught us basic French. I was awestruck
when she announced, 'when Catholics die zay will know everyzing
about ze universe'. I was already enthralled by astronomy and the
escalating space race. To encourage our education my parents
subscribed weekly to *'Knowledge'* magazine. 'A little knowledge is a
dangerous thing' was certainly true as I eventually decided science
could answer my questions about the universe long before their
posthumous revelation by the Almighty.

I'd been sent to St Mary's for 'a good Catholic education'. As
recent English converts, my parents were 'staunch' or, I now think,
over-zealous. My friends' families, mostly from Ireland, were more
relaxed about religion. Much later, as a teenager, I was mortified
when my parents berated my headmistress, a nun, for sanctioning
a Halloween/Guy Fawkes disco which they banned me from
attending. The disco was apparently doubly evil in celebrating
pagan beliefs and the burning of a Catholic. Ironically Dad never
knew that buried deep in his Tudor ancestry was a family member
burnt at the stake as an extreme Protestant, who believed the Pope
was the Antichrist!

I found St Mary's church a troubling place, smelling of Holy Water
and incense, with its flickering votive candles and impenetrable
shadows. We sang hymns for requiems, including twice at the
funerals of school mates. The whole school attended the 'Mass
of the Angels' for which the priest wore white vestments. I was
mesmerised by the small white coffin, thinking of the child inside

241

so unbelievably dead. I was also terrified by a lady who suffered from 'St Vitus' Dance', who practically haunted the church, seeking comfort I suppose. Under the red sanctuary light by the altar rail she twitched uncontrollably in ragged clothes with her rosary jangling. She frequented my nightmares.

On All Souls Day we knelt for an excruciating eternity in church, praying competitively on our rosaries. The more prayers completed the more souls would be released from Purgatory to Heaven by 'Plenary Indulgences': just like the 'get out of jail free' card in Monopoly, my favourite game. This prayer-factory approach to moving on the souls of the 'Faithful Departed' seemed pretty unlikely to me.

Apart from Christmas, my favourite religious festival took place in May when we brought flowers to school to fill a grotto for a statue of Our Lady in the 'big boys' playground'. One delicious sniff of lilac still sends me back to the precariously wobbling Blessed Virgin being carried over the tarmac by four junior boys. Class by class, we processed up the steeply sloping lane to the church singing 'Oh Mary we crown thee with blossoms today, Queen of the Angels and Queen of the May'.

Learning the Catechism by rote was utterly boring and whenever I prayed my imagination wandered off in fictional directions. I believed more sincerely in Enid Blyton's *Magic Faraway Tree* books than anything biblical. Completely convinced the magical characters, Silkie and Moonface, were real I arranged to meet them in the Enchanted Wood with my school friends every night.

The Jesuits were right: by seven many aspects of my adult self were in place. I'd been exposed to lifelong influences, but as a free spirit I'd reacted in unforeseen ways. I invented sins at my First Confession, reasoning that I hadn't been unduly wicked. It felt weird to go into the confessional with a priest and I hoped, from its wardrobe-like appearance, it was the portal to Narnia instead. Mum bought me a pretty white dress and veil for my First Holy Communion from the Catholic Repository. I tried it on behind the sweet counter. After Communion I felt irreverently disappointed that the host tasted like an inferior version of a Flying Saucer sweet: it lacked the sherbet fizz.

As I moved up to the Juniors there really was no hope for me.

My Prague Spring – Indian Style

Jeannie MacMeekin

(Market Lavington and Easterton)

After graduating I taught with VSO in Kolkata where I met and married a Peace Corps Volunteer. We have three daughters and four grandchildren. I spent most of my teaching career working with children who speak English as an additional language. I am a keen patchworker.

People of a certain age always know what they were doing when they heard that President Kennedy had been assassinated. But for me, I know exactly where I was when the Prague Spring collapsed. I was on a plane going to India debating with other would-be volunteers (VSOs) as to whether or not the Russians would invade Czechoslovakia. Within a month, all those issues of world affairs had been kicked into the long grass where they largely remained for the next year and a half.

To some extent my arrival in Kolkata simply confirmed what might await me after a week's bizarrely amateurish "orientation" experience (dark warnings about how the hot climate effects your emotions, the need to have a clean pair of white gloves readily available for every social occasion, don't use locally produced tampons, don't eat street food etc. plus a lesson in Hindi for those of us going to West Bengal where they speak Bengali).

We arrived at 11pm at Dumdum airport to find everything there closed , no-one to meet us and nowhere to change money. The High Commission had got the dates muddled up, and we had the luxury of eventually finding ourselves put up in the luxurious Great Eastern Hotel for a night, before unceremoniously being bundled round the corner to the Red Shield Guest house. How emblematic of Indian society even now, where the achingly rich live side by side with the disastrously poor.

After a couple of days lazing around, wondering what on earth we had let ourselves in for, we were gradually hived off to our various destinations. I was taken in the ubiquitous Ambassador black and yellow taxi to the Indian Statistical Institute, in what was then the wilder outskirts of Kolkata. This prestigious academic institution continues to produce highly valued statisticians found lecturing all over the world. Not that I knew its reputation then. The idea of me, a humble English and History graduate, working in such a place would have been rather daunting.

Three months after graduation, I found myself thrown into a new world which would change my own old world irrevocably. I found myself in a tiny office bearing the title "Visiting Professor", given several thousand rupees to reorganise the library, and about 10 hours lectures a week. My students were either first year Indian undergraduates (some who spoke English as a first language, others who had never heard English spoken but could read it fluently) or high-powered civil servants from all over the Far and Near East on UN training programmes. After only a week's TEFL course, it was something of a baptism by fire. However, it did teach me a great lesson - that with enough work, all things are possible.

Initially all my students looked the same to me. Then one day another VSO visited me when I was out. The other students tried to describe her to me, but ended up by saying "you all look the same to us". It was a chastening experience which made me re-examine my poor efforts to recognise all my students. Not only that, it made me re-examine what constitutes the familiar, and how the unfamiliar can be made familiar with a bit of effort.

The food was another issue. I had to eat in the foreign student hostel initially, where the cooks assumed that all non-Indian food had to be overcooked and completely tasteless (shades of "Goodness Gracious Me"). At the same time, I had to walk past a butcher's shop to get to work every day. In the morning, two forlorn goats would be tied up, bleating away. At lunchtime, only one would be there, with the bloody head of his friend hanging from a hook. By home time, there would just be the two bloody heads. I became a vegetarian... I eventually managed to convince the powers that be to let me eat in the girls' hostel which meant a very swift change of diet to include refried chapattis and cold curry for breakfast everyday, a great improvement over Indian cornflakes and hot milk. Whilst I returned to eating meat after a couple of years, I still find it hard to eat meat every day, although I adhere to the Bengali concept of fish as a "swimming vegetable".

In the midst of all this rapid acquisition of teaching skills, there was the glamour of the Queen's birthday bash at the High Commission, full of people eager for a free lunch, and a chance to network with other expats and interesting locals. I found myself standing next to a small walnut brown old lady in a plain white sari with a blue border. She had the most piercing eyes imaginable and her bony hands were startlingly powerful. With her was a motley crew of shabby children come to watch the magic show put on for our delight, although watching their unrestrained joy was what really entertained us all. In a passing conversation with the unknown lady I found myself boxed into volunteering to help out when I could. This was the start of an illuminating acquaintance with Mother Teresa.

Her shabby mother house on Lower Circle Road was a constant hive of activity and my first anxious arrival there found me immediately dishing out sulpha tablets to a line of leprosy patients who thrust the remnants of their hands through the little window in the gate house and were given a tablet which we had to ensure they took immediately.

Another task was sorting out the mountain of donated clothes which were constantly arriving, usually from the USA. Mother

Teresa was already spending the monsoon season away from
Kolkata, drumming up support for her charity so that by the spring
there would be plenty of gifts to sort through. Clothes which
had spent months in the docks waiting to be released for the right
exchange of "bakshish" were piled up to ceiling height in small side
rooms. The smell of damp clothing was powerful, but less of an
issue that the constant slight sound or movement always present.
As one garment was yanked from the bottom of the pile, a wave
of insects would scuttle out and the pile would heave dangerously
nearer. Within this sea of cast-offs were many things only suitable
for cleaning floors, plus dirty worn misshapen garments, fur coats
and plastic macs. It was a challenging experience which left me
often enraged by the way so many donors presumably felt that
the poor were only worthy of receiving things for which they
themselves had absolutely no more need. Mother Teresa was
much more gracious, always looking positively to what others could
ingeniously do with such dross.

We often in fact had differences of opinion. She and her nuns went
round collecting babies from rubbish heaps and putting them in
their intensive care unit-orange boxes with light bulbs suspended
above them. I knew that other nuns pointed women towards free
family planning clinics, and I argued vigorously that she should
do the same. Her infuriating response was to say, sex was the only
free entertainment and pleasure these people had, and she was just
happy to deal with its inevitable consequences. Which did not in
any way answer my questions.

Nor could I understand how she could accept money from people
she knew exploited their workers or were involved in very shady
business activities. Why didn't she challenge their behaviour as she
was already much revered throughout Kolkata society although
largely unknown in Europe at the time? She always replied that
it would be wrong to rebuff people's desire to give, to be generous
to others less fortunate. Again, not to my mind a very satisfactory
response. It was difficult to square her obvious success in raising
awareness among the rich of the terrible circumstances in which
many of their fellow countrymen lived, with the way she showed

not the slightest interest in using her moral clout to actually do something about the causes of such terrible poverty. The ambiguity involved in "greatness" was an interesting lesson. Watching the way her life has been sanitised and simplified has been fascinating, as well as a little alarming, since the implication remains that saintliness is more to do with spin than actual outcomes.

It was a turbulent time in general to be living, with the Prague Spring in the West and a powerful Naxalite Maoist guerrilla movement in India, especially West Bengal. There were constant attacks on isolated government offices and when Robert McNamara, then head of the World Bank, arrived, being a Westerner became quite dangerous at times. Fortunately, with long black hair and dark complexion I passed easily for a Kashmiri and faded quickly into the background. However, the smell of teargas and burning flesh hung over the city for months. The Naxalites at one point set fire to a tram just a couple in front of the one I was one. As we got off and hurried past the burning wreck, the smell of burnt bodies was unforgettable: the guerrillas had prevented anyone leaving the tram. How in many ways justified political outrage at inequality and corruption can itself produce hideously unjust results was a tough lesson.

A few days later there was a riot on the Maidan, the big open space where once the British army camped and marched about, establishing their superiority. Police with huge wooden lathies surged forward, smashing anyone who got in their way. Watching from the safer confines of a shop, it was a reminder of how close to the edge our lives can often be, and how the kindness of strangers can restore our faith in human nature. As a foreigner, I had been immediately ushered away to safety, with my needs put before those of my helpers. None of this darkness and violence stopped my exploration of the wonderful vibrant country. Kolkata was an exciting, buzzing place, full of street markets selling everything from avocados to xylophones. No need ever to feel a bit peckish: always there would be a street vendor with piles of hot chickpeas, fresh jalebis, chai in bio-degradable terracotta cups. The colours and smells were so new and varied. They altered forever the way I ate and my feelings towards colour and texture, making me much more expansive in both areas.

I joined other VSOs on wonderful trips beyond Kolkata. On one we accidentally caught the slow train instead of the express and spent an extra five hours in a train full of chickens and baskets of fruit which stopped at every station, often apparently in the middle of nowhere. It took a long time, but it gave me a powerful insight into the vastness and remoteness of much of the country. We did eventually arrive at Puri, at the time a sort of Indian Bournemouth where for a few shillings one could rent a room which opened onto a pale lemon beach. Middle-class Indian families were already enjoying the whole holiday experience, although swimming costumes were not socially acceptable: one went in swimming fully clothed. By then, we were all happy with that, compromising by wearing long T-shirts over our costumes when we plunged in. The great sense of hospitality I always encountered has often made me bitterly embarrassed and ashamed at the harsh rejection of the outsider which Westerners often exhibit.

VSO was supposed to be about me contributing to a developing country, whereas in reality India changed my life forever in unexpected ways. Being a stranger in a strange land made me look at so many things that I had accepted as set in stone, and helped me to appreciate different ways of doing things in a way that might have taken me a lifetime to develop otherwise. Whereas the Prague Spring may have been swept away in Europe, my own "Prague Spring" swept away much of my past certainties and changed forever my approach to life.

Strong Women
Eleanor Hughes
(Llangasty)

*I am a retired family therapist who grew up
in Hampshire. Following retirement from the
Berkshire NHS I moved with my husband to Brecon
where I enjoy singing, gardening, grand-parenting
and the WI.*

There were four women who stood out from the crowd: my
mother, my grandmother, Edith and Miss Moon. They defied
convention and followed their passions. In post-war Britain, when
most middle-class women were rendered ghostly through lack of
personal fulfilment, this was unusual.

Mum's passions filled the house, surrounded us with colour and
provided her with welcome distractions from parenting. She taught
herself folk guitar, collected a vast array of folk tunes from around
the world and laid on small fundraising concerts. My sisters and I
were obliged to sing, dance and play ukulele and recorder to add
volume and interest to the performance. We took to this with varying
degrees of excitement and dread till teenage rebellion set in.

Some folk songs were amusingly risqué. Shocked titters would
break out as we sang lustily about sailors having sex with mermaids.
An interesting spin-off was the guitar lessons offered to local boys

251

who would troop in by the back door mistakenly hoping to learn skiffle. On one occasion an attractive teenager was surprised to find himself cradling my eldest sister who had lost her grip in the sycamore tree by the gate and fallen on top of him. What timing.

Perhaps because of the trauma of her father's death when she was six years old, and her family's sudden loss of status and comfort, Mum had great sympathy for those who had been marginalised or abandoned. She arranged regular contact with a group of elderly women from a long-stay ward in our local psychiatric hospital and with an isolated elderly lady who was registered deaf and blind.

My sisters and I were drawn into these unconventional relationships and I enjoyed the challenge of making a genuine connection under difficult circumstances. These ladies were far more interesting than most adults in our village, and middle class rules of social engagement could be relaxed. I remember the expression on my father's face – a mixture of embarrassment and dismay – as Mum's hospital friends busily devoured her scones and fruit cake whilst puffing on their fags.

On one occasion Mum's desire to challenge complacency left me deeply shocked. She had arranged a coffee morning at our house in aid of the NSPCC, and large black and white posters of children found in appalling conditions invaded our living room. At this point I wondered who was more important – her children or the faces in the pictures?

Perhaps Mum's greatest gift was her enjoyment of female friendship. I understood this from her raucous laughter when close friends visited and the way she fell on the regular letters from her much-loved cousin in South Africa. It gave me a sense of the freedom and affirmation which may be found in the company of other women which has been a source of strength throughout my life.

Every summer my mother would take my sisters and me to stay with my grandmother in Devon. Widowed at 38 with four children under seven. Granny was relentlessly practical and, apart from a devotion to gardening, uninterested in the creative arts. While Mum cooked with sensitivity and imagination, her mother threw things together with some odd results. I remember, on holiday on Dartmoor, a particularly disgusting lumpy soup which Mum let us surreptitiously tip down the outside drain.

The annual trip from Exmouth to Dartmoor in Granny's Austin 10 was an experience. She had learnt to drive at the age of 60 and had never quite mastered the clutch. Her profile was tense as she gripped the base of the steering wheel in her upturned fists, lower lip jutting forwards in grim concentration. The car lurched round corners and up steep hills. Sitting on the back seat, inhaling the smell of peeling leatherette, my stomach would heave. "You'll have to wait!" she would bark as I croaked feebly and, to my sisters' exasperation and disgust, vomited into my lap.

On arrival the car would be parked on the crest of a hill and boxes and bags of provisions lugged down to 'The Hut.' It was a 1930s holiday bungalow on the edge of farmland with an unobstructed view of the moor. With an 'Elsan' toilet, open fire and ramshackle furniture, some might have considered it a hovel. But it was Granny's Getaway and to us it was magical. At night I would curl round the familiar lumps in my mattress and annoy my sister by jabbing a finger into her mattress above. We could hear our mother and grandmother next door getting ready for bed and anticipated the numerous rituals of life on 'The Moor'.

These included a daily visit to the neighbouring farm with enamel pails for fresh milk, the collection of drinking water from a natural spring on the hillside, wooding, picking tiny blueberries ('worts') in abandoned open tin mines, and early morning naked dips in the stream.

There was something religious about Mum and Granny's devotion to these rituals, perhaps influenced by 1920s and 30s ideas about the natural world as a source of inspiration and liberation. It was also a re-creation of my mother's holidays as a child, when Granny took her family to camp on the same site but in a Nissen iron hut

– until one night in the 1920s, when it blew down in a gale. Our 1950s experience was cushy by comparison, and moaning about discomforts was not tolerated.

Between the chores we were able to enjoy a deep connection to the natural world: the softness of summer moorland wind and rain, the rich scent of bracken and peat bog, the call of the curlew. Best of all was the morning dip in a secluded pool edged with foxgloves and ferns: the shock of the freezing water followed by a rush of warmth. It was sensory heaven.

Like Granny, Edith was practical and down-to-earth. She was the youngest of three sisters, none of whom had married, and who perhaps, as a result, took an interest in the families of their friends. She ran a college refectory and a cub pack with energy and dedication and was also a tireless fundraiser, ornithologist and walker. She sometimes played tennis or walked with my diminutive father. The sight of their retreating backs was comical - Edith was over six foot tall (we would measure things in 'Ediths').

A trip in Edith's car was another sick-making experience, careering through the lanes at high speed with the windows tight shut and a reek of wet dog. Despite this recklessness she showed a genuine concern for children and talked with a directness that I liked. I admired her independence, unconventional behaviour (she ignored class distinctions and enjoyed a beer) and outspoken frankness. This last was a refreshing quality which rather shocked my parents. Later in my teens, when my mother became ill, her honest presence would bring comfort to the house.

A short walk from our house was our small village school attended by children of agricultural workers from the surrounding farms. There the head teacher, Miss Moon, provided a surprisingly good all-round education. There were three classes, Miss Moon teaching the junior class of 7-11 year olds in a large room with high windows. There were four rows of desks, one for each year. Each row worked at their own pace on Maths and English, while other subjects were taught jointly. The years at the school were very happy ones. Miss Moon was as gifted at teaching music and handicraft as she was at her special subject of biology.

Full advantage was taken of our location in the countryside. On winter mornings we went for a run up the frozen lanes inhaling the cold biting air and pungent smell of kale and silage. In the warmer months we were taken for nature walks when children would take the opportunity to eat hawthorn leaves ('bread and cheese') and stuff rosehip seeds ('itching powder') down each other's shirts. During summer playtimes we would have access to the partly mown school field. On hot days we would lie in the long grass popping plantain heads from their stalks or sucking the sweet stems of grass flowers. In addition there was 'kiss chase' with both girls and boys in pursuit. I remember pinning down a boy with blue eyes and a mop of black hair - and the first whisper of lust.

A lack of restraint in the children meant that fights occasionally broke out. Both my sisters and I had fierce confrontations. On one such occasion I lost my temper with 'Bunter' Green, a solid boy who kept disrupting my girls' game. I slapped his face and he hit me back. Our blood was up and other children, shouting and yelling, gathered round to watch the performance. After what seemed an eternity, a teacher's flushed face burst through the rabble and brought things to a close. The fight seemed to clear the air and thereafter we got on well.

Miss Moon herself was not a stranger to aggression. She administered the cane on the palm of the hand to anyone who persisted in stepping out of line. On one occasion the mother of a particularly naughty boy turned up at the school in a rage and threatened to "Knock (her) block off" if she caned her son again. As far as I know Miss Moon did not lose her cool on that or any other occasion. It was her ability to steer a calm ship, make learning effortless and allowing us to resolve our own disputes that made her such an important figure in my life.

The capacity of these women to provide interest and excitement during the somewhat austere years following World War Two was greatly valued by my 10 year old self. My mother's creativity, love of friendship and difference, my grandmother's stunning example of independent old age, Edith's kindness and honesty and Miss Moon's calm ability to take control, have remained fine examples of female strength that I shall carry with me for the rest of my life.

Brought to Book

Geraldine Cox

(Leverstock Green)

I worked as a primary school teacher in London, England and Ontario, Canada. I took a break in 1965 to travel the 'Hippy Trail', before returning to teaching and later becoming a head teacher. I married a sea captain, have one son and now live in Hertfordshire.

A dead rat lay in a sawdust-filled gutter in a featureless, grey road. This deprived area of London contrasted dramatically with the leafy suburb of my home, but I did not realise that a greater impact awaited me in the shape of an all-powerful, autocratic and bizarre head teacher.

I was the first member of my family to achieve higher education. It was September 1958, and I was just twenty - a newly qualified teacher, in search of the infant school where I was to begin work the following week.

I hurried along the treeless road. On one side, olive skinned men wearing what appeared to be pyjamas sat on the steps of tall Victorian houses calling suggestively to me. On the other side, a notice proclaimed the presence of a wood yard behind a grimy brick wall. I passed a high spike-topped wall and eventually

257

reached the end of the road but could not see any sign of a school.
I anxiously retraced my steps several times but eventually returned
home in despair.

"How can I report for work if I can't even find the school?" I
wailed to my family.

"Don't worry" my brother reassured me. "We'll go out on Sunday
and find it."

Riding pillion on my brother's motor-bike, I coasted down the
street that I had walked the day before. From my new vantage
point the high spike-topped wall revealed itself as the playground
wall, and an arch inscribed "1870" curved over a heavy gate that
beckoned grimly to a tall rectangular three-storey building.

Very early on the following day, I crossed a drab playground
passing brick out-buildings and a covered, open-sided area before I
entered the school. It was deserted, and a strong smell of varnish
and disinfectant hung in the air. Rows of black metal coat hooks
and clean roller towels led me to a silent, central hall leading
to four curtained classroom doors, all firmly closed. I waited
apprehensively, and at last a jolly looking person appeared. With a
casual wave of her hand she indicated my room: Class 6.

I gazed around Class 6. High, narrow windows filtered light
onto walls of brown glazed tiles, with green paintwork adding an
institutional air. Bare display boards at adult eye-height towered
over shelves covered with thin cotton curtains. Two disconsolate
trays of sand and water stood empty in one corner, whilst in
another stood a board and easel. Front and centre, a teacher's desk
and chair faced scarred, wooden children's tables.

I walked slowly around the room and searched the curtained
shelves: grey plastic trays of junk and old Plasticine abounded, but I
failed to find any pencils, paper or other useful materials. A folding
bookcase revealed dirty, torn copies of *Janet and John* and *The Little
Blue Jug.*

258

A sharp rap on my door from my friendly neighbour summoned me to the playground where line Number 6 and I gazed eagerly at each other. Small girls dressed in stiff serge pinafore dresses and thick woollen cardigans stood next to boys in grey flannel shorts and heavy pullovers. All wore black-laced shoes and knee-length socks. My first class: I would discover them to be sweet natured, studious, boisterous and even naughty.

In the classroom a pile of paper and a box of pencils had been left on my desk, and I organised the children into writing about themselves. The hall, from where a constant buzz could be heard, was full of children with their parents. Periodically my door would open and a child would enter. Some wept, others clung to their mothers. They had just arrived from Cyprus; their first language was Greek and they did not appear to speak any English. Finally, Class 6 had forty-four pupils, and the hall was empty.

I gathered my little pupils together and we began to play singing games. Suddenly my door was flung open and an enormous woman, dressed in black, with dyed frizzy ginger hair, yellow protruding teeth, and an huge bosom, threw herself into the room, struck an operatic pose and sang loudly, "Lah!". She swung herself towards me, flapped her hand, trilled "Lovely dear, lovely," and left with a flourish.

I had met the headmistress. It was a bizarre experience, and proved to be the first of many as the year progressed. A trembling fear and unease of her unpredictability never really left me throughout my time at the school.

She rarely arrived before 10.30 am when she immediately locked herself in her office for the greater part of the day. Every afternoon she had a little nap, emerging at 3.30 pm. Very occasionally she would appear quite unexpectedly and demand that the whole school assemble in the hall, where she would play the piano and sing with the children. She was a marvellous pianist and had a huge repertoire of lovely songs, but many of the small participants found the experience upsetting as her ear-piercing screams at innocent mistakes often accompanied the songs. Return to the classroom frequently revealed damp underwear.

Clink! Clink! Coins mounted on my desk: it was Monday, Dinner Money Day and National Savings Day. The line of children shuffled forward. "Miss, my mum put milk in our water today," confided one small boy as he waited his turn. This level of hardship was beyond my experience. Money, and for some decent housing too, were in short supply. School dinners, charged on a sliding scale from 3d to 9d, were cooked on the premises and were a greatly anticipated part of the day. Nearly every child brought a shilling or sometimes two in order to buy a stamp for their National Savings book. Their parents had lived through the Second World War: shortages and rationing had created a generation for whom thrift and saving were part of life. Only a few children possessed plimsolls, and usually the class capered around in daywear outside and underwear in the hall. One or two little girls were sewn into their liberty bodices, but nearly everyone was as clean as possible. Drip-dry, Crimplene and easy-care fabrics were still just around the corner. No-one had central heating and everyone found laundry problematic. Most families dried their clothes on a clothes horse in front of a coal fire, or hung them to dry on an airer in the kitchen.

Every day I set out about twenty of my personal childhood books as part of the general activity sessions, and occasionally I added a book bought from my meagre weekly £7 salary. The lack of books, and of attractive ones in particular, remained a major problem and so I arranged to take my class to the public library. I gathered my forty-four infants into a crocodile (no-one was ever away) and we set off along the school road. The children were very well behaved and we arrived without incident at a major arterial road. As I debated how to negotiate us all safely through the relentless traffic, a mounted policeman appeared. He cheerfully raised his arm in an imperious gesture: the traffic halted and in no time we were in a warm, bright library.

A delighted librarian and several smiling assistants welcomed us and soon the library was full of excited chatter. Beautiful books entranced the children; some simply stroked smooth pages whilst others explored the myriad of choice upon the shelves. Our visits became the highlight of the week. We became a familiar sight wending our way along the road, and a mounted policeman was always waiting to steer us across the main road.

One afternoon, a tall man wearing a dark pin-striped suit fell in at the end of our line. He too crossed the road under the watchful eye of our policeman. He entered the library with us, but there was no sign of him as we blissfully explored wonderful and exciting books, and he remained unseen when we left.

The following morning I arrived to find a lone figure standing in the deserted hall. He smiled at me and I recognised the man in the pin-striped suit. He continued to wait patiently until the Head arrived, when they engaged in earnest conversation. Just outside my classroom door, two tall beech cupboards had remained permanently locked. Now I was summoned into the hall. The Head rattled her heavy bunch of keys and with a flourish unlocked them. I was speechless. Beautiful, brand new books filled the shelves. Pin-striped suit looked very pleased and with a friendly nod he left us. I was told that in future my class would use "The Head's Library".

The following day, clean dining tables were arranged on three sides of the hall and I was ordered to wipe them all again before taking my class to wash their hands. They filed meekly into the hall where the Head inspected their hands, back and front, and slapped any that were not spotless. The children sat in silence. A book, chosen at random by the Head, was placed in front of each. Pages were turned disconsolately. One child licked his thumb to turn a page and the ensuing shriek, accompanied by a heaving bosom, terrified us all. The books were collected, the cupboards locked, never to be unlocked again. Our love affair with the library was over.

"A present from County Hall!" announced our Head one day. She lovingly stroked a TV on a stand before outlining the dire consequences that would ensue should any accident befall such a gift. It was carefully wheeled into a safe corner of the hall, where it remained disconnected, its dead screen a silent reproach and its programmes forever a mystery.

Autumn turned to winter. Relentless rain hammered against the windows. Discontented children returned from a break time spent huddled under the covered area, and a restlessness filled the classroom. Soon the aroma of warm, damp bodies with a faint overtone of urine permeated the air. "Chalk and Talk" was considered inappropriate for infants, and my board and easel had remained unused. The moment had arrived to betray my training. I announced that we would all write *Incy Wincy Spider* together. Carefully I wrote the date and title on the board. Chewed lower lips, pink tongues tracing each letter, forty-four children copied in absolute silence before gazing expectantly at me. I sketched a friendly looking spider behind the text and invited them to follow suit. We were all highly delighted with our efforts. Praise resounded: "Wonderful", "Perfect!" Chalk and Talk had a place after all.

I became great friends with two colleagues. Shared meals and lively parties filled many evenings and weekends. From them I learned that it was common practice to strip a classroom of anything in reasonable condition whenever a teacher left the school. Education and learning, pupil progress and teaching skills were never discussed at any time. There was no sign of a curriculum and I was left entirely to my own devices. Each classroom was a separate world where teachers sought to protect pupils and themselves from the vagaries of the Head.

I became an expert at sourcing free materials, and in time my classroom became a warm, safe haven. In spite of the limited opportunities the majority did learn to read.

At the end of my first year the Head entered my room. Without preamble and without any classroom observation, she announced that I had passed my probationary year.

There were many joyful moments, but a further unsupported year, no resources, another class of forty-four, and a very low wage convinced me that teaching in such a barren environment might not be my vocation after all and I resigned.

Throughout my time I had failed to register the number of men in suits who arrived unheralded and clutching briefcases, but I learned later that they were from Her Majesty's Inspectorate. The Head who had made my life such a misery was retired early the following year. Too late for me.

Double Vision
Gillian Dykes
(Horsmonden)

I am current president of our TWILite memoir writing group, a 'resting' accountant, a previous Akela and occasional pantomime dame. I compete for living space with one dog, two guinea pigs, three teenagers, and a tolerant husband. I love story-telling whether on stage, screen or page. This is my first attempt at writing my own.

3rd August 1937

Charlie couldn't concentrate on the vegetable patch. The garden fork stood upright in the soil and served better as a coat rack on this warm summer's day. He sat back on his daughter's swing, filling the pipe bowl with St Bruno from his leather tobacco pouch. Unlit, he sucked the stem and nervously waited for news of his wife's confinement.

Night-gowned and exhausted, Lily was struggling to cope. This labour had been more difficult than with her first child. In unpaid attendance, her sister-in-law, Nell, had competently organized plenty of towels and hot water.

"Here, I've lined this with cotton wool. Squat down on it - that should help," the District Nurse coaxed.

"I'm doing no such thing. I don't want my baby born in a tin bucket. Get me back on the bed."

"In which case, use this roller towel if the pain gets too much. I'll place it at the end of the bed, my love."

Lily gazed uncomprehendingly at Nell. The next wave of contractions engulfed her.

"Oh Lily, you've pulled the sleeve clean off my dress"

"No matter now. I can see baby's head. Nearly there."

Eventually Lily delivered a baby girl, Irene, but she grew anxious as she watched the Nurse cajole the infant into life and administer brandy to her blue-tinted lips. Then she whispered conspiratorially with Nell in the corner of the bedroom. What was wrong? Did it matter that the doctor had wrongly diagnosed appendicitis instead of pregnancy in the early stages or was it to do with too many limbs being detected at the last examination?

Nell broke away, "I'm sorry, ducks, but I'm afraid there's another one coming. You're going to have to do it all again."

Fortunately, the birth of Maureen, the second girl, took very little effort. Later, Lily likened the process to being as easy as using the normal receptacle found underneath the bed.

Charlie rubbed his auburn locks and lit the pipe. The neighbours had been keeping Doreen, his eldest girl, occupied. He launched small stones at their backdoor.

"I've not got one, I've got two more daughters. Heavens knows how me and the Duchess will manage."

"Don't you worry we'll be up to sort that laundry and get it dry over the range. You'd best start a fire too, to get rid of all the other......"

23rd November 1984

I'm in an untypical room located in a concrete warren of student accommodation. No posters of androgynous idols or Athena prints blue-tacked to walls. No discarded tucker boots or cocktail glasses and leaking remnants of Malibu littering surfaces and, unlike my room, no constant soundtrack of synthesized pop.

This bed-sit is calm and uncluttered except for piles of pharmaceutical texts. Muted shades of Indian cotton are thrown over the bed and a hint of spice hangs in the air. No doubt from culinary supplies sent from home to enliven dull college catering.

"Did you know Hindus are taught palmistry? This girl on my course is very good. She'll read yours," my friend had enthused.

I'm reluctant to hand over my palm - not sure I really believed she can hold my life in her hands.

"Don't worry, I can see your lifeline clearly, but I never reveal anything about death. I'll tell you the usual - how many children you will bear and whether you will marry."

The golden bangles on her wrists tinkled as she inspected the relief map of my hands.

"You will marry young and you will marry ahead of your peers."

I scoffed. I couldn't possibly marry someone without at least a two-year trial run. If I was still to be deemed young, I needed to get a move on. My current relationship was definitely not a going concern. My twenty-second birthday was next month and I was about to be a 'third-time never the....' bridesmaid. I started to doubt the validity of her prediction.

Continuing, counting imperceptible bumps, she deduced "One, two....you will have three children".

"Oh no, I would never have three children - I don't like odd numbers....unless, of course, I had twins."

As that third-time bridesmaid, I attracted some attention from a lad I'd known for years. By the time I was twenty-four, he and I were married.

7th November 1995

My cousin-in-law waddled to the table with the tray. My mother-in-law intervened and took command of the tea pot. I resisted the urge to quote Nan's curse of the second pourer: "you'll get ginger twins"

"Ach, I'm bored with all this waiting. I just want to get this baby born."

Watching my toddler investigating anything within reach in her neatly-ordered cottage, I smiled.

"Have you tried this yet?" Threading her gold wedding band on a length of cotton, she proceeded to dangle the ring over my cousin's full-term bump. "I promise you, I'm not making it move. Look at it - back and forth - that's a boy."

I surprised myself at how easily I was persuaded to indulge in this bit of home-spun divination. Unconvinced, I let the thread hang over my four-month bump. Without any momentum exacted, the pendulum whirled round in a circular motion. I stopped, concerned that the hopes of my observing parents-in-law were being raised erroneously. They already had three grandsons.

Mother-in-law, enthralled and needing to satisfy her own doubts, held the cotton over us again. The unprompted movement alternated between swinging and swirling as before. She then held it over her own stomach and much to everyone's relief, the ring remained stationary. Applying the device one last time and without a shred of corroborating evidence, she concluded: "Well, that's just the sex of the twin that's lying on the top…"

Six days later, our cousin had a baby boy.

20th December 1995

Don't ever try to stencil low-level Teddy Bears while heavily
pregnant. For one thing, your bump prevents the close proximity
required to colour the templates accurately and for another,
kneeling on bare floorboards is agony!

Four years ago, we had swapped our terraced town house for a
country cottage. By the time I went on my first maternity leave, I
was eager, armed with paint-technique manuals and match-pots, to
transform the spare room into a pastoral nursery.

The resulting room has a black iron fireplace surrounded by
turquoise Fired Earth tiles, hand-painted alphabet dado rails and
the obligatory stripped-pine rocking chair. The pale lemon walls
are a backdrop for those bears that sit, clutching bold-coloured,
bunches of balloons, or stride across the scene, six inches above the
wooden skirting-boards. Higher up, an occasional escaped balloon
can be seen, headed for the emulsioned polystyrene coving.

Now, heavy with second child, I stand admiring the newly-acquired
bunk-beds. Our toddler spent his first night in a big boy's bed, under
a circus-themed duvet and he's delighted with himself. The vacated
cot, pushed into the alcove, pleases me too. The bunks can separate
into single beds if necessary so we are all set for the next basket to
bunk transition. The cost-efficiency gives me a smug glow.

Out of nowhere, a premonition hits me. What if we are having
twins? We're a bed short then.

"Ready", my husband calls up the stairs, interrupting my
deliberations. Today, we've a hospital appointment for my twenty
week ultrasound scan.

"Babies" points out our son, as the monitor screen is turned
towards us. The outline of one tiny head momentarily eclipses a
second one.

"Is there a history of twins in the family?" are the Sonographer's
first words.

"Yes" we answer in unison.

"You seem to be taking this very calmly", she continues, "not the usual reaction from newly diagnosed multiple-birth parents."

"Well, I'm trying to be rational. I've got such a head start compared to my Nan. I've time to plan and besides, I think I've always known my fate."

6th February 1996

My midwife timed two different heartbeats today. From her first booking visit, a heartbeat has always been easily detected. This is unusual but, perhaps two were being amplified as one?

Both were similar in pace indicating same sex twins. I'm a little disheartened. Although I would never say, I'd prefer a girl and a boy.

I'm unable to prise the ring from my finger so I slip the gold cross and chain over my head and start that dangling process. Back & forth it swings. I move the chain further down. It falters then rotates in a small circle. I double check the directions. It's my turn to have my hopes raised.

25th April 1996

We know one twin is breach so their birth has been scheduled for first theatre slot this morning. I wake early to be greeted by the familiar face of my community midwife. Her continued concern for my internal breathing space has ensured constant monitoring whenever I come within a wheeze of her blood pressure cuff. The babies are indulging in a spot of synchronised swimming but one heartbeat is getting fainter. They start to move us quickly.

Partners are not allowed in the anesthetist's room. For the first time, I feel anxious and alone. The well-meaning student stroking my hand is a poor substitute for my husband. They wheel me into theatre, clipping more monitors to me as they go. Where is he? The room is full of people – two of everyone to help deal with a double delivery. Then he appears clad in hairnet, clogs and scrubs:

a vision in blue polyester. He mumbles something about another blood test and consent forms but I'm not to worry now.

My lower body is covered with green drapes and a blood-stained gauze is tied to a metal frame just above my head, The Obstetric surgeon, imparts comforting words as she works swiftly.

At 10.07 hrs, a baby cries. Who's brought a baby in here? I realise it's one of ours. As Twin One is taken to be weighed and apgar-ed, Twin Two is lifted from me.

"Well that one's a boy, he's peeing like a fountain. Let me check there are no others before I sew you back up"

"That's not funny. What sex was the first one?"

"Oh I forgot to look."

As we wait, 'Jesu, Joy of man's desiring' emanates from the CD player. A bundle of white cellular blanket is handed to me. A tiny face, eyes tight shut, is just visible under a knitted bonnet. He needs warming so I'm encouraged to cuddle and feed him amongst the tubes and wires. A second similarly wrapped parcel is placed in her father's arms. Daddy's girl, with bright red lips wide, vocalizes her disapproval at being woken so early. Our secret prayers have been answered - a perfect pigeon pair. We feel very blessed.

The extra blood tests and consent forms mean the twin placentas can be used in a hospital's burns unit. Our bequest has enabled sight restoration to blinded fire victims.

28th April 1996
I've been professionally coached in coordinating nappy changes, grabbing sleep whenever possible and simultaneous feeding. To be fair, I can't see myself performing the latter al fresco, necessitating as it does, a comfortable chair, a large V-shape pillow and ideally, stripping to the waist. I've no desire to develop a new spectator sport.

"I've been married for sixty-eight years today" my Nan, Lily, announced on her visit. She lost my granddad, Charlie, sixteen years earlier but in her heart, death had not parted them.

"Twins are hard work but you will both work together. We did. Don't forget to make time for each other though." She advised us. "Oh, but I'm so pleased to be able to meet you two little darlings"

* * * *

A photograph of that first meeting sits on my window sill and daily, I bask in the warmth of that pride in Nan's smile, as she cradles my babies. Now, she has gone too, but they remain her enduring legacy to me. I wonder, with foresight, if I need to start writing an owner's manual for my own unborn grandchildren?

Beds, Bathrooms and Sick-Bags
Sue Callaghan
(Horsmonden)

A retired blackbelt and karate instructor, former brownie leader and foster mother, I am my WI's secretary during its formation year. A member of my village drama group, I volunteer for local charities. Currently studying with the Open University, I love anything chocolate and live in Kent with my husband.

"Wait...wait." I flapped my hands and hopped from one foot to another like Homer Simpson. "I can't think with no clothes on!"

I rushed into the other room of our hotel suite and looked round for a t-shirt or something, leaving my boyfriend of just three weeks lying crumpled on the floor after falling out of bed.

Once I'd covered up, I returned to Mike. Moving his wheelchair gave me a better view of the situation. His right arm was pinned under his slight but solid 5'5" frame, his left leg had disappeared under the bed, and the radiator was making what would be a cool-looking pirate-type scar on his lightly-freckled oval face. His blue eyes, a couple of shades darker than mine, twinkled under his newly cut sandy brown hair. Actually his hair is almost as ginger as

273

mine but 'sandy brown' are his words so we'll just go with them.

A quick glance told me he was conscious and not bleeding, and who knew how relieved I'd be to know those two things? Mike's unshakable sense of humour and determination not to let his Muscular Dystrophy control his life, made returning him to a more recognisable human shape take twice as long, because his comically inappropriate remarks kept making me laugh causing us to return to square one.

I'd met Mike on-line four months earlier in May 2002 when I was working as a Learning Support Assistant in a secondary school in Somerset, and Mike worked, as he still does, in IT in Kent. I needed a project to replace PE for a lad with brittle bones who'd broken his arm. A friend suggested a pen-pal and a website for people with disabilities. The lad and I trawled through the weird and the tragic before stumbling across Mike's strangely 'normal' posting.

In a fit of giggles we sent a garbled message, and to my utter astonishment Mike answered the same day. Daily emails followed, then texts and phone calls. In September 2002 I took my 1st Dan Blackbelt in Karate, and Mike suggested I recuperate at his place, which I accepted. Apart from a communication problem about the train station, which is a whole other story, we had a wonderful weekend, which is why three weeks later he booked an accessible hotel suite in Somerset, and I discovered that I can't think like a grown-up if I haven't got any clothes on. I realised then that beds were going to play a huge part in our relationship, but not for the reason you'd expect.

Until I started travelling with Mike, I was completely innocent of the fact that beds come in a range of heights but wheelchairs don't! When we stayed in Charing Cross, the bed was so high I had to lift Mike in stages - after dropping him on the first attempt - using objects from around the room. Finally, standing on tiptoe gave my 5'2" freckled frame the extra inch or so to be able to lift Mike onto the bed. Well, to be honest, it wasn't so much a lift as a throw and a fall.

274

Low beds aren't any easier as it means fighting gravity first thing in the morning, never an easy thing, made worse by the fact I'm not a morning person. Lifting Mike has become slightly easier since we got the lifting belt because once it's on him, Mike has handles. Unfortunately the belt itself, about four inches wide and three foot long, slightly padded, with alternating vertical and horizontal woven handles fastened by webbing with a three prong safety clip, has given us a few problems. I once fastened it round Mike's waist and the wheelchair, without noticing, and then wondered why I couldn't lift him. When I realised, I laughed so hard my face hurt.

Taking the belt through Airport Security has not been plain sailing either. I usually pack it in our hand luggage, just in case I need it. Mike gets taken to one side to be pat-searched and have the wheelchair swabbed, leaving me with both bags, two pairs of shoes, two jackets, passports and all the paperwork. After the bag was x-rayed at Gatwick on our way to Cyprus, I was called over to empty it, and asked what 'that' is. I garbled an explanation pointing at Mike, and after I had actually demonstrated the belt on myself, we were sent on our way. I later realised that the lifting belt must look like a shop-bought suicide bomber's belt. I always lay it out separately now.

Airport security always brings surprises. As we flew out of Las Vegas via McCarron Airport, Mike's shoes tested positive for nitroglycerine, which caused him to be sidelined and cordoned off. It turned out that the show we had attended the night before at the Excalibur Hotel had used indoor fireworks, and Mike's shoes had absorbed the offending explosive chemical. On our way to Tenerife through Gatwick, I was almost arrested under the anti-terrorism act for carrying a now-illegal Martial Arts weapon. I was using the kubatan, which is the size of a pen and solid metal, as a key-ring.

Bed heights and airport security aren't our only problems. Sometimes just getting into the hotel room is a hurdle. It turns out that wheelchair accessible doesn't mean the same thing to everyone. In a hotel in Bristol we were upgraded eight times but Mike still couldn't get in the bathroom. After a long, and on my part heated, discussion with the hotel manager, it turned out that they could say the bathroom was accessible because they got their wheelchair in it. When their chair arrived it turned out to be child-sized. We agreed to use it only because we were staying one night on our way to Paris for my birthday, and the manager had offered us free dinner and a bottle of wine to seal the deal.

Travelling itself is my biggest hurdle. I have labyrinthitis, a permanent inner ear infection, which means that I can get travel sickness from walking. If I have an attack I am violently sick and then pass out. I take travel-sickness tablets every day, so every bag we travel with has some form of sick-bag in it.

Mike, however, is a fantastic traveller. He didn't even flinch when we went to Pearl Harbour to see the USS Missouri, and the passenger lift arrived on the front of a fork-lift truck. It had a wooden pallet floor and chicken wire walls! As it juddered ever upwards I held the wheelchair so tight my knuckles turned white. I had my eyes squinched shut and held my breath the entire journey. I took the stairs on the way down, which was not an option for Mike.

It isn't all fun and laughter travelling with a full-time wheelchair user. There's not enough room in our car boot for the suitcase, because of the wheelchair. Mike can't stand, so he requires carry-on assistance which means we are first on and last off, and the aircraft toilets are never accessible.

When we were unfortunate enough to be involved in a road traffic accident that forced us onto the central reservation on the motorway, on the way to my sister's 40th birthday, we finished up at an angle in the middle lane with the traffic stopped behind us and smoke pouring from the bonnet. I had the unenviable decision of whether to leave Mike in the smoking car, drag him out and onto the tarmac but with no way of getting him to safety, or risk taking the extra time to get the wheelchair out first, even though there was nowhere safe for us to wait if I did.

Luckily a group of bikers pushed the Jaguar with Mike still in it onto the hard shoulder. The traffic cops cleared a back seat space for him and then drove him to the train station. I travelled in the tow truck with the wheelchair. We had to come home by train as there was absolutely no way I could lift Mike into a seat in the tow truck. I'd had enough trouble getting in it myself.

Mike's positive attitude to life, regardless of his physical limitations, has encouraged us to travel far and wide. We have stayed in hotels in Somerset, Wiltshire, Bath and Bristol, suffering single beds, impossible inclines to entrances, and the wrath of elderly ladies. To celebrate our second wedding anniversary – cotton – we stayed in a converted cotton mill in New Lanark, Scotland, and whilst it wasn't completely accessible we managed to have a great time.

Mike's work commitments have taken us to Leicester, where he fell off the ramp getting into a taxi; Lisbon; Portugal; where the pavements were so bad we couldn't leave the hotel; Lytham St. Annes, where we had no roll-in shower even though we had specifically asked for one; and Kent, where our largest cab company doesn't have a working accessible taxi. And many London hotels have very high beds or very long corridors with deep pile carpet that makes steering the wheelchair really difficult.

My birthday trip to Paris saw Mike having to wee in the bidet in a cupboard, because the toilet was behind the door in the tiny bathroom. New Year in Hamburg, Germany, saw Mike having to be carried, in his chair, up and down the hotel entrance steps. We have holidayed in Cyprus with my sister and her two boys, where they delighted in the game of crash testing dummies with a manual and an electric wheelchair. A short stay in Brussels wasn't short enough as they have no dipped kerbs and no accessible taxis at all.

We honeymooned in San Francisco and Las Vegas, where we queued in the street for a bus, with everyone else. In San Francisco, the receptionist rang to check if we were ok, because we had spent the day in our room. Well, we were on honeymoon. A three day stay in Washington DC saw Mike being accused by a homeless woman of stealing her shoe and then of fathering her baby.

Hawaii and Oahu were perfect places to relax. We even toyed with the idea of hiring a beach wheelchair, which had wheels about the size of a Mini, but we weren't quite brave enough. The year before our wedding, we spent a fortnight with my almost-parents in Jacksonville, Florida. They had prepared for our arrival by building a long ramp into the house. Unfortunately they also ended up having to remove the bathroom door so Mike could access the facilities, and hanging a curtain for privacy.

Travelling in Britain has been made much more practicable by the fact that our local train companies have supplied all trains and stations with usable ramps, although not always with the key to unlock them, or the personnel to assist. All London taxis are accessible and 99% of cab drivers are more than willing to help. The 1% that aren't have been reported by the 99% that are.

Travelling, either at home or abroad, with a full-time wheelchair user isn't easy, as it requires a lot of planning and the need always for a plan B. But don't let that stop you. No matter where we've been or intend to go in the future, beds, bathrooms and sick-bags will always be our biggest hurdles. But just because travelling with a wheelchair user is littered with problems doesn't mean we aren't planning more adventures, and as a by-product mis-adventures, in the future. After all, life is for living.

The Reluctant Toreador
Cynthia Hinsley
(Marlow Bottom)

I was born in 1929. Once married I travelled extensively, accompanying my husband, who was in the Diplomatic Service, to faraway places. On returning home, we settled in Marlow Bottom and I carried on with various activities, including the WI, serving for many years as President.

Sadly, Cynthia passed away on 28 June 2011, so her contribution to this collection has a special poignancy.

As my husband was in the Diplomatic Service for many years, we travelled to several countries. One of the most interesting was Pakistan. Over four and a half years we were posted to Lahore, Islamabad and Karachi, and while we were in Lahore, India and Pakistan went to war and we were evacuated back to Britain, ending up spending our Christmas on the Isle of Wight with my father. The war didn't last very long, and after five weeks we were sent back to Pakistan.

Pakistan is very colourful and while we were there I felt inspired to write a little poem about it, so here goes:

> Ladies in saris and shalwa kameez
> Gents in their dohtis, down to their knees

Hundreds of people around the bazaars
Business men driving around in their cars
Camel carts, taxis and rickshaws galore
Tongas and donkeys and bikes by the score
Well laden buses all listing to port
All of them carrying far more than they ought
Gay painted lorries go speeding along
"I'm bigger than you so I can't be wrong"
Many new road signs but what use are they?
Most of the drivers can't read what they say

Highways and byways, side streets and lanes
Potholes and ditches and sewers and drains
Pedestrians swarming like bees in a hive
In spite of these hazards they seem to survive.

This poem shows what life was like in the old cities of Karachi and
Lahore, but Islamabad was a new government city.

When we were there our youngest daughter was about nine and
went to the British school. So when Mr Bhutto suddenly declared
a day's holiday, as he sometimes did, this school had to keep open.
On those days, they organized a long walk up the mountain and
they asked some parents to help. First of all we drove as far as the
road went, and then started off in a long crocodile of children,
some parents and three people from the British Council.

At the bottom of the mountain was a rocky, dried-up river bed,
and a little way away were some buffalo. As we crossed I was
suddenly aware of people grabbing children and running away. I
turned round to face an enormous buffalo coming towards me. He
then charged me and knocked me over on to the rocks and then
had the cheek to circle around and charge me from the other side.
Suddenly the owner appeared and chased him away.

After giving my daughter our very squashed sandwiches, I was
taken off to the doctors, but apart from extensive bruising, no
bones were broken.

When I had recovered I felt the need to write about it and called
the poem

THE RELUCTANT TOREADOR

If only someone had told me, I never would have gone
I went out hale and hearty and came back pale and wan.
"Buffalos here are docile" is what I'd often heard
But to say this one was gentle was utterly absurd.
I'll start at the beginning…………..it was a lovely day
Though overcast at early morn, the clouds had blown away
The children from the British school, mums, dads and
teachers too
Started walking up the hillside and looking at the view
We all were chatting gaily as we slowly strolled along
But across the dried up river, something was clearly wrong
A buffalo was standing there, his face was fierce and wild
He looked at me, straight in the eye – he was really very
riled.
The next I know, he'd hit me hard and thrown me to the
ground
And then, what do you think, he quickly turned around
And kicked me on the hand and back, his hooves left quite
a scar
And then his owner came along and drove him off afar.
The hazards of the Service are manifold we know
But few can boast of being charged by an angry buffalo !

Part 6

Inspiring People

Memories Of Nana

Valerie Richards

(Much Marcle)

I am a wife, mother and former nurse. Ever since I started writing leaflets for patients in order to convey important information succinctly and intelligibly, the written word has interested me greatly. Memoir writing is a new discipline for me and has proved an interesting challenge for my retirement.

The photograph was taken, in 1905, during the reign of Edward VII. The girl stands proudly, dressed in an ankle-length, shiny, satin dress with a tight waist and long sleeves. One foot, shod in a neatly-laced boot, is pointed out in front of her. Her long, dark hair hangs almost to her waist and she wears a large hat decorated with feathers. She stares confidently at the camera and I can detect a slight resemblance to my sister. Although she is unfamiliar to me I do know that her eyes are different colours; one is blue and the other is a hazel. The girl is Rebecca and she is sixteen years old. Forty years later she became my grandmother.

On that day, more than 100 years ago, when Rebecca dressed for her visit to the photographer's studio, the thought of grandchildren probably never entered her head. The youngest of 15, she was, at birth, already an aunt to several of her siblings' children. Her father was a jobbing builder and her mother took in washing to make ends meet. The large family lived in a small terrace house.

Her upbringing was essentially Victorian where hard work, common sense, a strong religious and moral code, family ties and parsimony were the values she was taught and by which she lived. She also had a good sense of humour, laughed easily and was extremely sociable. For most of her young adult life she would have been aware of the fight for women's suffrage yet she would not have been entitled to vote until 1928, at the age of 29. Perhaps that is why she held strong opinions and was well-informed on current affairs.

By the time she reached her grandmotherly status, Rebecca had lived through the worries and sadness of two World Wars. My grandfather, George, was in the trenches during the First World War. He survived but was a victim of mustard gas which eventually affected his health. I like to think that my arrival, her first grandchild, brought her joy amid the horror of the Second World War, in which her children - my father, his sister and brother - all saw active service. Certainly I was completely overjoyed with my first grandchild, and I like to think that Rebecca, or Nana as I called her, felt the same about me. She believed that 'actions spoke louder than words' and although she never actually told me that she loved me, she always made me feel extremely special.

My main memories of Nana are when she was in her sixties and I think of her more and more as I, too, have reached that age. I spent some of my school holidays with her whilst she nursed my grandfather, who had cancer of the oesophagus, and when she became a widow I stayed more frequently. She was extremely practical and did all the housework, gardening and cooking herself. It was accepted in our large family that children, especially the girls, made themselves useful with small tasks such as laying the table, drying and putting away crockery and cutlery, helping to fold sheets and table cloths before they were ironed, and, as we got older, ironing handkerchiefs (no paper hankies in those days) and dusting. Things were no different when I stayed with Nana. I didn't dislike these chores as I felt very grown up working alongside her and listening to Mrs. Dale's Diary and Workers' Playtime. We used to clean the brass and silver and, when I clean some of the items I've inherited from her - the silver backed brush and hand mirror, the silver tureens and the brass coal scuttle - I reflect on her maxim of "use plenty of elbow grease" as I shine them up.

Life in my grandparents' household was very ordered. The baker, in his brown overall coat, called every other day bringing from his van an enormous wicker basket full of a variety of bread and rolls. Nana usually selected a milk loaf but occasionally she chose a crusty wholemeal. The milkman called for his money on Friday and was invited to sit at the kitchen table for refreshment and a chat. In the winter, Nana made him a cup of 'Camp' coffee and in the summer he had either 'Kia-ora' orange squash, or 'Stones' ginger beer. Groceries were delivered weekly after we had visited the shop in the High Street and ordered bacon, sugar, butter, tea, broken biscuits, rice, flour and soap powder. The laundryman called every week when a wicker basket full of dirty linen was exchanged for one of clean, starched, white sheets, pillowcases and fluffy, big bath towels. All these items had to be individually labelled and Nana taught me how to sew on name tapes, which was a very useful lesson for later life.

Sometimes, on a Sunday, the shrimp man called. He pushed a two-wheeled barrow, shouted his wares and sold shrimps by the pint glass. It was the children's job to shell the shrimps, which we would have for tea along with celery sticks, kept fresh in a crystal jug full of water, and very thinly sliced brown bread and butter. Sunday tea was a ritual with friends and relations sitting around the big, oval table covered with a white, lace cloth. The best blue and white Spode crockery was set out along with silver tea knives, teaspoons, jam spoons, butter dishes and knives. Friday was baking day and Nana made shortcakes, fruit cake, biscuits and sponges. Throughout the year she made jams, jellies and marmalade, which were stored in the larder. Nana took great pride in presenting a good spread.

"The devil makes work for idle hands to do" was another of Nana's sayings and she rarely sat, especially in the evenings, without some piece of work in her hands. She liked to embroider and made many tablecloths and antimacassars, favouring the Jacobean style

of embroidery with intricate flower and fruit designs. During
both World Wars she knitted socks and gloves for the troops and
then made fair-isle jumpers, woolly hats, gloves and socks for her
grandchildren. I loved to sit by the open fire watching her fingers
manipulating four needles as she turned the heel of a sock or
knitted the fingers of gloves. She taught me these skills and I loved
to emulate her. Wool was reused; sweaters were washed, dried and
taken to pieces. The wool was rewound, first into skeins, one end
of which I had to hold an arm's width apart whilst Nana wound
it into balls. Sometimes, before my bedtime, she would play the
piano and sing A.A. Milne's poetry, which had been set to music.
I particularly liked "They're Changing Guard at Buckingham
Palace", and more especially the last verse, when Christopher
Robin asks

"Do you think that the King knows all about me?"
"Sure to dear but it's time for tea", says Alice.

Now, when I sit on her round, piano stool at my dressing table,
I often remember how, as a child, I used to swing it around and
around raising and lowering the height, just for fun. Everything
seemed so matter of fact and secure. As did the warm bath and
rose scented talcum powder applied with a soft, swansdown puff.
I was indulged, and being the eldest of four children, relished the
individual attention I received at Nana's. I slept in my own room
and loved to lie quietly in the feather bed dreamily looking at the
floral wallpaper and curtains, and imagining faces and patterns out
of the intricate swirls of foliage.

In the sitting room there was a settee with the arm labelled "Press"
on the side. Most afternoons Nana did just that, to lower the arm,
and take her 'nap' for thirty minutes, whilst I had to be quiet as
a mouse. Dutifully I sat in a corner and looked at copies of the
'Woman's Journal', with its glossy black and white photographs of
beautiful debutantes on the first page, and the National Geographic
full of colour photographs of strange and wonderful foreign lands.
Once the household chores were complete, and lunch and the 'nap'
were over, it was time to go out, usually to the shops. Sometimes we

went to the cinema or theatre. Once we saw Mario Lanza in 'The Student Prince', which we both enjoyed and especially the tea and scones served on trays during the interval. We often went to a smart restaurant for afternoon tea, served by waitresses in black dresses with frilly white caps and aprons. We usually had hot, buttered toast and small fancy cakes. My favourite was a sponge one covered with green and white marzipan shaped like a small cauliflower.

Dressing up to go out was a ritual. Nana was attractive, tall and confident in her manner. Her short dark hair was greying at the sides and swept back from either side of her face and held by two tortoise-shell combs. Before going out she would brush her hair vigorously, apply Elizabeth Arden cream to her face and then dab 4711 eau de cologne behind each ear and inside her wrists. How she must have revelled in being able to buy these luxuries. Nana always wore pearls believing that pearl ear-rings, in particular, were flattering and that their lustre was enhanced by wear. Her several pairs of pearl ear-rings - cream, white, pink and black - were of the screw on type and it bothered me, despite her assurances, that they were painful to wear. Of her several pieces of jewellery, a gold necklace made from the chain of her father's fob watch and a cameo brooch depicting the Three Graces were her favourites. Having chosen which piece of jewellery to wear, then it was the question of which hat - for like many of her peers Nana normally wore a hat and gloves to go out in. She favoured cloche type hats which looked extremely elegant on her. Although we often took the bus, Nana loved to walk, and she generally wore sensible shoes - not flat but always with a medium heel.

On Sunday we often went to St. Andrew's, the local parish church, where I can remember people turning round to stare as Nana let her wonderful contralto voice soar above that of the congregation. It always embarrassed me. Because she loved to sing so much we also tried other churches: Unitarian, Baptist and Methodist as well as the Salvation Army, just to get a variety of choral experiences. Nana frequently sang at charity concerts and enjoyed dressing up in her lovely evening gowns, long white gloves and soft mohair stoles. How I loved to watch her getting ready for these events.

As the years passed we rarely met, as my career and marriage took me away from Norfolk, where she lived. Nana continued with her knitting and made many garments for my children. Eventually she succumbed to Alzheimer's disease and became almost blind, deaf and unable to walk. She died at the age of ninety-three.

When I reflect on my memories of Nana, I realise how important she was in my childhood. She helped to shape my idea of the world and my outlook on life. Looking back I admire her fantastic energy and enthusiasm for life. She enjoyed company, entertaining and looking after people. My grandmother made me feel comfortable not only physically but also emotionally. Her legacy was to set me the example of how a grandmother should be. When my grandson told his mother "it is comfortable at Nana's house" I felt elated and as one with my own Nana.

The Young Years

Sue Mitchell

(Horsmonden)

I'm Sue Mitchell, 37, allegedly middle-aged, but very 'young at heart'. This is my first attempt at writing. I love singing and amateur dramatics. At home in Pembury, Kent, I have a menagerie of eight chickens, two guinea pigs, Catface the cat and a fantastic nine year old daughter.

Love is..... never telling an animal-loving child that you were once a butcher. I had always wondered why Young and Jim's only daughter, Jill, had a fear of birds and, particularly, feathers. I recently found out why. Jim had been a butcher for nearly all of his working life. At Christmas, the turkey carcasses would be hung up in Jim's workshop, and Jill fearfully had to battle through them if she needed to get anything from inside. Yet when I decided, aged 13, to become vegetarian, they never passed judgement. While sceptics, including my Mum, warned me I'd be ill, Young and Jim accepted my decision without question. And I never expected anything different from them.

My first childhood memories include Mum nipping five doors up the road every morning. She'd say, 'I'm just going along Youngs!' and would disappear for ten minutes. I had always assumed that Mrs Young, or Joy, was simply called 'Young'. I never thought it

was an unusual name and, although a little fun was made over my
misnomer, the name stuck and this wonderful couple were ever
after known as Young and Jim. Even when I speak to Jill now, she
refers to her Mum by this nickname. They dubbed me Tootsie, or
Toots for short.

Young was a willowy, bespectacled woman, with wispy, white curly
hair. I always remember her wearing a blue and white nylon
checked housecoat, which she only took off if she was going out,
or had company. Jim, always smiling, had balding grey hair, bushy,
dark eyebrows and tufts of hair on the end of his nose. He was
slightly shorter than Young. He always wore a shirt and trousers,
and a tie if he was going out. His sleeves were invariably rolled
up as Jim constantly had work to do. He had a pacemaker, which
could be seen sticking half an inch out of his chest: that always
intrigued me.

Living in the small hamlet of Colt's Hill, with no friends of my
own age, I spent many happy hours at Young's. Goodness knows
what my grandparents thought: they lived next door. I'd merrily
hop and skip up the road, past my Nanny and Granddad's house,
and into the welcoming garden of High View. There was nothing
particularly wrong with my grandparents, but they were almost
20 years older than the Youngs and, to me, nowhere near as much
fun. Even if I had started off at Nanny and Granddad's, I'd soon
be clambering through the hole in the privet hedge that had been
there since the war. I would run to the back door and barge in like
a whirlwind. Young and Jim were always pleased to see me and
whatever they were doing, there was always something for me to
'help' with. Young would let me polish the brass with Brasso, or
Jim might hand me a piece of kindling wood and a knife for me
to 'whittle' while he tinkered in his workshop, (no turkeys in there
by then). I have memories of countless jam jars, with their lids
screwed to the undersides of the shelves, containing various nails
and screws, and the pungent smell of engine oil coming from the
Jerry cans underneath. All the hand tools had their place, hung
orderly at the back of the workbench. Jim let me drill bits of wood,
held fast in the huge cast-iron vice on the bench. If he was toiling

in their well-ordered flower and vegetable garden, I'd happily help with the weeding, or have great fun playing with the 'woodies', or woodlice as they are more commonly known.

Inside the Youngs' cosy, modest bungalow, the Parkray fire was always lit. There was a real warmth in the living room and not just from the fire... I loved my cuddles with Jim. I remember being jogged on his knee, singing the 'Going for a ride on a horsey' nursery rhyme. This was affectionately coined our 'fun hour.'

Quite often, Young's widowed brother in law, Uncle Jack would be visiting. He was a portly, kind man with a beaming smile, who smelled of Old Spice. Usually, I'd be treated with a perfect cup of sweet tea from a china cup and saucer, accompanied by a digestive biscuit. As I got older, I graduated from serving out the biscuits and sugar from the sideboard (which now graces my living room) to actually making the tea. Well, pushing the button to dispense leaves from the automatic tea caddy on the wall, at least. I seem to remember I was never allowed to do such tasks at home; either that or I had no interest in doing them. I rarely ventured into other parts of the house. The front 'sitting room', which contained their best furniture, remained unused unless there were special house guests. I didn't like their bathroom much either... strong smells of Imperial Leather and scratchy Izal toilet paper were a distinct repellent.

I loved to hear stories of the olden days, including their friendship with my grandparents. Apparently, Granddad, a market gardener, was a bit of a joker. Young's other next door neighbour was rather less green-fingered, so Granddad thought it would be fun to tie a cucumber on to the old boy's plant. He was so excited to have found his fruit, he called out, 'I've got one, I've got one!' He didn't notice the piece of twine, still hanging from the cucumber, which Young deftly removed when she was inspecting the prized item. I suppose Jim must have been away at that time. He was stationed in Holland during the war, in the Army Catering Corps. Whenever he returned, he would bring sweets home for my mum. Once, he brought home a foot-long shell case, which had been elaborately engraved with the words, 'To Diane, From Holland.' Mum was obviously well-loved too.

I hardly ever remember Young or Jim being upset with me, but there was a rare occasion. One day, when I was about six, I found a pair of my sister's out-grown shoes in the wardrobe in our shared bedroom. The little mirrored cupboard contained (and still does) myriad memories. These beautifully shiny, brown leather shoes had been kept for hand-me-downs. I proudly donned them and ran joyfully along to Young's, to show them my find. Ever the show-off, but hardly sylph-like, I started performing my own special form of gymnastics on their living room floor. Young raised her voice: 'Be careful, Toots!' just as I fell awkwardly from a handstand. The heel of my sturdy shoe went straight through the glass door of their Parkray. I was utterly horrified. They had warned me to be careful, but I was so intent on impressing them, I'd made a complete fool of myself, not to mention causing them great expense. I couldn't bear the look of disappointment on their faces; I cried and cried, with head in hands. They never told my parents... that's love, I guess.

Reaching my teens, I spent far less time with my surrogate grandparents. Young and Jim now had their own grandchildren and I was less the centre of attention I craved. My real grandparents had passed away by the time I was nine. Mum passed her driving test (with Jim's help – he sat with her for years) so I was able to be ferried around to friends' houses and escape Colt's Hill. I'd also discovered music and would shut myself in my room for hours: listening, writing, singing. In 1990 I bought a moped on which I would ride to school. I used to keep it in Jim's workshop, so I'd see them daily, but only rarely stop for a chat. The fun hour was sadly becoming a distant memory.

Jim's health started to fail. He developed dementia, which was largely blamed on the shock of their being burgled – an unheard of crime in Colt's Hill. The Youngs were devastated, as I was for them. Jim started acting strangely soon after. One horrible day I received the news that Jim was in Pembury Hospital with an enlarged heart. I didn't understand the seriousness of his condition and was afraid to visit, not knowing how I'd find him, or even if he'd know me. So I left it and left it, until it was too late. Jim died in 1993 and I was heartbroken. I felt so guilty for not being there for him that I vowed I'd always be there when Young needed me.

Young coped admirably on her own: at 78 she was still quite sprightly and, having lived through two World Wars, certainly had a 'Keep Calm and Carry On' attitude. In the age of labour-saving devices, the nearest she got to owning a washing machine was a Baby Burco boiler and a spin drier. I carried on seeing her as regularly as possible, although by this time I had 'A' Level studies and a boyfriend to keep me busy. I now wonder if perhaps I was distancing myself to prepare for losing her, as I had been so hurt to lose Jim. Conversely, I fantasised about moving in with Young to look after her in her old age. I still kept my motorbike in the workshop, but by that time I had my own key, so I wouldn't disturb her if I came home late.

As time passed, Young lost interest in her personal appearance: her nails were dirty and the drip on the end of her nose made my eyes water. Sometimes, she would forget whether she'd had a meal. Young's health deteriorated over the years and she suffered several mini-strokes. After one fall too many, she was hospitalised. When I found out, at 10 p.m, I went straight to the hospital to be with her. The doctors discovered that she had osteoporosis and had broken her hip some years earlier. She had just carried on regardless: no wonder she hobbled about. Young was too ill to return to High View and was booked into a residential home. When Young died in March 2000, I was devastated.

My story doesn't quite end there though. In 2001, I was married and expecting a baby. Jill asked if I was interested in having High View, and, yes, I was desperate to buy the house that I'd had so many happy memories in. There was no way we could obtain a mortgage for the full price, but I had a plan. I persuaded Jill to rent the house to us while we amassed a deposit and then lend us some of the money to buy the house.

So, I found myself 12 weeks pregnant and moving into a new home. It was exhausting, but a dream come true. We busied ourselves with decorating and preparing for the new arrival. I had planned a home birth, but as my baby was two weeks overdue, the midwives insisted I was booked into the hospital for an induction, which was incredibly disappointing. However a beautiful daughter, Tegan Verity, was finally born to overjoyed parents in May 2002. I discovered a wholly different, exciting new chapter in my life developing at High View and hoped to recreate the happy home that I'd experienced there. I still had many mementoes of the Young years though: the wooden electric clock on the mantelpiece; pictures on the walls; even the sofa from their sitting room ensured that Young and Jim were still a part of my life. I felt them watching over me and hoped I'd made them proud.

I really wish that Tegan could have met Young and Jim. Very fond memories of my rôle models live vividly on. Often, when I have a dilemma, I ask myself what they would think or tell me to do. Even though they are no longer with us in body, their spirit will never leave me.

Ripples

Cynthia Kirk

(Horsmonden)

I am an advisory language teacher who has relished the opportunity of developing my writing skills. Apart from reading (and now writing), I enjoy playing the piano (Mozart to Van Morrison), the company of my partner and adult children, and walking in the Kent countryside with my dog.

D ear Neil

You are the brother who died before I was born, so it may seem strange that I'm writing this letter to you. There is so much I'd like to know about you and the events which took place on June 12th 1949, when, according to your tombstone you 'Died suddenly aged 15'. I know some of the story of how you came to drown in the River Cherwell, but it didn't end there. Your struggles from the river's murky depths caused ripples which have disturbed the lives of our family ever since.

I am writing this on the 62nd anniversary of that Sunday. It is cold and threatening to rain, so very different from that scorching hot day. Mum would have given anything for the weather then to have been like today, as events would have turned out very differently.

What were things like for you on that day? I expect it started like any other, with you feeding the chickens in the makeshift shed which Dad constructed out of corrugated iron and chicken wire. Maybe you fed them Mum's pungent mixture of boiled potato peelings mixed with bran which they would gobble up. Keeping chickens was a throwback to Mum's childhood on the family small-holding in Wales, but unusual in the garden of a semi-detached council house on the outskirts of Oxford. As a child I never tired of watching them, and when they clucked at each other I'd fondly imagine that they were talking to me. I gave them names and it was unbearable when eventually they were served up for Sunday dinner. I would mutinously refuse to eat them, but to no avail.

Sunday mornings usually meant going to the old village church. With its impressive square tower of Cotswold stone it remains a solid and dependable presence at the heart of the old village and another link with you. You were the cross bearer in pristine white robes solemnly leading the procession of brightly clad clerics at the beginning and end of services. Was it daunting or did you enjoy the sense of drama and expectation you created?

After Church there would be Sunday lunch. Did you have a roast dinner on that last day and, like me, did you have jobs to do like shelling the peas or broad beans? My favourite job was making the mint sauce to go with mum's delicious roast lamb. I loved the refreshing aroma produced by the mint leaves when I picked them, but chopping them up was tricky. After adding sugar and putting it into a little jar with some vinegar, I would proudly place it on the table.

Or maybe, because it was such a hot day you had salad with a mountain of crispy lettuce from Dad's allotment. Did you, like me, inspect each mouthful carefully before you ate it, just in case one of the little, anaemic-looking slugs had survived being washed and was hiding amongst the leaves? There would be the occasional slice of tomato and cucumber as well, but not much as these had to be bought.

Maybe you had rhubarb crumble and custard for pudding. Making the custard was another of my jobs. There was always the anxiety of whether the custard would thicken or 'turn' as Mum would put it, when adding the hot milk to the custard powder and sugar mixture. I got the proportions wrong on many occasions and the custard obstinately remained thin no matter how much I stirred it.

Much of what we ate came from Dad's allotment and the taste of those home-grown vegetables has never been surpassed. It was a refuge for him and he took great pride in tending it. But it was going to Dad's allotment on that fateful day which started the chain of events which was to end in such a tragic way. Dad wanted you to help him – probably grumbling that you never did. I expect Mum stuck up for you, but you went to keep the peace. It was a bone of contention between them ever after because if you hadn't gone to the allotment you wouldn't have bumped into your friends and been persuaded to go to the river with them.

I expect you really wanted to go as it was so hot, but Mum said 'no' at first. You pleaded with her and she gave in; a decision she was to regret for the rest of her life. After that she'd never change her mind about any decision, especially if we begged her, like you'd done. Once I was desperate to go to an outdoor activity centre where there was canoeing, but knowing the dangers of a river, Mum wouldn't let me go. I railed against her decision, but it made no difference – the more I pleaded the more adamant she was that I would not go.

So you went off on your bike and that was the last Mum saw of you. I can imagine her standing at the gate and waving you off – watching you out of sight – something she never did when any of us left the house after that. There were also other things which we couldn't do because Mum felt, in some strange way, that they'd contributed to the events of that day. Once I picked some fragrant sprigs of lilac blossom for her, expecting her to be pleased. Instead she was devastated telling me to 'take those out of here – they're bad luck.' I felt crushed and she explained that you'd brought her some lilac not long before you died. Strange that we did the same thing, but it brought back disturbing memories for Mum.

Mum thought you were only going to the local 'brook' to play with your friend's dinghy. Why did you decide to go further? Was it because the brook was hardly deep enough for a dinghy? Cycling the few miles to the beauty spot on the Cherwell was much more appealing. On that scorching June afternoon it would have appeared a quiet, peaceful and lazy river and there were so many people enjoying the sun and the water. You must have had a great time messing about on the river, but why oh why did you stay behind on your own to have a swim, and why on earth did your friends leave you?

It was many years before Mum was able to visit that place. I remember coming home from school once and finding her very upset because she had walked to see it. She had been overcome by the menace of the river. She said 'I never knew it was like that - if only I'd known.' I think she always blamed herself for allowing you to go.

I know you wanted to practice for the school swimming gala. Why was that so important? Having spent the war years evacuated to a village in Wales, you didn't have the opportunity to swim, so were you worried about being shown up? I suppose it was important for you to make a good impression at school. Slipping into the cool water when it was so swelteringly hot must have been delightful and you never thought of the dangers. It seems incredible that no-one heard your struggles as you were lost to us for ever.

When you didn't come home and Dad discovered your friends had already returned, a night of unimaginable anguish ensued. They searched everywhere desperately hoping that you would turn up at any moment. Next day your clothes were found by the bank and later your body was discovered entangled in the weeds. That was when Mum felt her life had ended. She used to say 'I wondered how the world could carry on turning.' But she did carry on for the sake of our sister Maggs and your baby brother who was born four months later - another son to help alleviate the terrible ache of losing you, though nothing could really do that.

We didn't talk about you very much, not because you were forgotten, but because it was too painful. Mum often looked wistful and we knew she was thinking about some event which involved you. She'd get upset at any reminder of you. Dad never talked about you. Maggs couldn't show how upset she felt because she didn't want to add to Mum's distress, so she kept her feelings locked away, and to a lesser degree we all did the same.

Mum kept many of your things in her chest of drawers and I was told firmly 'not to go in there.' I felt resentful and frustrated because I wanted to know you and share things which had been yours, but they were too precious. Later, when I felt brave enough, I did go in the drawer and found your old postbox money-box. I even slid a knife through the slots to extricate some of the money – mostly old pennies which lay cold and heavy in my hand. Strange to think that you had put them in there and I had taken them out. What were you saving for? Your old school books were also in there. To a little girl, they seemed strange treasures to hide away from prying eyes.

Even though we didn't talk about you, your presence loomed large in my life. Your photo hanging on the wall in Mum's bedroom was a constant reminder. It came from your last team photo and it only shows your head and shoulders. You seem to be surrounded by a hazy mist and I thought this added to your mystery. You smiled down at me all through my childhood and I used to stare back at you. Looking at you now, I see a diffident youth on the verge of manhood, with a thick mop of dark hair and the strong chin we all inherited from Mum.

I used to go to the cemetery with Mum, although I didn't enjoy these trips, as she became very distant as she busied herself tidying your grave. I felt excluded and would wander round aimlessly looking at other graves with strict instructions not to step on any of them. I read about the people buried there and read your inscription too, 'Blest are the pure in heart' and wondered about having such a perfect brother. I felt very naughty in comparison. Fetching the water in a little tin watering can was the highlight of my visits there.

We have some things in common - a brown mole on the side of our tummies - Mum would look wistfully at mine sometimes. We nearly shared the same birthday – yours is only two days before mine. In fact, when the doctors wanted to induce Mum because of her high blood pressure, she asked them to wait as she didn't want us to be born on the same day. I don't think Mum felt very much like celebrating my birthday as it was so close after yours, but she always made an effort and made a sponge cake with butter icing which she would decorate by running a fork through the icing to make wavy patterns.

Your death at 15 was such a tragic waste. Mum tried to make sense of it by saying that you were 'too good for this world'. I know that the people who are left behind often believe 'only the good die young'. Maybe this is the case or perhaps they only remember the good bits. It seems to me that you were a victim of circumstance – a lethal combination of events which came together on that fateful day with such dreadful consequences.

I hope you don't mind me sharing all these experiences with you and asking all these questions. Even though I never knew you I've always felt an affinity with you and wish so much that things could have turned out differently.

Your Loving Sister
Cynthia

The Birthday Card

Christine Churchill

(Horsmonden)

Describe me in 50 words I said to my husband. What a mistake. I always knew he should wear glasses. I love my family, friends and a chilled wine. I can't say 'No', and end up joining all sorts of activities, often way beyond my physical and mental capabilities.

My Nana, Evelyn, had a birthday card from the Queen last year.

Nana attended a family birthday tea held in her honour. She smiled politely and laughed when we read her the cards and good wishes. Gradually you could see the confusion in her face as she shed a few tears and decided she wanted to be wheeled back into the lounge of the nursing home. She really didn't know who many of us were.

This was a heart-breaking moment for me, as I found it hard to comprehend how this woman, my Nana, who had given me so many happy childhood memories, had really no idea who I was anymore.

I was the eldest of four grandchildren for Evelyn and Les, and the only girl. My Dad and his brother sound as if they were extremely boisterous as boys, and when I came along, I believe, I was greeted with delight.

With a big age gap between me and the other grandchildren I did not have to share Nana with anyone else for a very long time. She was a slim, tanned woman who when indoors, always wore a half apron or a housecoat. She wore, I remember, plain, rough-feeling nylons (even when working on the allotment) and she certainly never wore trousers.

She was only 47 when I was born, younger than I am now, but her clothes were typical of the 60's and often home-made. Little make-up other than a dab of powder and a touch of lipstick, and her hankie was always folded under her gold expandable watch strap.

Her favourite hobbies were gardening, the allotment, preserves and knitting. So this is where my happy memories begin as she involved me with her activities when she used to look after me.

Mayfield Road, where we lived, backed onto the allotments where Granddad and Nana had a plot. Before they had a car they would walk from their house, a good 30 minutes, past my home, to take me with them to the allotment. I loved it there. I was given such freedom, though looking back on it; I was probably an absolute nuisance and was therefore given tasks that took me ages to complete. One task I adored was to go back and forth with a watering can to an old cast iron bath that was filled to the brim with sludgy rain water. I remember the delight of swirling all the green slime with my arm before I dipped the watering can in. The watering can would become so heavy I would drop it in the bath and have to search around to find it. Once found, I had to heave the can out and it would invariably spill all over my brown Clark's sandals and white ankle socks. I would then splash back to the patch of allotment that my grandparents were working on with of course a half-empty watering can.

Nana was never ever cross with me. She would laugh, take off my sandals and socks and then I would repeat the whole process all over again but completely bare-footed. Why I wonder did I never take my sandals and socks off in the first place?

I can't pass strawberries, blackberries, blackcurrants, raspberries or any soft fruit in a shop without thinking of Nana. She would grow the juiciest and sweetest of fruits and I was only allowed to sample a few as they were hurriedly taken home, destined for the preserving pan. However much you begged for just one more strawberry, you knew that they were destined for the jam jar. This was obviously the mentality of having to live through a war. She certainly would have got through another war as the back bedroom in their house contained a wardrobe with shelves groaning with pickles, salted runner beans and the jams made of all those berries. She would have swept the board in a WI competition.

I do know that she was a regular winner at the annual Thornton Heath Flower and Produce Shows held every September. I have some memories of how she would carefully place the required number of Gladioli, Chrysanthemums or Asters in vases. She would arrange and rearrange flower displays. Then in the orderly manner required by the rules place her beans, onions, potatoes, and carrots neatly on the trestle tables. Then of course there were the jams and her wonderful cakes, which often won prizes. She must have spent ages cooking and preparing for this event.

I recently had to make one quiche as part of a village competition, and in the fright of letting my friends down made several before the big day, as well as getting up extremely early to make a fresh one for competition day. In fact I sat looking at the cooker for 45 minutes in case I burnt it. I have also made jams and pickles like Nana, but never year after year as superbly or as seemingly effortlessly as she did.

I was so proud of Nan when we would go back after lunch to see where she had come in the competition and collect her prize money. This was just a mere fraction of what the event must of cost her to enter.

Spring is here and the Camellia is looking splendid in the garden.

Good job I bought the right soil to feed it through the harsh winter we have just had. I feel so proud it is still doing well with me. In Nana's back garden in a large pot she had a beautiful pink Camellia that she had probably grown from a cutting. When Nan had to go into the nursing home I took the Camellia home to live with us. I always take a couple of the flowers to her and try and explain that her Camellia is still going strong. I don't know if she understands what I'm saying, but she always smiles and thanks me. To me it signifies the end of the dreary winter and the start of warmer weather to come. Funnily enough Nana gave Keith and me some gooseberry bushes for a plot in our garden just after we got married. I had a baby nine months after that.

Both my birthday in August and Christmas used to mean one thing - knitted jumper time. For both these celebratory events those immortal words "hold your arms out" meant time for a measure-up. Nana would see how much more puppy fat I had on me or if I had grown, and would take the new measurements for my cardigan or jumper or even a trendy tank top. Of course the tank top never looked like the one in the Jackie teenage magazine. That would have been made from 100% acrylic in a factory. I had one made from 100% wool from a pattern that was for a sleeveless cricket top. However hard I tried to think otherwise, it was just not a tank top.

After the ritual of the measuring - which would be noted on a Woolworths pad of lined paper - it was the choice of colour. Again, there never really was a choice of colour, as it would be the colour available at the best price from the wool shop. Even my school jumpers, which of course were considered as a birthday or Christmas present, never quite were the blue everyone else seemed to have from a shop. I remember dark brown was a popular colour choice as a casual wear jumper, as was emerald. Neither colour does a lot for me now, and as a child with puppy fat I must have looked like a sausage or nuclear disaster.

The knitting went on earnestly. The August birthday meant a very quick turnaround for the Christmas surprise jumper. The wool would come in skeins which Nan and I would wind into balls. She would patiently sit in the winged chair holding the skein while I would run around the room supposedly making a ball. But we would end up playing Cowboys and Indians and I would tie her to the chair with the wool. I hasten to add that I did not do this when I was older and wanting the trendy tank top.

The wool would have been in such a knot, but she would laugh - probably through gritted teeth - and we would stop the game and have a cup of tea and a piece of home-made flapjack. Added to all this mayhem would be Nana's dog, Chum, who would also get tangled up in the wool and pull it all over the room.

I bet Nana was pleased when it was my bedtime, but that was such fun too. She would fill the bath up so deep I remember thinking I could swim. It always had scented bath salts in it that scratched your bottom if they hadn't dissolved properly. I was allowed to slide up and down the bath causing a mini tsunami all over the place. Nana seemed to enjoy it as much as I did.

Out of the bath and time for bed. Nana had a big double bed in her spare room which seemed to be extremely high, and it had crisp white sheets with many blankets and then an eiderdown on it. I remember feeling so tiny in this huge bed. It would of course have had a hot water bottle put in it which you had to find with your feet to keep warm. The only company you had in this room were the hundreds of jars of pickles and jams. But there was a game to be had in here too. Nan would tuck me in one side and as soon as she went to the other side of the bed I would untuck the side she had just done. This game seemed to go on for ages while we both laughed and laughed. She must have been near to hysteria with me by now. It was a good job I used to fall straight to sleep. I suspect she did too.

I had a phone call this morning. An unknown voice said "Evelyn Warne passed away at 11.20. You were named as next of kin to contact as your parents were away."

What could I say? All the family knew it was imminent. She had been 101 years old and her body had had enough. But it was still a shock, and I am disappointed that I had not finished my memoir of our time together because I had wanted to read it to her.

In any case, at the end of your life, my lovely Nana, I was the first to know that you had died. I feel privileged that it was me.

Fraulein Goldstein

Iris Roberts

(Handbridge)

*Since joining the WI in 1963 I have lived with my
husband and children in Lancashire,
Gloucestershire, Berkshire and now Cheshire.
In each place I joined the WI (six in all). I have
made many friends, been on committees, laughed
a lot, learned a lot, attended area and national
meetings and studied at Denman College. Great.*

In 1946, at the age of 10, I became a pupil at Stand Grammar
School for Girls at Whitefield, North Manchester. Three other
girls in my form had passed the 11-plus examination a year early
and from the first day we were known as "the four of you" and
treated differently from our classmates.

A few months after we started we were summoned to the office of
the headmistress, Miss Grace Lobjoit, and informed by her that
we were to begin to study our second foreign language earlier than
usual. A new language tutor would arrive the following week and
the four of us would be her only pupils because she had been very
seriously ill, was far from fully recovered and needed lots of rest.

At Monday morning's assembly, the head announced that a
new tutor would arrive later that morning and added that any

309

girl seen to be staring at her or discussing her would be expelled immediately. It was therefore with some trepidation that we waited in the designated classroom for the arrival of Fraulein Goldstein.

After a short time there was a knock on the door and in walked a skeleton with women's clothes hanging from it – a skeleton covered with wrinkled, dark grey and sallow yellow skin and with hardly any flesh between the skin and bone. On the skull were small, sparse clumps of very short hair, indeterminate of colour. She could have been 20 or 70 years old, there was no way of telling.

This was Fraulein Goldstein – charming, courteous, patience personified, highly intelligent and obviously well-educated. She was always interested in our lives outside school, our families, holidays, etc. but never spoke of hers. In time, we gradually learned that by the end of the war all her immediate and extended family were dead, and then to her great joy she had discovered that one brother had survived and been shipped to America at the end of the war. They corresponded regularly and she was so happy when she received one of his letters.

After a time, she began to smile a little and even, occasionally to laugh – a short, strange sound which seemed to surprise her as much as it surprised us. Despite her outward appearance she obviously must have had immense inner strength and courage to carry on when she thought she had lost all her family and was alone in a foreign land. We greatly admired her for that.

Fraulein Goldstein taught the four of us all through our school years, adding Spanish to our French and German lessons. Other subjects we studied with the rest of our form mates. She gradually put on a tiny amount of weight but always felt cold and wore ankle socks over her stockings all the year round. Her hair slowly grew and was short and grey. We estimated from the snippets she told us about herself that she was in her mid twenties when we first met.

Over the years, conversing regularly and very easily chatting together, the words "concentration camp " and "Jew" were never spoken. We left school in 1953 and on our final day, Fraulein Goldstein gave each of the four of us an envelope full of American postage stamps, carefully cut from the envelopes containing the precious letters from her beloved brother. They had still not met since the start of the war in 1939, fourteen years previously.

I do not know if or when she and her brother were reunited.

Homage To My Invisible Father

Lis Neighbour

(Marlow Bottom)

*I left my home country at 18, never to return on
a permanent basis – when you live in a foreign
environment you are no longer reminded about
your past in your daily life and it slips away.
These memoirs have helped to minimise my guilt
for so carelessly letting my father slip away –
unremembered.*

I am 10 years and two days old - the year is October 1947 and
it is a Saturday - I am playing in a side street off our own road,
Rugaardsvej, with some of the children from the apartment blocks.
An ambulance's siren sounds and for a minute I wonder who it has
come for – then I carry on playing and running around the block.
At home my father has been unwell in bed for a couple of days, but
then that happens now and again, so that does not worry me. As it
is, however I should have worried, because that ambulance causes my
father to disappear in body as well as in my mind.

When I later get home my big sister tells me that father has had a
heart attack and won't be coming back home. "So when mother
returns from hospital, we must be brave and help her by not crying."
I cannot recall crying but I have one memory of standing with
mother, holding her hand, whilst people move past us talking to
her and pitying us. It is as vague as a dream and I have a sense of

313

being oblivious to what is going on. I feel however the place is the cemetery where we often go later. I have no memory of missing him or being sad and crying. Father could not have been a remote parent to me, he worked from home and I spent ten years with him day in and day out. I am told that two days before he died, at my 10th birthday party I sat between his knees whilst playing games with my friends – however I cannot picture it in my mind. Father was gone and that was that!

My father only lived for 47 years and 10 days but when he died the doctor is supposed to have told my mother that his heart was like an old man's heart. He was born with a concave chest cage, maybe due to rickets whilst in the womb and/or women's fashion in those days for narrow waists. It was said that one could lay a fist in the hollow of his chest, which meant that there was not enough room for the internal organs. This caused him to suffer from breathlessness and bouts of bronchitis all his life, which must have sapped a lot of his strength – he was handicapped. According to Mother he often 'admired the views', on their evening strolls, rather than admit fatigue. It is therefore even more of a wonder to me that he managed to start and build up a business from scratch. Everything he undertook must have needed more effort than a healthy person required.

Everything about him is erased from my memory like he never existed and however much I try I cannot bring him back. If a 'picture' of father pops up, I soon wonder if it is a 'real' memory of mine, I question if it is something somebody told to me or a picture I have seen somewhere. It is a great shame because what I have learned in later life from my mother and sister makes me feel that he and I are very alike. Mother, my sister and I carried on living in the factory environment after his death as mother kept the business going for 5 more years. Perhaps through his achievements I can bring forward a picture of him.

Father lived in Odense in Denmark – the fairytale teller Hans Andersen's town – and this is my very different fairy tale! Initially he made soap in the backyard of an apartment building in town, with the help of his father and brother; however his younger brother, single and in good health, left for grander schemes. Then in 1930, with a four year old daughter and a wife, my father decides to take out a bank loan in order to purchase a plot of land from a farm on the outskirts of Odense. Here he has a house built with a low factory extension at the back, cellar rooms underneath plus a low office building on one side, intended as an office. In order that he can accrue a little income, the upstairs is designed as a self contained flat, although the bathroom has to be shared as there is only a toilet downstairs! A photograph showing him in the drive by a shining new gate and sign with 'Odense Soap Factory' clearly tells me of his pride in this achievement. At that time most businesses were small and people's expectations simpler; however, it still seems to me a brave undertaking given that he had a wife and child to support and was not in the best of health.

He started small with probably only one person helping him with the manufacturing. Mother helped him with his accounts and office work whilst looking after home and child, but later on she had a local girl to help her in the house. Then one day, seven years later in 1937, I arrive – unexpected and not asked for, quite a disaster in fact, eleven years between children and still with tenants upstairs. However, they survive and at some stage later they take over the whole house; by then father has two men working for him, a lady in the office, a car in the garage and a maid. Like an 'Avon Calling', father went into the country visiting farms and shops taking orders for his soaps, soapflakes, creams, lotions, toothpaste & Vaseline. He would usually overnight a couple of nights and then come back with the orders, make them up and deliver them again - all in a little Ford Junior. He probably also used the railway as there was a small line near our house.

In the private part of the house father had a small room which he used as his office when he was a little unwell and didn't want to go into the factory. He was able to communicate with his men through a square hole in the floor by his desk – neatly finished off and with a lid for when it was not needed. Some years later he would acquire a couple of great big internal telephones. These worked by turning a handle to crank them up. The factory to the back had three rooms;

here the soap manufacturing took place. There was a big cauldron in which they made the raw soap; they would stand and stir this 'porridge' with great big wooden sticks and test the consistency by placing it on the tongue. When cooled it would go into a machine where it would be pressed into a long rectangular rod, which came sliding out on a rail. This would then be cut into long sticks and stacked for the next processes. Some would be pressed into bars of soap and others grated into soapflakes for washing clothes. Back then it was mostly soapflakes but he did also produce some washing powder which he called 'Snowwhite'. For me it was exciting to go into the factory; on soap making days there was a real sense of danger in the room where the cauldron was. The floor would be wet and slippery and the soap making materials all around; however, on those days I was not allowed to enter, only to open the huge iron sliding doors and pass on a message for the men. When the grating was taking place in the other room soap filled the air, getting in your throat, but I particularly liked to see the bar of soap being pressed into being – especially when they were making the one that bore my name - Lisa! Not everyone can boast a bar of soap named after them – my claim to fame!

All over the factory there were machinery and gadgets tucked into corners; father would make most things himself. He would have a guillotine to cut the cardboard for boxes, a machine would dent the cardboard so it could be bent into shape and finally a foot operated machine would fix corner staples to secure the box and its lid. He did a lot of his printing himself and his setter's box with all the rubber letters and numbers was of great interest to me. He learned how to make lotions and creams with help of a big industrial recipe book and one of these, a 'barley milk lotion', was very successful. When a nurse praised it he asked her permission to quote her comments on advertising material and even made her a kind of trademark by having a clay bust made of a nurse in Florence Nightingale uniform! On the bust was an inscription: 'The best soap for adults and children' signed 'Cosmetic Laboratory Odense' - i.e. the upstairs kitchen! He bought Vaseline in bulk and filled it into little tiny tins and toothpaste into tubes. They were simple products and simple ways but the times were different and people not so demanding. He had the ideas and had a go.

There was an office building attached to the side of the house, where he and his typist would sit at either end of a long desk, and here he would receive any visitors. In the yard there would be containers of all shapes and sizes, some made of glass with protective metal cages, containing all the raw materials. Two garages were also there, a bike shed and in the autumn the world's most delicious pears growing up against the house. In this yard I would play, sometimes with friends, within reach of dangerous substances, and in the summer father and mother would spend the lunch break in deck chairs quite happily without any worry about Health & Safety issues. How innocent they were. Sometimes through the years we owned dogs, another time pigeons in the top roof, also about a score of canaries housed in a large cage built into one of the factory windows. At one time there was also a sandpit for me to play in.

Father was fortunate in having enough intelligence to set up his own work environment, where he could incorporate his 'off' days. Self employment suited his ill health and he had enough enthusiasm to give him the energy for it. I do wish I could remember him. Why did a ten year old forget a person so dear to her? I think children's overriding need to be happy causes them to push away events that are too traumatic, a kind of safeguard they have - they bury it. That is what I must have done, so well that I could not dig it back up again. You can imagine my dismay and disbelief when fifty six years later my son-in-law dies, leaving his 10 year old daughter and 12 year old son. Will it happen again, will they opt for safety and bury their past to stop the sorrow? History seems to be repeating itself.

Today, eight years on, I can still hear my granddaughter saying: "I don't want to talk about it, it is hurting so much in here," touching her chest. I pray that with my daughter's knowledge of my dilemma my grandchildren have been able to hold on to their memories.

The Biggest Hug

Evelyn Carter

(Marlow Bottom)

*I was born in 1941 in Berlin and, after completing a
Business Course, came to England as an au pair and
never left. I raised a family and worked with and
for various community groups, for single mothers,
disabled income groups and deaf young people. I
also organised a year's sabbatical, travelling to the
Far East alone to get under the skin of yet other
cultures. I retired 11 years ago.*

I went to the Royal British Legion in Marlow, feeling a bit like a
stranger - and came away with the biggest hug ever in my life.

But I am getting ahead of myself. It all started a long time ago.
"Mummy, I am sooo hungry. Can I have a 'Brotchen'?" I am
seven years old and have not eaten all day.

"You go out and play for a little while and when I come back we
will have a nice sandwich, yes?" came the cheerful reply.

So I did.

The roar in the sky becomes louder and louder. I drop the ball I
have been knocking against the wall and look up. Here it comes: a

319

massive, menacing looking plane, barely avoiding the roof tops as it quickly disappears in the distance.

I pick up the ball.

Here comes another one, just as huge and scary looking and flying in the same direction. And another one - followed by yet another one.

This time I don't stop playing. I have seen it all before.

It is 1948 and Berlin has been decimated by the war. At the end of WWII the Allies divided Berlin into four zones: the British, French, American and Russian zone - all surrounded by the Soviet Union. Berlin had become an island. Borders were strictly patrolled and movements between zones virtually impossible. Life had been tough, but it was just about to get even tougher.

Russia wanted to take control of Germany and in June of that year decided to block all transport into the city by road, rail or waterways. Like any city, Berlin needed a constant supply of food, medicine and fuel, plus industrial materials, to function. Even the electricity was cut off. This was obviously designed to force the three Allies into submission as Berlin had only enough supplies to survive for 36 days. (I was starving like the rest of the population and still remember foraging through the scraps of our land-lady's bin for potato-peelings. Mother scrubbed them clean and made a rather watery potato soup. Better than nothing.) But, survive we did, all 3 million of us, in spite of the fact that the 'Blockade', as it was called, lasted an unbelievable 11 months.

I guess it must have had something to do with the strange food we had. Soups and stews were made with dried, chopped-up vegetables which needed to be soaked for a long time. To me they tasted delicious. As I munched away I was rather intrigued by the precisely diced vegetables and when Mum was not looking would try and build little houses with them. Even today when I have Scotch Broth I am reminded of the vegetables all those years ago, but I no longer play with them.

320

Meat - such as it was - came out of tins. I don't know how mother managed but it certainly tasted "good enough to eat". Of course, the fact that we were rather hungry must have had something to do with it.

We did not have many fresh eggs, but the egg-powder was just fine for baking and scrambled eggs. But, the best was the dried milk powder. Many a time I crept into the larder and helped myself to a spoonful, just as it was, straight from the bag. It tasted rather sweet and when we mixed it with water to make it into a drink, it was so much better than the watered down milk we had during the war.

There was one thing I could not understand for many years. Who was sending those little white handkerchief parachutes, with chocolate bars and bon-bons attached, down from the sky for the children? Did I imagine it all? Was it a dream which seemed so real to me with the passage of time that I could even taste the sweetness of the fruit-drops with the 'hole in the middle'?

One day, when there was a rather large crowd celebrating in the street, I asked my mother if it was because of her birthday. "No," she laughed, "something much, much better. Today they lifted the Blockade." I did not really know what that meant, but I joined the brass-band which appeared from nowhere, sung my little heart out and danced in the street like everybody else. I was even allowed to wear my one and only best dress, a 'dirndl', which had been extended top and bottom for many years to accommodate my growing body.

Things became normal after that and I eventually started school, still wearing THAT dirndl as we did not have school uniforms. We carried on with our daily lives the best we could. The help and support the three Allies had given formed the topic of conversation for many years to come. I learned a little more each time and realised, over the years, how the British, American and French people enabled us to survive through the 'Airlift' against all the odds.

So it probably comes as no surprise that I felt the need to attend a talk, given at the Royal British Legion two years ago, entitled:

"The Berlin Blockade 1948". The Speaker was a British pilot who flew supplies into Berlin all those years ago. He was now 86 years old, and when he explained that the planes, on a good day, landed every 90 seconds, it brought it all back to me as if it was yesterday. I could actually see and hear the roar of the planes again and sat enthralled, listening with great interest as he filled in so many missing pieces.

I learned that there had been no agreement on ground routes when WW2 had ended, but there was a signed document that there would be three 20 mile-wide air-corridors giving free access into Berlin. And this provided the Allies with an opportunity: ".....to fly-in much needed supplies through the 'Airlift', right down to the materials needed for the production of light-bulbs," the Pilot said with much pride in his voice.

When he mentioned that even the children had been catered for, I could hardly contain myself and my ears pricked up as he explained: "Gail Halverson, one of the many pilots, was making a film about the Airlift and met some children at the end of the runway. The children asked lots of questions about the aircraft and their flights, and, as a goodwill gesture, Gail handed out his last two sticks of Wrigley's Gum and promised that, if they did not fight over it, he would return and drop off more. One child ask him "How will we know it is you?" He replied "I will wiggle my wings."

The next day, on his approach to Berlin, he rocked the aircraft and dropped some chocolate bars attached to handkerchief parachutes to the children waiting below. "Hier kommt der Rosinenbomber" cried the children and ran to collect the booty. (Now that I could REALLY relate to) "In time other pilots also got involved and when news reached the USA children all over the country sent their own candy to help out. Soon major manufactures joined in. In the end over three tons of candy were dropped in Berlin."

The smile on my face grew wider and wider. It was true, I had not imagined it. And what a great story.

He also explained that nearly 700 aircraft were engaged in the Berlin Airlift and that the cost of the operation was approximately £4 billion by today's value.

Sadly some pilots lost their lives as they were being attacked whilst flying over "enemy territory" but all those involved were determined not to give up. It goes without saying that the Berliners have been eternally grateful to the Allies and several memorials which have been erected in the city testify to that.

One member in the audience that evening asked "Did the Germans ever appreciate what you have done for them?" I was pleased when the speaker replied: "Yes, very much so. We have been invited to several functions over the years in recognition of our contribution."

And this is when I finally was able to put up my hand and say: "I was seven years old at the time and I was there...... and I have come here tonight to thank you personally for keeping me and my family alive.......and I can assure you, we NEVER forgot what you did for us".

It was not the applause from the audience which took me by surprise, but the reaction from the pilot. He came bounding over to me and said with deep emotion in his voice, "You have made my day."

And that's when I received the biggest hug ever in my life from a stranger.

Ghost In The Rubble

Pat Morrison

(Market Lavington and Easterton)

After many years as an itinerant naval wife, mother and teacher, I settled in Wiltshire. Four years ago, the children having flown the nest, I retired and started the next phase of my life. I learned to sail, took up the flute and started to write. Who knows what comes next?

Outrageous. They are going to demolish my old school. I haven't been back inside it for over 45 years. In fact I only see it once a year now, on my visits north. But there it is, a squat red brick hexagon surrounding an inner courtyard with imposing red wooden double doors on its front façade and long, narrow windows at regular intervals all the way round. These days it is surrounded by tall, rectangular glass and concrete blocks in various stages of decay, like a brood of scruffy, lanky teenagers gathered round a dowdy mother. They are going to pull it down to build a smart new academy but, captured inside that old ugly building is my young self in the years between 11 and 16, the people I knew, the lessons I learned – both literally and emotionally. I drive past, wave to my young self and salute the teachers who, in many ways, formed so much of what I am today. I need to rescue some of those memories before they disappear, buried in a pile of builder's rubble.

The school was a short bus ride from my home in an area
of Lancashire nestled between Manchester and Liverpool.
Surrounded by coal mines and cotton mills, it was typical of many
schools built in that area between the 1930s and 1940s. Having
failed 'the scholarship' I was expected to disappear through the red
doors to emerge at 15 equipped to work in a factory, a shop or an
office, depending on my performance in the Leaving Certificate.
Most of all, I was being prepared to become an efficient housewife.
There was no inkling of ideas about careers, only 'jobs'. What
I didn't know in 1958 at the age of 11, was that I was about to
become part of a social experiment.

The school was about to establish a voluntary fifth form, where
pupils might elect to stay on and take GCE exams if their Leaving
Certificate results were good enough. The result in my first
two years in the school was an influx of bright, ambitious, and
politically motivated young teachers. They were on a mission, anti
the 11-plus and out to make a point.

There were about 400 pupils in the school. The boys who were,
shall we say, not academic, knew there was plenty of work for
them as they followed their fathers into the pits or the factories
or, in some cases into farming. Big, amiable lads, they spent most
of their time tending the school's chickens or learning practical
skills in woodwork. Oddly enough, the only one of my school
contemporaries to come close to being a millionaire was one of
them. He was blonde, always full of jokes, and I don't think I ever
saw him break into anything more than a gentle amble. He went
into the scrap metal business on leaving school and now lives in a
lovely house with sheep grazing on his extensive lawns so that no
one has to be bothered to cut the grass. Not academic maybe, but
not, I think, stupid either.

However, the wind of change was already blowing. Many of the
old teachers were retiring and the new Headmaster had plans
which were gradually being implemented. This gentle wind
continued to blow as new staff arrived, until, at the end of my
second year, a hurricane hit the school. The name of the hurricane
was Miss Jones.

Marion Jones was the only daughter of a Welshman who had
lost his way out of the valleys and found himself in Lancashire.
Politically active in the Labour Party and the Trade Union
Movement, he and his wife gave birth to a firebrand who was
determined to change the world, starting with our Secondary
Modern School. Marion was clever, and on leaving school went to
Cambridge where she studied English. She was also heavily into
student politics. At 21, instead of entering academia or a genteel
Grammar School, she returned to live with her parents and became
a probationary teacher at her local Secondary Modern School.
She also became a major influence on my life and that of many
of my contemporaries. Miss Jean Brodie would have paled in
comparison.

At five feet two inches Miss Jones was smaller than many of her
students. This was no problem to her. It was not unusual to see
whole classes of tall, adolescent boys shuffling uneasily from one
foot to the other as they lined up outside a classroom to suffer a
tongue-lashing from a small, articulate and angry virago for some
misdemeanor or other. I remember one boy saying "I'd rather have
the cane than two minutes of her temper."

However, once she had established that she was not to be messed
with, her lessons were inspirational and fun. She was young and
pretty and not above flirting chastely with the boys, who hardly
knew what had hit them. At the same time she had the knack of
making the girls feel that she was on their side. We worshipped at
her feet and longed to be like her. She wore exotic perfume every
day while most of us were used to our sensible mums who felt
daring if they dabbed a bit of 'Evening in Paris' behind their ears
on the rare occasions when they went out in the evening. A friend
of mine who joined the school half way through the third year
didn't know what to think on his first day when he was greeted with
'Well I'll give you enough rope to hang yourself. Just be careful how
you use it.' And later in the day during a reading of Shakespeare
she exploded "That was bloody awful. Let's try again."
None of us had ever come across anything quite like her and we
loved her for it. Passionate about poetry and Shakespeare, she

could read the former to us with all the resonance of her Welsh ancestry and the latter with a realism that brought it to life. She did admit that she might have gone too far with one class when her description of Lady Macbeth hastening to the gate to admit Duncan while removing her hairnet and curlers, was quoted back to her in an exam. All the older ladies we knew went to bed with their curlers held in place by a hairnet. I have to admit that to this day, in my mind Lady Macbeth is more Hilda Ogden in Coronation Street than she is Shakespearian heroine.

Not content with just classroom teaching, Miss Jones also organized trips to the theatre - the Manchester Playhouse and the Everyman Theatre in Liverpool in its early, heady days when I was young and impressionable. This was the start of a lifelong love for the theatre. Another passion which she and two or three other young teachers handed on to us was fell walking. They would take groups to the Lake District and for the duration of those holidays teachers would become companions. We all struggled up Skiddaw and got soaked in the inevitable rain. We shared dormitories in Youth Hostels and sometimes got cross and scratchy. We learned a different kind of respect in shared laughter and experience. Somehow, once you have compared blisters with someone, you continue to see them in a very human light afterwards.

Under the influence of a forward-thinking Headmaster and these young teachers, the school continued to change. Uniform was introduced and worn with pride, a choir was started, clubs developed, we entered a local Drama Festival and won prizes for the best production, best actress and best actor (the producer - M Jones). Confidence grew and there was an air of purpose and excitement in the school. Of course there were flaws. After the age of 13, girls dropped science for shorthand typing. Chalk and board dusters flew around many classrooms, aimed with deadly accuracy at the head of any miscreant. But, as 11 year old 'failures', we were given a sense of self-worth and ambition. My class produced a number of graduates as well as a Headmaster and various university lecturers. The fact that many of us are still in touch bears witness to the spirit which was engendered by the school.

Marion Jones left the school soon after we did. She married and moved to Scotland, and we lost contact. When we hit 60 we organised a reunion, the first full one since we were 16. Realising that she was only in fact eight years older than we were, we set about tracing her. Sadly we found she had died of cancer the previous year. I wish I could have told her face to face what a very positive effect she had had on my life.

On reflection, maybe she knew. All those ghosts in that building actually escaped many years ago and they are strong enough to survive any amount of builder's rubble.

Cave Lane

Joan Greenwood

(Crantock)

*I am a retired forensic social worker. My husband
is a retired hospital consultant and we are currently
building a house overlooking a beach in North
Cornwall. I enjoy writing, painting in oils, playing
the piano, swimming and walking.*

I had driven to Yorkshire for a family visit, but couldn't leave
without going back to Cave Lane. I parked near the school at
the top of the hill and walked down. The slab steps up the high
wall were still there, a shortcut along Gypsy Lane to the shops. Mrs
Lewis's substantial property used to be half way to 'our' house but
was now empty and windowless, on the edge of open land. The
row of five terraced cottages where I was born was gone.

Olive, my father's older sister, had lived in the last house in the lane.
My parents rented the house next door, a two-up-two-down with
no electricity or indoor plumbing apart from a single cold tap in the
kitchen. This is where I was born, but we left to live in Leeds when
I was a baby.

Olive's house remained an important part of my childhood. My
aunt was a busy, cheerful lady who was happiest when she had
someone to mother, but wasn't able to have her own children. She

331

moved to Cave Lane as a bride in 1936 with her husband Arthur, a miner. His upright walk made him look taller than his 5ft 8in. He started work in the mine aged 13 and had lost two fingers in an accident. Out of his pit clothes, he looked and acted like a gentleman and had beautiful copperplate handwriting. During the war he was a senior civil defence warden and, it was said, won medals for first aid. He was known as "The Hairy Ape" in his amateur wrestling career, which I couldn't understand as he was bald when I knew him.

I spent my school holidays with my aunt and uncle. Their home was a haven of comfort. Fuel was rationed, but miners had a coal allowance and fires burned in both downstairs rooms. The panelled walls and furniture were polished to a bright shine. On the wall hung a brass plate depicting Walter Raleigh covering a puddle with his cloak for Queen Elizabeth I to step on. On the sideboard was a silver coloured box which played 'Danny Boy' when the lid was opened. The Irish GP who occasionally called always opened it and said it was his favourite tune.

Arthur left for work before it was light. He would walk with a neighbour across the fields to Lofthouse Colliery. I liked porridge for my breakfast and asked Olive if she had time to make it. Olive said she "grew time (thyme) in the garden." Another mystery to me. Fresh bread, cakes and pies were baked daily in the fireside oven, their rich smell filling the house. Once she put too much sugar in the cake mix and let me eat the result. It was deliciously sweet, crunchy and golden.

Arthur's pit clothes were impregnated with coal dust, and Olive washed them by hand. A copper boiler was attached to the range fireplace. Water was boiled and the clothes were scrubbed on a washboard, rinsed, passed through a mangle and then hung out to dry.

As she worked, my aunt told me family stories. I learned that she had baked her first loaf of bread when she was 12, the day my father was born. Dad as an infant had had golden ringlets and a brown velvet dress with a lace collar. Railwaymen like my grandfather were given green corduroy suits and red neckerchiefs. Two red squares could be used to make a child's dress. (Small boys also wore dresses then). Dad was a boy scout and the proud owner of a drum.

In 1926, 200 unemployed men marched from Jarrow to London to the Houses of Parliament. Some local men joined them and borrowed the drum for the march, but it was broken when they returned. One bonfire night my father and other boys got into trouble because a neighbour's cart was put on the fire when they ran out of wood. Cars were a rare novelty and the boys would beg for rides, sometimes walking miles back home.

Olive left school on her 14th birthday and then stayed at home to help her mother with the housework and caring for my father, Arthur, who was a lively toddler. He was precious because, before he was born, his sister Ivy May had died aged four.

When Olive's housework was done, we would walk along Gypsy Lane to the shops. Butcher Bill sold rationed meat and could be persuaded to add an extra sausage or two. The Co-op was impressively large. There were wooden counters behind which were many drawers and cupboards labelled with their contents. I watched butter being cut from a large slab and deftly wrapped in greaseproof paper. Once there was a child's outfit on display, a red coat, buttoned leggings and bonnet which Olive bought for me. I was with her so often that people assumed I was her child and she did not correct them. We did not have to carry the shopping home; it was delivered later by a boy on a bicycle.

Sometimes we would call on my aunt's friend, Mrs Lewis, for a cup of tea on the way home. Mrs Lewis kept poultry and would give me a tiny bantam's egg for my tea. When I started learning music she seated me at her piano and asked me to play. However, I couldn't play anything without my own music and was upset because I felt I had disappointed aunty Olive.

If the weather was fine, I would walk across the fields to meet Arthur on his way home from the mine. He would be completely black from coal dust, apart from his red-rimmed eyes and white teeth. In the late 1950's pithead baths were introduced, but until then Olive had to have a tin bath of hot water before the kitchen fire ready for him, screened by clothes horses draped in towels. Clean and smartly dressed, Arthur was a different man. His shoes were highly polished, his coat brushed, and in cold weather he always wore a hat and gloves to walk up the lane to the Working Men's Club for his pint of beer.

After tea we would sit by the fire in the cosy light of the gas lamp. Arthur read his Daily Express, with its emblem of a knight in armour, and showed me the Rupert Bear cartoon. Olive would sew or knit. My favourite occupation was going through her sewing box. This was a large cube shaped wooden structure with spindle legs. Inside, the lid was padded with faded green satin. It held reels of thread, scraps of fabric and ends of ribbon. Best of all, at the bottom was a treasure trove of coloured buttons and occasional beads. The only sound at night would be the distant noise of a steam train on the Leeds to London line of the Great Northern Railway. A similar noise still gives me a feeling of security and comfort.

Behind the house was a tiny garden with a square of grass and a flower border. My uncle decided to build a swing for me there. One at a time, he carried heavy discarded pit props from the colliery to make the frame, which could have supported the weight of an elephant. Ropes were attached to metal hoops in the cross bar. The poker was heated in the fire until it was red hot, then two holes were burned in a plank to make the seat. The ropes were passed though these holes and knotted underneath. I was delighted with it, and it was very popular with the other local children.

In 1953 came a big change. Electricity was installed. Not only did we have the magic of electric lighting at the touch of a switch, but Olive and Arthur raided their savings to buy a television set. No-one I knew had ever seen television and it caused a stir in the neighbourhood. It was bought especially for the Queen's coronation, when I was eight. Our whole extended family and several neighbours squashed into the sitting room in the dark with the curtains drawn, watching the ceremony on the tiny black and white screen. I have a photo my uncle took of the TV at the moment of crowning, a postage stamp of light on a black background.

I visited Cave Lane less often as I got older, but when I was 14 my parents decided to move back to that area. I was attending a girls' grammar school in Leeds and had to transfer to a mixed grammar school near our new home. I went to stay with Olive and Arthur so that I could start the term at my new school as the move was two weeks later.

I started the week confidently, but was shocked by the rudeness and aggression of the pupils. I wasn't used to male teachers who shouted. One of them threw a wooden blackboard eraser at a boy who was misbehaving which hit and hurt me. There was no acknowledgement or apology. I missed my parents and my friends in Leeds and felt increasingly lonely and anxious. The children all spoke in a broad Yorkshire dialect.

I was small and thin, and a very large girl called Sophie who was over 6 feet tall, took pleasure in tormenting me, making fun of my accent and clothes as I didn't yet have the full uniform. Seats at lunch were allocated, but one or two people like me were "spare" and I had to look for an empty place and run to claim it. I once slipped on some spilled potato and fell onto the grubby floor. Laughter erupted all around me. I ran out of the room, locked myself in the toilet and sobbed. When a prefect found me I pretended I felt sick and was sent home.

I walked down the lane wondering what I would say, too ashamed to admit that I couldn't cope at this school. I was crying when I got to the door. Olive didn't say anything. She put her arms around me, made me a hot drink and put me on the sofa by the fire with a blanket over me. When Arthur came home, she wouldn't let him question me but said firmly that I had a cold and would stay at home the rest of the week. This was just what I needed, a few quiet days to adjust in a place where I felt safe.

The next week, I went back to school feeling stronger. Sophie emptied my school bag down a stairway. I was normally timid, but I was so angry I ran after her to where she was sitting on the grass. I jumped on top of her and yelled in her face. I thought she would hit me, but she seemed frightened and cowered away from me. We weren't friends, but she never bothered me again. I had learned a valuable lesson about standing up to bullies. School gradually improved, and I moved back to live with my family in our new house.

In 1966, the terraced houses in Cave Lane were demolished. Olive and Arthur moved to a house two miles away, purchased with their savings. Sadly, Arthur died two years later, just as he retired after spending 52 years at the mine. Olive was a frequent visitor to my homes in London, Wales and Norwich and was much loved by my children. She was a wonderful role model and I have tried to recreate the warmth and security of her home for my own children and grandchildren.

Wartime Oranges
Fiona Sparrow
(Rydal)

I left Ambleside in 1958 to travel abroad with my husband. We have two children. We lived in Africa, Eastern Europe, France and Canada before retiring to Ambleside in 1994. I gained a TEFL certificate in Paris and taught English as a Foreign Language while living abroad.

The orange trees and the fertile landscape were a welcome change for the British soldiers when they landed in Sicily in 1943. So my father, a Major in the Royal Army Medical Corps, told me. The change was welcome after hard months of fighting in the North African desert. The time spent in Sicily allowed the soldiers to recuperate before the invasion of Italy, which was to prove drawn out and hard-going. My father described Sicily with nostalgia whereas he would speak only reluctantly of his other wartime experiences.

Like others he probably wanted to forget the things he had seen, things not easily spoken of in everyday conversation. It is left to poets with their transforming gifts to make the horrors of war bearable. The Scottish poet Edwin Morgan served in the desert campaign at the same time as my father. He had volunteered as a non-combatant orderly with the RAMC. The poet and my father had a common purpose in caring for the wounded. Edwin

Morgan recollects how he 'dreaded the stretcher-bearing' and how he helped to carry in the desert, that dead officer drained of blood, wasted away, leg amputated at the thigh.

My father maybe had such amputations to perform but he did not want to talk of them on his return home.

Home was Ambleside in the Lake District. When war came he had recently moved there as a GP. Ambleside was 'another country' for both my parents. My father, born in 1906 in Buxton, had always wanted to be a doctor. He looked south to realize his ambitions and after studying at Cambridge, completed his training at St Thomas's Hospital in London. It was there that he met my mother. She had joined the Training School for Nurses, founded in 1860 at St Thomas's by Florence Nightingale. My mother was proud of being a Nightingale nurse and she was also proud of being a cockney, born in 1907 within the sound of Bow bells. She first saw my father across a hospital bed and it was love at first sight. Their engagement was announced and a London wedding followed. The journey north was an exciting prospect, into unknown territory.

My father had answered an advertisement for a junior partner to join a medical practice in Windermere. Someone was needed to open a surgery in Ambleside. My father's application was successful. My parents moved north in 1934 and I was born the next year in Ambleside on a fine Sunday evening in July, as the church bells were ringing for Evensong.

Ambleside 'lies between the mountains and the lake.' The two mountains which protect Ambleside to west and east are Loughrigg and Wansfell. They are sheltering landmarks, their contours and paths known to me as far back as I can remember. Their names are used everywhere in Ambleside to identify houses and roads. My father's first surgery and our first home was Loughrigg House. The year before the outbreak of war we moved across Ambleside to a house in Wansfell Road. I have no memories of my father dating to the pre-war years. Indeed it was not until my father returned from the war in my tenth year that I came to know him at all.

The war years were not easy for my mother. When my father left she had two small children, my brother had been born in 1937 in Loughrigg House. Having just settled into our new home, she had to move out to make room for the locum found to look after my father's patients. This was, of course, before the National Health Service altered the way a GP managed his own independent practice. The locum came complete with a family and they needed somewhere to live and anyway the surgery was run from the two front rooms of the house in Wansfell Road. So we moved out and for the first two years of the war we lived with grandparents. First with my father's parents in the Derbyshire plague village of Eyam, where my sister was born in 1941, and then with my mother's family in Weston in Hampshire.

As a child I was aware but strangely untouched by the way the war disrupted, even destroyed, the lives of grown-ups. The tragedy that hit my mother's family must have caused great heartache. When I was born my mother had two brothers, but the elder died in an accident in 1937 and then the younger, newly married and having just finished training as an RAF pilot, was shot down in 1940 over Germany. My grandmother did not recover from the shock and she suffered a stroke while planting roses in a garden she was making in remembrance of her lost sons. She was left paralyzed down her right side, totally dependent on my grandfather. I can only remember her as crippled, but as a child I marveled at the way she learnt to write with her left hand, in a distinctly curled and uniform style which I learnt to recognize. My mother's grief over the loss of her brothers, and she had been particularly close to the elder, compounded by my father's absence, was deep but she did not allow it to interrupt my carefree days. Through a happy summer I played untroubled with my brother and our now fatherless cousin.

My earliest recollection of being with my father relates to the time we lived in Weston. I must have stood near him at my sister's christening in Eyam but the only part of that service I can remember is fidgeting with the decorative greenery that hung down from the font as I stood next to my brother, the strange proceedings going on over our heads. My father was there but I cannot recall any details concerning him. His visit to Weston, however, is a precious and unique memory for me, fixed in time as though it were one of the old black and white photos that constitute our family record of those years. As I struggled with a dictation exercise, seated with my mother at my grandparents large polished dining-room table, we both looked up and saw through the window my father walking up the path to the front door.

Why was I doing dictation with my mother? Well in 1940 when I turned five the question of my schooling had arisen. My mother signed on with the Parents' National Education Union, which had been founded in Ambleside by Charlotte Mason. This system helped parents living abroad or on the move to oversee the education of their children. There were one or two PNEU schools in Britain and I had been able to attend one, at Grindleford, when we lived in Eyam, but at Weston my mother had to take over and my father arrived during one of our daily lessons. The dictation came to a halt when we saw the uniformed figure on the path. My mother's feelings I can only imagine, mine were confused. He was a stranger, but I knew who it was and that he belonged to me in an unconditional way.

Soon after that we returned to Ambleside as we were able to share our house with a new locum, a single 'lady' doctor. My second sister was born there in 1943 and then we just waited and followed the progress of the allied forces, eagerly examining the maps that appeared daily in the newspaper, detailing a pincer advance on Berlin. I now attended the local PNEU school. Charlotte Mason had founded a Teacher Training College in Ambleside to promote her methods and she then set up a small preparatory school under the supervision of a headmistress where her college students were able to practise. One day I was summoned to the headmistress's study to be told that my mother had rung to say my father was coming home and I could leave early.

So the great day of his homecoming had arrived at last. What emotions I wonder did it hold for my father? He was returning to take up his responsibilities as a doctor in the community and as father to a ready-made family, a quartet of growing children, who needed feeding, clothing and educating, in those difficult times of rationing and readjustment. He was never loquacious but he had a dry humour. His patients talk to me now of his gruff manner but they trusted him and many loved him. I can understand that. He was never demonstrative and as children we were half afraid of him. It was never in his presence that we quarreled, sulked or complained of 'having nothing to do'. That was an aggravation we loaded on our mother but we would be severely reprimanded if he caught us answering her back or disobeying her.

I still live in Ambleside and I delight in hearing stories about my parents, told by the patients whom they cared for, as together they built up his practice and then adapted to the introduction of the National Health Service. I take a strange delight in hearing of fish hooks carefully extracted from throbbing flesh or playground wounds neatly stitched up. Many of my father's patients tell me he brought them into this world. My mother always played an important part; she cleaned his surgery and fielded emergency phone calls. She woke me one night and showed me a newborn baby, which my father had just safely delivered in a taxi outside our door. The driver, realizing that he could not make the maternity hospital twelve miles away, had stopped at the doctor's, just in time.

As I grew older I learnt to rely on the unqualified support and love I was given by both my parents. My mother's I had always selfishly taken for granted and maybe undervalued; my father's, I think, because it came later, I did not take for granted and therefore perhaps unjustly gave it a higher premium. The fact that he died young, shortly before his sixtieth birthday, while my mother lived on without him for thirty years, means I invested heavily in my memories of him.

Even while I admit this, I remember him as the soldier father who returned from the war and won my devotion. How did he do it? It was with few words but with many small connecting moments. The first of these and I think the one that will remain with me

longest has to do with an orange. Soon after his return he came
up to the room at the top of the house where we as children slept
and played. His surgery and waiting room were downstairs and
we were banished upstairs during surgery hours. He found me
there alone. It must have been winter as I was next to our hissing
gas fire, probably with my head in a book. He had an orange for
me. Oranges were not at that time as scarce as bananas but to have
one for myself was a treat. Still unused to having him around I
remember feeling shy as I took it from him and looked uncertainly
at it.

'Let me,' he said as he took back the orange. 'This is how to peel
it. I used to do it often in Sicily.' Taking out a penknife from his
pocket, he cut, with surgical skill, a round off one end and scored
the skin into quarters, then neatly peeled off each section. Nothing
remarkable in this one might say but to me it was magical. We
shared out the segments and though we did not say much, it was
the beginning of a close and happy relationship. Every time I have
peeled an orange since then, I have thought of him. Long after his
death I went to Sicily and looked with his eyes at the Roman ruins,
at smoking Mt Etna and above all at the laden branches of the
orange trees.

After The War

Margaret Smith

(Brightwell cum Sotwell)

Growing up in Kent during the war years and now living in Oxfordshire Margaret has enjoyed the opportunity to compile her memoir to share with others. She feels that it has given her incentive to write more as a record for her family which they will hopefully treasure.

One of the happiest periods of my life was when I lived half at home and half with my grandmother who rented a house immediately opposite. I didn't so much as live with her, rather that I slept with Gran at her house. My grandfather had left my grandmother soon after the war and although she had her son Jack living at home she wanted other company. She said that she could not possibly sleep alone and that one of my mother's four girls would have to go over each night to sleep with her.

The eldest of a large family living in a small cottage my grandmother had never slept on her own in a bed and found the very thought terrifying. Even when in service from the age of fourteen until her marriage she had shared a bed with another servant. Apparently, according to my mother, during the first world war whilst my grandfather was away, a young girl who lived in the village came each night to sleep with Gran for company. This of course would not be acceptable these days - what a story for the media!

However I, being the youngest, was chosen on this occasion much to the disgust of my second sister who had believed herself to be my grandmother's favourite and could see my getting all sorts of privileges that she would have liked for herself. I was to suffer for this oversight several years later.

And so we settled into a routine which was to last for the next four and a half years. I slept at my grandmother's house but my meals were taken at my home across the road. I usually went over to Gran's after I had finished my homework spending a few hours with her until bedtime.

My grandmother also had a morbid fear of thunderstorms. Whether I had the same fear I can't remember but after living with her for quite some time gave me plenty of opportunity to acquire one. At the very first distant rumble in the night she would wake shaking me to get up. We would then cover everything that reflected light and might draw the lightening. All of this would have been carried out in the dark. Once my grandmother was satisfied all was secure we went down to the cupboard under the stairs where we would remain until the storm had passed.

It was very dark in the cupboard, smelling of old coats and gas. We would huddle tensely together waiting for the next clap of thunder. The only sounds were the ticking of the gas meter and our laboured breathing as we waited in fear, trembling for the storm to end. My grandmother was absolutely convinced that her next breath would be her last. It wasn't of course and she lived to the good old age of eighty-nine. Myself, I began to fear storms as much as she did. I also had terrifying nightmares of dark shapes jumping on me in the night, probably those smelly old coats in the gas cupboard. It took many years to conquer this groundless anxiety and I still cower in a corner when there is a particularly bad one.

During the school holidays I spent the daytime at my own home as my grandmother was working. This was often difficult as my sisters were not too happy at having a younger child around who was in their opinion a spoilt brat and nothing but a nuisance. To avoid their torments I made my escape to the allotment that my father rented at the bottom of our garden.

Previously an orchard, a number of apple trees remained and it was one of these that became my retreat. Away from the noise and bustle of the house, most often with a good book, I dreamt away the hours until my mother came to find me.

In the late summer evenings I often watched my father busy with his gardening. Watering, weeding, nurturing the plants. Rejoicing in the good crops of potatoes the ground yielded or cursing the white butterflies whose caterpillars devastated his cabbages. All of the ground was used for the cultivation of food except for one small corner where he grew gladioli for my mother. At the first showing of colour at the bottom of the spike he cut them close to the ground and carried them into the house for my mother to enjoy.

These were the only flowers he grew as generally he preferred the wild flowers of the countryside. In the springtime he always found the first bluebells and wood anemones fixing them to the saddle of his bicycle to bring them home. They were displayed in a jug or a milk bottle on the sideboard. They would not last long. Very soon the lace runner was littered with fallen petals and the water sticky with the sap from the long stalks.

Life was simple then. The country was recovering from the deprivations of war. There was little money for holidays, certainly not travel abroad. There were no package holidays. A day at the seaside was a rare treat and so we looked to our immediate locality for our pleasures and entertainment. Most Saturday evenings Gran went to the cinema with her sister Kath. She took with her little luxuries to eat and any that were left she gave to me later in the evening. There were often a few grapes or cherries when in season and if I was really lucky there were some of her favourite sweets rattling around at the bottom of her bag. Fruit bonbons by a company called Pascal, they were oblong fruit drops with a soft fruit filling, wrapped in a double paper; a piece of grease proof inner and a white decorated outer which carried an illustration of the fruit flavour centre. They were really yummy and even more so because I used up my sweet coupons at the start of the month and it was a very long wait before I could buy sweets again.

When she wasn't working and cooking for my uncle my grandmother liked to potter around in her garden. There wasn't a great deal. Being an end of terrace cottage the rear garden was a long narrow strip the width of the house. Two thirds of the this was used by Uncle Jack. A gravel path ran to the bottom of the garden to the Anderson shelter and it was the narrow border on the side of the path where she grew her flowers. Every year she bought a few packets of seeds from Woolworth's. Always the same. Clarkia, Larkspur, Love-in-the-mist, Godetia and Marigolds. These were the names we knew them by. No doubt 'Gardener's World' would name them differently. The seeds were scattered along the strip of ground and left to fend for themselves. Throughout the summer there was always a wonderful display of delicate pastels rising up from the rich orange and yellow marigolds.

Uncle Jack was my grandmother's eldest son. He was a plasterer by trade and not in the services during the war. In his spare time he grew chrysanthemums. During the war the main section of the back garden was used for growing vegetables. It was the only way to guarantee a supply of fresh food for the table. As life became easier after the war he was pleased to be able to concentrate on growing his flowers. He worked busily, dis-budding and staking , weeding and spraying, producing some of the finest blooms in the village. Incurving and mop-heads in rich butter yellow and glowing coppery russets. The flowers were never seen in my grandmother's house. They were sold at the 'Working Men's Club' where Jack spent his evenings. Once the season was over the plants were tidied up and prepared for the winter, strewn over with straw to protect them from the frosts and snow.

In the early years of the war our house was damaged when a bomb fell on the nearby hospital and we all lived at my grandmother's for a while. It was a typical Victorian cottage. There were three rooms down and three rooms up. There was no hallway. The front door

opened straight into the sitting room which was only used on high
days and holidays and for laying out the dead. The living room
had a Kitchener stove for heating the room. It was also used for
cooking, although my grandmother had a gas stove in what was
known as the scullery. The cottage was divided by the staircase
which went up diagonally between the sitting room and living
room. There was one large bedroom at the front and two smaller
at the back. The very smallest was reached by going through what
was known as the middle bedroom.

It was whilst we were all living at Gran's that the whole family was
struck down with a contagious infection of the blood. Several of
us, including myself and my mother's youngest brother Billy were
quite seriously ill. Of course there were no antibiotics then. Two
years before, Billy had damaged his spleen in a bicycle accident.
Sadly because of the injury he was unable to fight the infection and
died aged just nineteen. It was a very sad and traumatic time for us
and especially for my grandmother. Billy was one of those special
people with a kind and generous nature. It took all of us a long
time to come to terms with his untimely death. We had him laid
out in the parlour for about a week. I didn't really understand why
I was not allowed to see him.

On Saturdays my grandmother sent me to the house of Mr and
Mrs Prescott to buy flowers for Billy's grave. Being in the last
of a terraced row built for mill workers they were fortunate in
having a good strip of land adjoining their home. On this land
they supplemented their meagre income by cultivating flowers for
cutting. With a shilling to spend one could buy a nice big bunch.
Sometimes Gran asked for a particular flower but more often
than not I was left to decide. And what a choice. Sweet Williams
and old granny's pinks. Gaillardias, Scabious, Shasta daisies and
Brompton stocks and always to finish off a couple of pieces of
Gypsophila. Up and down I wandered behind old Mrs Prescott in
her flowered overall her hair bun bobbing up and down as she bent
to cut this one and that one. When the bunch was sufficient she
tied the flowers with some raffia and exchanged them with me for
the shilling. They were taken to the churchyard the next day and

placed on Billy's grave.

There were many changes in the years that I lived at my grandmother's. I spent more and more time there. My Uncle George came to live there with his wife Peggy until they were able to buy their first home. Soon after they moved out Jack re-married and moved from the small back bedroom to the big one at the front. Happily that freed up the room for me and as I had passed my eleven-plus I was quite delighted to have a room of my own. It was furnished with a single white-painted iron bedstead and a pine chest of drawers, on which was placed a charming set of Victorian china. I had by now abandoned the apple tree in Dad's garden and spent many happy hours lying on the bed reading with the company of my fluffy black cat.

Sadly good times don't last forever. Years pass and people's circumstances change. My idyll at my grandmother's ended abruptly one day when Aunt Kath, suddenly homeless, moved into my small back room and I was sent home to share once again with my second sister. A situation that we both found abysmal.

Acknowledgements

We would like to thank Ruth Bond and Jana Osborne from the NFWI and all of its participating members for making this project such a wonderful success. Our heartfelt thanks also go to David Chesterton and Katie Williams for their generous time in editing this book and to Sarah Allen for her commitment to the production and design.

"This has been an extraordinary journey. We encouraged women across the UK to write their own stories after the success of our own writing group The Contemporary Women Writers' Club. A year on and the WI members have surpassed all of our expectations. We are proud of them and of our imprint, Queenbee Press, for producing such a significant collection of stories which give us great insight into contemporary women's lives over the past 80 years. For me it has been unputdownable."
Lucy Cavendish, Novelist and co-founder of Queenbee Press

"The WI members who took part in Women's Memoirs truly embody the WI strap line 'Inspiring Women'. This collaboration showcases the huge talent across the WI's diverse membership, and as with our Love Your Libraries campaign, demonstrates just how close written stories are to members' hearts. Hopefully this project will inspire these brave, budding authors to greater literary heights and kindle the same bravery in those thinking of taking up writing to pick up that pen and start."
Ruth Bond, Chair of the National Federation of Womens' Institutes

Lightning Source UK Ltd.
Milton Keynes UK
UKOW041900140212

187305UK00006B/3/P